The Healthy Gourmet Cookbook

MARY HARRISON CARROLL
Writer

HAL STRAUS
Editor

KEITH OVREGAARD
Photographer

KAREN HAZARIAN
Food Stylist

AMY GLENN
Photographic Stylist

CALIFORNIA · CULINARY · ACADEMY

Mary Carroll has been teaching the principles and techniques of healthy cooking for a dozen years. She is the founder of Cuisine Naturelle, the West Coast's first natural foods cooking school, and is a nationally known writer on healthy cuisine for such publications as *American Health* and *Medical Self-Care*. Her recipes and unique approach have been featured in *USA Today*, Time-Life Cookbooks, and many television programs. She is the author of the California Culinary Academy cookbook *Elegant Low-Calorie Cooking* and a national syndicated cooking column, "Cuisine Naturelle" (formerly "Laurel's Kitchen"). As the cook for the Preventive Medicine Research Institute in San Francisco, she created the recipes used in a major study of the effects of diet on reversing heart disease. Mary currently resides in the Minneapolis area, where she teaches healthy-cooking classes and writes.

The California Culinary Academy In the forefront of American institutions leading the culinary renaissance in this country, the California Culinary Academy in San Francisco has gained a reputation as one of the most outstanding professional chef training schools in the world. With a teaching staff recruited from the best restaurants of Western Europe, the Academy educates students from around the world in the preparation of classical cuisine. The recipes in this book were created in consultation with the chefs of the Academy. For information about the Academy, write the Office of the Dean, California Culinary Academy, 625 Polk Street, San Francisco, CA 94102.

Front Cover: Duplicate the feeling of a French bistro with an intimate, nutritious, gourmet dinner for two: Salmon With Mustard Sauce (see page 46), Pasta With Miso Pesto (see page 116), steamed asparagus, and a rich-tasting Peach Strudel With Vanilla Sauce (see page 106).

Title Page: The ingredients of the healthy gourmet dinner shown on the cover form a palette for the creative cook.

Back Cover

Top Left: Leeks, carrots, potatoes, onions, garlic, and herbs are just some of the ingredients that go into a rich veal stock (see page 31). This stock can later be used in a variety of ways for everything from soups to sauces.

Top Right: Try Curried Prawn and Pasta Salad for a light, tasty lunch (see page 37).

Bottom Left: A splendid finale to your next gourmet dinner is chilled Compote of Winter Fruits in Red Wine, with a dollop of yogurt (see page 104).

Bottom Right: Four Cornish game hens are arranged artfully on a platter with baby carrots and green beans. Among the lessons to be learned from professional chefs is that the way food is presented is nearly as important as how it tastes.

Special Thanks to: Staff and students of Cuisine Naturelle; Tony Moore; Cottonwood; Fillamento; Sue Fisher King; Vignette; Virginia Breier; Fioridella; Judy Goldsmith; Bernie Carrasco; Barbara Brown; Nancy Glenn; Ward Finer; Hal Freedman; Willi Rudowsky; Karen Kuhn in San Francisco; Elica's Paper Plate and Fauxcus, Glendale, California; Bea and Marty Glenn, Miami Beach, Florida.

Contributors

Calligraphers
Keith Carlson, Chuck Wertman
Nutritional Consultant
Michelle Hanson
Additional Photographers
Alan Copeland, at the Academy; Michael Lamotte, back cover, top left and bottom right; Beth Marsolais, author, at left; Kit Morris, chefs, at left; Richard Tauber, pages 50, 77, 110, 111
Additional Stylists
Gina Farruggio and Eve Hinlien Shaw, assistant food stylists; Amy Nathan, food stylist, back cover, top left and bottom right; Sara Slavin, photo stylist, back cover, top left and bottom right
Photographic Design Consultant
Debbie Dicker
Copy Chief
Melinda E. Levine
Editorial Coordinator
Cass Dempsey
Copyeditor
Judith Dunham
Proofreader
Dan Ashby
Indexer
Elinor Lindheimer
Editorial Assistants
Deborah Bruner
Karen K. Johnson
Layout & pagination by
Tamara Mallory
Composition Coordinator
Linda M. Bouchard
System Coordinator
Laurie Steele
Series format designed by
Linda Hinrichs and Carol Kramer
Production by
Studio 165
Text separations by
Palace Press, Singapore
Cover separations by
Color Tech Corporation, U.S.A.
Lithographed by
Webcrafters, Inc., U.S.A.

The California Culinary Academy series is produced by the staff of Ortho Information Services.
Publisher
Robert J. Dolezal
Editorial Director
Christine Robertson
Production Director
Ernie S. Tasaki
Series Managing Editor
Sally W. Smith
System Manager
Katherine L. Parker
Address all inquiries to
Ortho Information Services
Box 5047, San Ramon, CA 94583

Copyright © 1989
Chevron Chemical Company
All rights reserved under international and Pan-American copyright conventions.

1 2 3 4 5 6 7 8 9
89 90 91 92 93 94

ISBN 0-89721-194-4

Library of Congress Catalog Card
Number 88-63841

Chevron Chemical Company
6001 Bollinger Canyon Road
San Ramon, CA 94583

C O N T E N T S

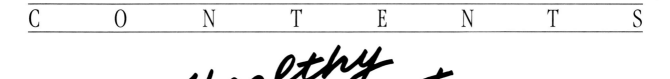

The Healthy Gourmet Cookbook

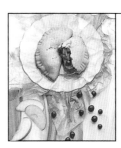

You can enjoy eating well and feeling well when you plan healthy menus, beginning with the basics: fresh fruits and vegetables, whole grains, and legumes.

Introduction to Healthy Cooking

Imagine serving dishes such as Cream of Zucchini Soup (see page 116), Sole aux Amandes (see page 47), and Baked Pear Gratin (see page 121). Too much bother, you say? And too rich to be truly healthy? Not true! Each of these dishes can be prepared in less than an hour, each is bursting with nutrients and flavor—and each contains less than 300 calories per serving. Once you read this chapter, these dishes—just a small sampling of the many healthy recipes in this book—will be a snap to prepare. This chapter also explains the basics of healthy foods and the cooking techniques that will transform these foods into delicious, nutritious meals for you and your family.

COOK RIGHT TO EAT RIGHT

If you love feeling well and eating well, there is good news for you: You can achieve both goals by adjusting your cooking habits.

Healthy cooking is the first step to healthy eating. When you cook your own meals, you can ensure that you and your family get well-balanced meals and the right nutrients. And study after study shows that eating right helps you feel and look better and also helps prevent certain diseases and conditions that are the natural legacies of an unhealthy diet.

Despite what you may have heard, healthy gourmet cooking need not entail complex techniques or expensive cookware. You can probably prepare most of the dishes in this book without spending one penny on new equipment. Almost all healthy cooking techniques are well within the ability of the beginning cook. The best news is that eating nutritiously does not mean giving up all the foods you like; you may only need to make subtle changes in cooking methods. In fact, you may already be using nutritious foods and not know it.

Healthy foods, prepared and served tastefully, can become new favorites in your cooking repertoire. In essence, you are embarking on an adventure in discovering new flavors and different cuisines and in feeling and looking better.

About This Book

This book is designed to guide you through this adventure. All the basics of healthy cooking are introduced in this chapter. Succeeding chapters present, course by course, recipes and menus that will please your palate as well as enhance your health.

Throughout the book, special features offer up-to-date nutritional information and tips on cooking techniques. As an added bonus, the last chapter spotlights recipe ideas for people who want to monitor intake of certain foods or substances, such as dairy products, fat and cholesterol, and sodium.

In general, this book follows the recommendations of many medical authorities and respected sources, including the U.S. Dietary Guidelines, the U.S. Surgeon General's Report on Diet (1988), the American Heart Association, the American Cancer Society, and the American Dietetics Association.

Although the details of these recommendations vary slightly in approach, certain general guidelines appear consistently in all of them.

☐ The average American diet does not contain enough of the following nutrients essential to good health: lean forms of protein, certain vitamins and minerals (such as vitamins A and C, calcium, and iron), complex carbohydrates, and fiber. To increase the nutritional value of meals, the recipes in this book use unprocessed whole grains and beans, lean meats and poultry, fresh seasonal produce, low-fat dairy products, and fresh fish and shellfish. All are rich in vital nutrients, flavorful, and pleasing to the eye.

☐ People in the United States typically consume too much saturated fat, cholesterol, calories, salt, and sugar. Numerous scientific studies have linked eating excessive amounts of these to various diseases, such as heart disease and hypertension. The recipes in this book avoid these substances whenever possible, using healthier substitutes (such as low-fat dairy products, yogurt, and herbal salt substitutes) and cooking techniques tailored especially for healthy ingredients and weight control (such as sautéing, poaching, and cooking in parchment).

To help you monitor your intake of important nutrients, a box at the end of each recipe lists the amount of calcium, calories, carbohydrates, cholesterol, fat, fiber, protein, and sodium contained in one serving of the recipe. This information, with the following guidelines (based on the U.S. Recommended Daily Allowances), will help you achieve your daily nutrient needs.

Calcium: 800–1,200 milligrams a day
Calories: 2,000 a day
Carbohydrates: less than 300 grams a day
Cholesterol: less than 300 milligrams a day
Fat: 67 grams a day
Fiber: 25–35 grams a day
Protein: 44–56 grams a day
Sodium: 1,100–3,300 milligrams a day

These are general guidelines; you might need more or less of each substance depending on your age, gender, activity level, medical condition, and so on. Figures for certain nutrients are often given as a percentage of daily calories: carbohydrate intake should provide about 55 percent of daily calories; protein about 15 percent; and fat no more than 30 percent.

About the Recipes

The recipes in this book focus on meals to serve yourself and your family, but many are ideal for entertaining. At your next dinner party, for example, try the Fireside Feast (see page 99), or take your friends on a Country Picnic (see page 41).

A wide array of international dishes is offered, but you will also see many favorites from the United States: Dorothy's Hearty Ham and Lima Bean Soup (see page 34) and Mom's Cinnamon Swirls (see page 96), to name only two.

Even the beginning cook will find the recipes easy to prepare. Because the techniques are streamlined to fit into a busy life-style, many recipes take less than an hour to make—including cooking time—and a good number can be made ahead. Preparation times are given for each recipe in the book, along with cooking, chilling, marinating, or other times, as applicable.

Serving sizes are normal: large enough to satisfy but small enough to minimize calories. Recipes yield four to eight servings but can be easily doubled or halved, depending on your menu needs.

SIX STEPS TO HEALTHY COOKING

The first steps you take toward healthy cooking will determine your success at making lasting, positive changes in your diet. The following suggestions, gathered from recommendations by medical and health professionals, will help to smooth the way.

1. *Learn the fundamentals of nutrition.* Know which foods your body needs—and which foods it does not need—to stay in good working condition.

2. *Apply this basic knowledge to your specific health needs.* Perhaps your family has a history of heart disease or you have heard that cholesterol contributes to heart disease. To create an eating plan that addresses these concerns, you must know which foods increase the risks.

3. *Become familiar with new cooking techniques.* How you cook is often as important to taste and nutrition as what you cook. Some cooking methods, such as stir-frying and steaming, work well with healthy ingredients by enhancing their flavor and retaining their nutritional value. Other methods, such as boiling or frying, destroy nutrients, tend to use unhealthy ingredients, or otherwise are inappropriate for healthy cuisine.

4. *Choose varied, flavorful dishes that are easy to prepare.* A wide assortment of tasty recipes enables you to stick with a healthy diet. These recipes also must fit your situation. It doesn't matter how many great recipes you have on hand if they are way beyond your technical skills and equipment, use exotic ingredients unavailable in a local store, differ so much from your customary menus that your taste buds are unable to adjust, or take so long to prepare that you never have the time to use them.

5. *Plan meals and menus ahead.* You are more likely to use the right foods and techniques if you plan and prepare meals in advance. An important part of healthy cooking is learning how to shop, read labels, and store foods so that they retain freshness and nutritional value. Organizing your kitchen logically and efficiently will make cooking enjoyable rather than a chore.

6. *Learn to enjoy healthy eating.* Once you learn the basics of light, healthy gourmet cooking, you will come to prefer the simple, delightful taste of fresh fruits and vegetables to the taste of packaged, processed, and frozen foods. You will also relish the feeling of accomplishment that accompanies the creation of beautiful-looking, delicious meals that you know are good for you.

Steaming and other healthy cooking techniques are vital for retaining the nutrients and flavor of fresh whole foods.

NUTRITIONAL BASICS

For a healthy diet, you should be eating the proper amounts of the following essential nutrients.

Protein—The Body's Main Building Block

All through life, protein functions as a building tool for the body to grow, nourish, and repair its cells. Protein carries oxygen to the cells and produces enzymes and hormones that regulate the metabolic process. It also helps fight infection and sustains the immune system by producing antibodies.

There are several types of protein, and consuming a variety of proteins is essential to good health. Since the human body does not manufacture or store protein, it must be supplied daily through the food you eat. Meats, poultry, fish and shellfish, eggs, dairy products, legumes (peas and beans), and whole grains all contain large amounts of protein.

Americans tend to rely on high-fat meats and dairy products for the majority of their protein. Although meat is an excellent source of protein, the high fat content of many meats is unhealthy. For healthy cooking, animal protein should be obtained from lean sources, such as leaner cuts of red meats, skinned chicken, fish, and low-fat or nonfat dairy products. Try such recipes as Minnesota Chicken and Wild Rice Soup (see page 31), Baked Salmon Provençale (see page 49), and Turkey Chili Burritos (see page 65). For more information on protein, see All About Protein on page 68.

Carbohydrates—The Body's Source of Energy

The main function of carbohydrates is to provide energy. The body also uses them as a source of B-complex vitamins. Carbohydrates come in two very different forms: simple and complex. Simple carbohydrates are found primarily in fresh fruit, fruit juices, and refined sugars such as those in candy bars and other sweets.

Fresh fruit is a necessary part of a healthy diet, since it provides essential nutrients such as vitamins and minerals, as well as carbohydrates.

Refined sugars, on the other hand, are less beneficial for the body. Although you may feel a spurt of instant energy after eating candy, the refined sugar contains an ample amount of calories. Sugary foods may fill you up (and out), but since they usually lack the nutrients the body needs to process the sugar, they contribute little to total body health. Because foods that contain refined sugar typically have little nutritional value, you are less physically satisfied when you eat them and so you consume more to compensate.

Scientists are divided on the harmful effects of sugar. Some believe that refined sugar is relatively harmless. Others think refined sugar does more damage than merely contributing to tooth decay. Some studies have found that sugar can place stress on the pancreas, causing it to produce excess insulin; others have linked excess sugar to hypertension.

Foods rich in complex carbohydrates, or starches, are the primary source of protein in many countries. Whole grains and legumes, such as rolled oats, cornmeal, whole wheat breads and pastas, and cooked beans and peas, are excellent sources of complex carbohydrates.

The average diet in the United States, which is low in complex carbohydrates, fails to take advantage of the benefits that these foods can provide, such as fiber, vitamins, minerals, and protein. Even in "restored" or "fortified" foods, such as certain breakfast cereals with added vitamins and minerals, the fiber content cannot be replaced. Fiber, bran, germ, and other nutrients in complex carbohydrate foods are the keys to proper digestion of these foods. They allow the body to burn the carbohydrate at an even rate, supplying energy as needed. When these nutrients are refined out of complex carbohydrates, as in the processing of wheat to make white flour, the body is

deprived of these nutritional keys. In this book, recipes that use complex carbohydrates include Pasta Shells With Peas and Chicken (see page 90) and Polenta Pizza (see page 94). For more information on complex carbohydrates, see The Value of Complex Carbohydrates on page 93.

Fiber—Digestion Aid and Disease Preventer

Fiber is the component of food that cannot be broken down by enzymes in the human digestive tract. All fiber comes from plants, and most types of fiber are complex carbohydrates. Since fiber is, for the most part, indigestible, it aids in elimination as it passes through the digestive tract. Fiber is highly regarded for its role in proper bowel function, fat and carbohydrate metabolism, and prevention of colon cancer. Many studies show that fiber may also help to prevent other diseases—diverticulitis, appendicitis, gallstones, and varicose veins.

Good sources of fiber are whole-grain cereals such as wheat, oat, and corn; oat and wheat bran; whole-grain breads and pastas; fresh fruits and vegetables; and beans, seeds, and nuts. Ukranian Sauerkraut Bread (see page 97) and Brian's Best Bran Muffins (see page 57) are recipes rich in fiber. For more information on the role of fiber in promoting good health, see The Benefits of Fiber on page 40.

Vitamins—Maintainers of Metabolism and Health

Vitamins are essential to almost all metabolic functions. They assist the catalytic action of enzymes, on which almost all body processes depend for chemical reactions and cell growth. Vitamins help release energy to the system, build tissue, and control the use of food by the body.

Vitamins are classified by their solubility in water or fat. Fat-soluble vitamins, such as A, D, E, and K, are stored by the body; water-soluble vitamins, such as the C-complex and B-complex vitamins, are not. The balance of different vitamins, and the total amount of vitamins are keys to

optimum health. Essential vitamins include A, B$_1$ (thiamin), B$_2$ (riboflavin), B$_3$ (niacin), B$_6$, B$_{12}$, biotin, C complex, D, E, folic acid, and K. See The Four Most Overlooked Nutrients, page 86, for more information on vitamins.

Minerals—Builders of Strong Bones and Teeth

Minerals perform a variety of functions in the body: building strong bones and teeth, strengthening enzymes, and maintaining the acid-alkaline balance. The most important minerals include calcium, fluoride, iodine, iron, phosphorus, potassium, sodium, and zinc. See The Four Most Overlooked Nutrients, page 86, for more information on minerals.

Supplementation

Over the years, changing agricultural, distribution, and storage methods have affected the amount of vitamins and minerals in food. Although it is best to obtain vitamins and minerals directly from food—where they exist in the proper balance and amount that the body can assimilate—many medical and health professionals encourage vitamin and mineral supplementation. Iron and calcium are two of the minerals most frequently deficient in the diet, especially for women (see The Four Most Overlooked Nutrients, page 86).

Supplementation, however, can have disadvantages. For example, excessive amounts of some of the fat-soluble vitamins, which are stored in the tissue, can produce toxic reactions. A rational approach is to choose a healthy eating plan and then supplement it if needed or medically advised to do so. Recipes packed with vitamins and minerals include Grated Vegetable Salad With Mustard Vinaigrette (see page 39), Greek Spinach Salad (see page 23), and Spicy Crabmeat Tacos (see page 22).

A well-balanced meal, such as one featuring Baked Salmon Provençale (see page 49), provides most essential nutrients and is low in fat, cholesterol, and other potentially harmful substances.

Fat—Blessing or Burden

Although fat is an oft-maligned substance, it does have a purpose in the chemistry of the body. Fats aid in digestion, are a source of energy, and carry certain fat-soluble vitamins into the system. It is important to understand the kinds of dietary fat: Some fats are good for you; others are not.

The three types of fats—saturated, polyunsaturated, and monounsaturated—are identified by the arrangement and number of carbon and hydrogen molecules.

Saturated fats come from animal products, such as meat, poultry, fish, lard, and dairy products, and from certain vegetable products, such as margarine, vegetable shortenings, chocolate, and coconut and palm oil. Saturated fats are usually, although not always, solid at room temperature, which makes them easier to identify.

Most of the fat in the American diet is in the form of saturated fat, the most difficult kind for the human body to handle. Saturated fats are also manufactured during hydrogenation, the process used to make margarine. Therefore, a polyunsaturated fat, such as corn oil, can become saturated through processing.

Polyunsaturated fats are most commonly found in vegetable oils, such as safflower and corn oils, but also exist in fish and nuts. Mono-unsaturated fats are primarily found in olive oil, nuts, and poultry. Studies done on polyunsaturated oils show they may reduce cholesterol in the body, whereas saturated fats tend to raise the level of cholesterol. Some nutritionists believe that polyunsaturated fats help the body metabolize saturated fats, which are more difficult to digest.

Many people consume 40 percent of their total calories in fat—an expensive way to travel. Fat contains 9 calories per gram, as opposed to protein, which contains only 4 calories per gram. That means you can eat twice as much protein as fat for about the same amount of calories.

Medical professionals are urging people to cut back on fat. The ideal is to consume no more than 30 percent of your total daily calories as fat, and preferably in the form of polyunsaturated or monounsaturated fats. Therefore, the healthy cook should cut back on fatty meats and high-fat dairy products, cook with safflower oil and olive oil instead of shortening, skin chicken before using, and add more complex carbohydrates to fulfill caloric needs.

Cholesterol—A Link to Heart Disease

Cholesterol is found in animal products and in the human body. It is manufactured by almost all body tissues and is used for a variety of body processes. The body manufactures plenty of cholesterol for its needs, however, and is often unable to

assimilate dietary cholesterol—that is, the cholesterol consumed when animal products are eaten. The excess cholesterol is often stored along the arteries, which can mean clogged blood vessels and atherosclerosis. As a result, cholesterol has been linked to coronary heart disease by many scientific studies. Foods highest in cholesterol include egg yolk, organ meats, butter, and some shellfish.

Cholesterol is not fat but is often found in high-fat foods. See Reducing the Cholesterol in Your Diet on page 63 for more information on how to reduce dietary cholesterol.

Sodium—Important in Small Amounts

Although sodium contributes to vital mineral balances in the system, many people ingest an excess of sodium in the form of table salt. Research has linked excess sodium to improper fluid balance (water retention), as well as to the more serious problems of hypertension and heart attacks. Many people are cutting back on salt, and cooking with herbal salt substitutes and low-sodium soy and tamari sauce, all of which can provide flavor, welcome variety, and change. See Seasonings Beyond Salt, page 123, for more tips on salt-free seasoning.

Preservatives

Food additives probably originated centuries ago when humans discovered that salted meats lasted longer. Most commonly, additives are found in convenience foods; they enhance flavor, stabilize sauces and thicken soups, prevent discoloration, and generally increase the shelf life of certain packaged foods. A diet rich in fresh foods avoids additive-laden convenience foods and promotes health with natural nutrients.

WEIGHT CONTROL AND HEALTHY COOKING

Maintaining your ideal weight may take work, but the benefits are worth it: more energy, a general sense of well-being, and a more positive outlook on life. And healthy cooking is a practical first step to controlling weight.

Calories—Measurements of Energy

Calories are not a substance but merely a unit that measures the amount of energy the body requires to metabolize a certain food. If your body is functioning normally, if your diet is relatively low in calories, and if you get a proper amount of exercise, then you burn off the calories that you consume.

Exercise speeds up metabolism of fats, proteins, and carbohydrates so that fewer are stored as excess weight. If you can exercise regularly, you can more easily handle occasional treats of empty-calorie foods—foods that provide little nutrition for the amount of calories the body must burn off to metabolize them. These foods include cakes, candies, and desserts made with white flour and white sugar; high-fat and high-salt snack foods such as pretzels, potato chips, and salted peanuts; and foods high in oils, butter, or fat-rich dairy products. Weight control is one of the benefits of healthy cooking. Because high-calorie foods are typically also high in fat and cholesterol, when you begin to cut the fat from your diet, you will simultaneously be introducing low-calorie recipes into your weekly menu plans.

Nutrient Density

Nutrient-dense foods are high in nutrients and low in calories. They give the body long-lasting energy, are assimilated easily and efficiently, and

COOKING WITH LESS FAT

Many foods, such as potatoes, start out light in calories, only to be cooked in too much shortening or loaded with fatty toppings. To reduce the fat in your diet, use cooking methods that do not require additional fat.

Braising To braise foods, wine or broth is used as the cooking liquid instead of fat, saving many calories. Start with a small amount of white wine, sherry, or defatted chicken stock (¼ cup per 2 cups of vegetables or meat to be braised), heat to simmering point, then add food to be cooked. Cover pan and keep heat on medium-high. Braise until food is tender or it reaches the specifications in the recipe. Braised vegetables absorb flavor from the cooking liquid and retain their bright color and texture as well.

Broiling Broil meats on a rack to let the fats drip off while cooking. Meats broiled correctly are crisp on the outside, tender and juicy inside. Marinate fish fillets in lemon juice or teriyaki sauce before broiling—the extra liquid helps prevent them from drying out during the cooking process.

Grilling When you grill chicken, potatoes, or squash, it is a good idea to bake the food for 30 minutes before setting it on the hot coals to ensure complete cooking. Baste grilled foods with mustard, lemon juice, or marinades while cooking (try the sauce from Grilled Sweet-and-Sour Tuna Steaks, page 46).

Poaching During the poaching process, food sits directly in a broth, wine, or fruit juice and absorbs the flavor of the liquid. Sweet poaching liquids, such as apple juice and dessert wine, are used for desserts (see

Compote of Winter Fruits in Red Wine, page 104). Savory liquids, such as stock and dry sherry, are preferred for fish and chicken (see Prawns with Peanut Sauce, page 51).

Sautéing As with stir-frying, medium-heat sautéing can be done with small amounts of butter, oil, or a combination of oil and wine. Since less fat is used than in frying, sautéed food must be stirred frequently to avoid sticking. Heat the pan until it is too hot to touch, then add the oil, butter, or liquid. Immediately add food to be sautéed, and stir quickly to coat the food thoroughly. This will seal in the nutrients, preserve color, and help prevent burning. Sautéing at medium temperatures develops a wonderful sweet flavor in most foods, especially those in the onion and garlic family.

Steaming Steamed foods cook quickly (heat from steam is hotter than heat from boiling water) and retain many nutrients that are lost in other cooking processes. Place a stainless steel or bamboo steamer in a deep pot above boiling water or broth, add vegetables, and cover. Steamed vegetables are ready when they appear bright in color and are tender when pierced with the tip of a knife. Fish fillets can be cooked in a bamboo steamer: Simply place the fish on a heatproof plate inside the steamer before placing the steamer in the cooking pot.

Stir-frying Favored by Asian cooks, stir-frying employs high heat and a rapid stirring process that prevents food from sticking and burning. Small amounts of flavorful oils, such as dark sesame or safflower oil, can be used, or a combination of sherry, *mirin*, and white wine. Woks or deep, rounded skillets are recommended for stir-frying because they conduct heat more evenly than flat-bottom pans.

The well-prepared, healthy gourmet cook keeps within easy reach a pantry stocked with whole grains, legumes, and fresh vegetables.

WHOLE FOODS: AN ESSENTIAL PART OF HEALTHY COOKING

Whole foods are unrefined, unprocessed foods, preferably fresh rather than canned, frozen, or packaged with preservatives. Once considered the choice of only health-food aficionados, whole foods are now sought by anyone concerned with health.

Whole foods include fresh vegetables and fruits, whole grains and legumes, fresh seafood, poultry and lean meats, low-fat or nonfat dairy products, tofu and tempeh, and certain condiments, natural sweeteners, and seasonings.

Many whole foods are available in supermarkets, but some are found only in local health-food stores or groceries specializing in natural foods. You might ask the store manager for a tour. Confronting bins of bulk foods may be intimidating at first.

Whole Grains

Providing abundant protein and other nutrients, whole grains are a standard ingredient in many of the entrées, soups, salads, and desserts in this book. Many whole grains require longer cooking times than refined grains, but the added nutrition is well worth the effort.

Barley cooks fairly quickly and is a nutritious ingredient of many soups and stews (see Hearty Beef and Barley Soup, page 30).

Brown rice comes in two varieties. Long-grain brown rice is appropriate for salads; the more starchy short-grain is best for croquettes and stir-fries (see Minnesota Vegetable and Wild Rice Pilaf With Cashew Gravy, page 79).

Bulgur is cracked wheat that is briefly steamed, then dried. This simple process makes it a fast-cooking grain. It is fluffy and tasty, and often used in salads or vegetarian entrées (see Minted Bulgur Salad, page 36).

add to the store of vitamins, minerals, and other life-enhancing substances.

Nutrient density has a direct relation to weight control: Compared with foods low in nutrient density, nutrient-dense foods are more likely to be burned as energy than stored as fat (as long as the quantity consumed does not exceed the caloric needs of the body). For example, a large baked potato and a small bag of potato chips may contain the same number of calories, but the baked potato has more protein, thiamin, riboflavin, niacin, vitamin C, and iron. Therefore, the baked potato is more nutrient-dense than the potato chips and is a healthier choice.

Nutrient-dense foods include fresh vegetables and fruits, low-fat or nonfat dairy products, cooked whole grains and legumes, whole-grain breads and pastas, lean meats, fresh fish and shellfish, and poultry without skin.

Foods with low nutrient density include packaged snack foods; high-fat dairy products; desserts, cakes, and candies made with white flour or white sugar; most commercial salad dressings; ice cream; and frozen dinners.

Cornmeal is the finely ground corn kernel. Polenta is a coarsely ground variation that is often cooked into a cereal, cut into wedges, and served with tomato sauce in Italian cuisine (see Polenta and Curried Vegetables, page 80).

Couscous comes from the Middle East and tastes like nutty pasta. It cooks in 15 or 20 minutes, and is often served with curried lamb or vegetables (see Couscous With Mushrooms and Curry, page 85). Packaged instant couscous is also available at many markets.

Millet has a fluffy consistency and a nutty taste, especially when roasted before steaming.

Rolled oats are ideal in cobbler toppings, thick creamy soups, and granola.

Whole wheat flour can be classified into two forms. Whole wheat pastry flour, a special type of wheat grown in the summer or spring, is essential for light and flaky pie crusts, pastries, and muffins. Whole wheat bread flour is a darker, richer flour made from red winter wheat; it has more gluten (bread protein) than pastry flour and is used in all the yeast breads in this book.

Legumes

Black beans are favored in southwestern cooking because they go well with chiles and cilantro. Cook them with onion and garlic for rich flavor (see Martinique Casserole page 80).

Kidney beans are excellent ingredients for chili and soups. They have a rich taste and lend a dark red color to tomato-based dishes (see Vegetarian Chili, page 123).

Lentils and *split peas* are quick-cooking and contribute a rich flavor to soups and stews. They give a thick texture to soup (see Swiss Lentil Soup, page 30).

Lima beans marinate well in salads because they hold their shape even after cooking. They are also good for soups, puréed spreads, and dips because of their buttery flavor (see Dorothy's Hearty Ham and Lima Bean Soup, page 34).

Natural Sweeteners

Many health professionals and nutritionists prefer using natural sweeteners instead of refined sugars because of their mineral and vitamin content. Cooking with them is easy once you learn the rules (see Substituting Unrefined Sweeteners, page 107).

Date sugar, made from finely ground dried dates, is a good substitute for brown sugar in pastries and pies. Because date sugar does not dissolve well in liquids, it should not be used in custards and soufflés but rather in crusts and cobbler toppings where its texture is an asset (see Tangy Lemon Custard Tart, page 111).

Honey is used instead of white sugar in many recipes in this book because of its flavor and aroma. Light-colored honeys, such as clover and wildflower, are the most versatile and available (see Hazel's Carob Cheesecake, page 109).

Maple syrup is delicious in desserts that feature fresh fruit, such as Cranberry Turnovers With Maple Glaze, page 105. Store maple syrup in the refrigerator; otherwise it may ferment.

Healthy Condiments and Seasonings

Choice of seasonings and condiments is important in healthy cooking. The following seasonings are made without preservatives or additives and add valuable nutrients to the diet.

Flavored vinegars (apple cider, raspberry, rice, balsamic, wine, and herb) are delicious ways to broaden your seasoning repertoire. Apple cider is a good all-purpose vinegar; raspberry lends a sweet flavor and fragrance to foods; rice is recommended for Asian cooking; balsamic and wine vinegars add robust flavor; and delicate herb vinegars are good additions to marinades and to salad dressings used over tender, fresh lettuces.

Herbal salt substitutes can greatly reduce your sodium intake. Use in the same amount as iodized salt when substituting in a recipe.

... ON WEIGHT CONTROL

Weight gain can be affected by emotional needs as well as by metabolic imbalances. Understanding the reasons for food cravings can make them easier to control.

☐ Plan ahead. Decide before a meal what you will eat and how much, and stick to that decision.

☐ Try a new low-calorie recipe every week. Experiment with different ones from this book, and write your results in the margins. Collect favorites that you can rotate during the week.

☐ Drink alcoholic beverages in moderation. In addition to its caloric content, liquor tends to dull judgment and self-discipline, making it too easy to cheat on a diet by eating impulse foods. Substitute club soda with a twist of lime or lemon, one of the new flavored sparkling waters, or even a low-calorie wine spritzer.

☐ Try not to arrive hungry to a cocktail party or dinner. If you eat a small low-calorie meal rich in nutrients before you leave home, you will be less likely to overeat the rich party food or nibble on too many cocktail snacks.

☐ Learn the difference between hunger and appetite. Hunger is a genuine need for food; appetite is tied to psychological needs. Fight the craving for snacks, or choose a low-calorie snack, such as fresh vegetables with a low-calorie dip, instead of high-fat crackers.

☐ Never skip a meal while dieting. You may compensate for the additional hunger by craving larger amounts of food at the next meal. Instead, train yourself to enjoy smaller portions of food at regular intervals.

Low-sodium tamari and *soy sauces* are other ways to decrease sodium intake. Tamari, the Japanese soy sauce, is richer and less diluted than commercial soy sauce, so you can use less in recipes (see Broccoli, Mushroom, and Water Chestnut Stir-Fry With Noodles, page 78).

Mirin is a sweet rice wine that is used in Japanese sauces and sautés. Dry sherry is also used in many Asian recipes. The alcohol evaporates during cooking, leaving a sweet, caramel flavor (see Szechuan Sautéed Tofu and Vegetables, page 76).

Miso is the by-product of making tamari or soy sauce. It is less salty than commercial soy sauce, tastes very much like a milder version of tamari, and is wonderful as a base for soups and salad dressings (see Japanese Miso Dressing, page 41).

Mustards, both stone-ground and Dijon, are good for hearty salad dressings (see Marinade for Bean Salads, page 41).

Vegetable oils—safflower, sesame, and olive—are preferable to saturated fats, lards, and hydrogenated oils because they contain polyunsaturated or monosaturated fats. Use safflower oil as an all-purpose oil for sautéing and salad dressings. Light or dark sesame oil is more heat-sensitive. Dark sesame oil is preferred for Asian stir-frying, light sesame oil for marinades or salad dressings. Olive oil, especially the first pressing, called extra-virgin, is ideal for salads and Italian dishes (see Pasta With Walnut-Garlic Sauce, page 80).

Low-Fat Dairy Products and Protein Sources

Cutting back on fatty protein, such as high-fat dairy products, fat-rich red meats, and egg yolks, is a step toward better health and reduced risk of heart disease. The following are good low-fat protein substitutes.

Low-fat cheeses (low-fat ricotta, farmer, and mozzarella) are gradually infiltrating the healthy cook's kitchen. For tips on low-fat dairy substitutions, see Low-Calorie Substitutions for High-Fat Dairy Products, page 117.

Nonfat yogurt, a good substitute for sour cream, may be used in many salad dressings and creamy, low-fat sauces (see Green Goddess Dressing, page 41).

Tempeh, similar in nature to tofu, is rich in vitamin B$_{12}$ and a good source of protein. It has more texture than tofu, and is made from soybeans inoculated with a culture similar to yogurt culture or the yeast that is used in making beer (see Tempeh Olive Spread, page 24).

Tofu is a white, cheeselike substance made from soy milk. In Asian cooking it is often a prime protein source. Soft or silken tofus blend well into sauces and dressings; firm varieties of tofu are used in stir-fries (see Szchewan Sautéed Tofu and Vegetables, page 76).

CHANGING YOUR DAILY MEAL PATTERNS

Scientific studies have shown the benefits of regular, moderately sized meals as opposed to the trend in the United States of no (or a small) breakfast, rushed lunches, big dinners, and before-bed snacks. Many people neglect to fuel their systems at peak energy hours—7:00 a.m. to 3:00 p.m.—and overload their bodies as they are winding down for sleep. People who seem to gain weight easily often follow this daily meal pattern.

The body handles food best in moderate amounts and early in the day. Food metabolizes best when the body is at its peak activity. The old adage, "Eat like a king for breakfast, a queen for lunch, and a pauper for dinner," is still true.

Breakfast

Breakfast is the most important meal of the day. Yet more people skip breakfast than any other meal.

Most medical and health professionals recommend a protein-based breakfast that includes a source of carbohydrates.

At this peak metabolic time, the body is most prepared to utilize protein to rebuild cells and to stabilize blood sugar levels, and carbohydrates

to provide energy. Accompany the protein with a source of vitamin C, such as fresh juice or fruit, and a whole-grain carbohydrate for energy. Variations in menu are limitless: Try low-fat cottage cheese with Orange-Date Muffins (see page 98) or Tempeh Olive Spread (see page 24) and a selection of fresh vegetable sticks for a quick breakfast. When you have more time, indulge in Eggs à la Suisse (see page 84) or French Buckwheat Crêpes With Mushrooms and Herbs (see page 79).

Lunch

Many people eat lunch out, order a big meal with several courses, and find themselves sleeping through the afternoon. A lunch loaded with nutrient-dense foods should supply you with a substantial portion of your protein intake for the day, plus give you an ample serving of vitamins, minerals, and fiber.

If you plan ahead, lunch can fit into your healthy eating patterns. Salads and soups are great lunch fare (try Hearty Beef and Barley Soup, page 30). Warm up a previously prepared entrée such as Fresh Trout Florentine (see page 49) or Salmon and Julienned Vegetable Sauté (see page 48).

Dinner

Lighten up for dinner. Although the evening meal is traditionally the time for family gatherings or socializing, it is also the time when the metabolic processes of the body begin to slow down, so you should eat less and ease your digestion. If you don't, your body may become tired from working throughout the night to digest food rather than resting as it should. When you enjoy a dinner with scaled-down proportions, you will sleep better and wake up hungry. Many nutritionists recommend eating a combination of complex carbohydrates and a lean protein source for the dinner meal.

The trick is to listen to your body. Eat when you have energy or need energy, not when you're tired and winding down. Eventually you will find your own balance in eating.

...ON PREPARING MAKE-AHEAD MEALS

The secret of efficient healthy cooking is spending a couple of hours of preparation time during the slow periods of the week.

☐ When you come home from shopping, take 15 to 30 minutes to wash and prep vegetables. Wash lettuce, dry in a salad spinner, and store in lock-top plastic bags for fast salads. Wash and grate beets and carrots; trim broccoli stems, asparagus, and bok choy; peel onions and green onions; and store all in lock-top plastic bags.

☐ Grate by hand or with a food processor any low-fat hard cheeses and store in bags in the refrigerator or freezer for quick addition to recipes. Wash, spin-dry, and mince fresh parsley; store in the freezer. Juice lemons and freeze juice in ice cube trays; drop frozen cubes into a bag—each cube equals about 2 tablespoons of juice—and store in freezer.

☐ Assemble two dishes up to the point when they should be cooked. Examples of easy make-ahead recipes are Roasted Chicken With Rosemary and Garlic (see page 62) and Easy Beef Fajitas (shown above; see page 68). Prepare one soup, such as Dorothy's Hearty Ham and Lima Bean Soup (see page 34), and two lunch spreads, such as Tempeh Olive Spread (see page 24) and Cream Cheese and Garlic Dip (see page 18). These dishes will form the basis for quick meals all week.

☐ Begin soaking two different grains or beans for meals during the week. Wash well, then examine for stones. Place each type of grain or bean in a separate bowl and cover with water. Soaking overnight reduces cooking time by one third. Cook grains or beans when you have an extra hour at home, and freeze or refrigerate.

☐ Organize prepared foods according to the day you will be serving them: The appetizer and assembled entrée for the Friday dinner party gets placed on the back of the second shelf; lunch items occupy the middle. Label containers or use clear plastic containers.

☐ Start a soup stock (see page 31 for easy directions), which can be simmering while you prep. Let the stock cool, then freeze in double lock-top plastic bags or in 2-cup containers. Good stocks form the basis for the best soups. You can also use them for poaching fish or chicken, steaming or stir-frying vegetables, and adding flavor to various sauces.

☐ Now take stock of what you have accomplished. You have the basics for many easy meals. Lunches will be faster with spreads ready to make into sandwiches, and hearty salads will take only a minute to assemble. An impromptu poached fish dinner can be made by defrosting a few cubes of lemon juice, some gingerroot and parsley, and a fillet of fish. Two entrées are ready for the evenings when you might not feel like cooking. Even entertaining will be easier with an appetizer (one of the lunch spreads on whole-grain crackers or vegetable sticks), a soup, and an entrée ready to go.

For a light meal, Spicy Crabmeat Tacos (see page 22) offers taste and charm, but avoids the fat and calories of the deep-fried version.

First Courses & Light Meals

The recipes in this chapter will serve triple duty in your menu planning—many can be used as a light meal, or as the appetizer course of a menu, or as a healthy snack. For a party, experiment with filo, a light, flaky pastry that is the equal of butter pastry in every aspect but calories. Try Filo Pastries With Smoked Turkey and Mushrooms (see page 20) or Filo Cheese Pastries (see page 19). For a tasty and nutritious meal-in-itself, try Spicy Crabmeat Tacos (see page 22) or Hummus in Pita Pockets (see page 25), a traditional Middle Eastern dish. A strictly American Super Bowl Grazing Party menu (see page 25) completes the chapter.

SAVORY APPETIZERS

Perfect for on-the-spot entertaining, these easy, yet elegant, appetite teasers pave the way for heartier main course fare. Many can be made ahead, frozen, and reheated just before serving. Rely on seasonally ripe produce for the best nutritional value and flavor, especially in recipes that call for fresh herbs or tomatoes.

STUFFED ARTICHOKE BOTTOMS

Artichokes are a delicious source of calcium, fiber, and vitamin C. In this recipe, the tang of marinated artichokes (usually packaged in jars) is highlighted by a creamy blue cheese filling. Make a trayful ahead of time, refrigerate after covering tightly with plastic wrap, and let sit at room temperature about 30 minutes before serving. For an exotic display, line a flat basket with banana leaves (available from most florists) and alternate Stuffed Artichoke Bottoms with Stuffed Snow Peas (see page 21).

    2 ounces low-calorie cream
       cheese, such as Neufchâtel
    2 tablespoons crumbled
       blue cheese
    1 tablespoon low-calorie
       mayonnaise
   12 marinated artichoke bottoms
       Paprika, for garnish

In a small bowl, mix together cheeses and mayonnaise. Spoon cheese mixture into artichoke bottoms and garnish with a dusting of paprika. Serve at room temperature.

Makes 1 dozen stuffed artichoke bottoms, 6 servings.

> *Preparation time:* 15 minutes
> *Per serving:* calcium 40 mg,
> calories 62, carbohydrates 3 g,
> cholesterol 11 mg, fat 4 g, fiber
> .45 g, protein 3 g, sodium 141 mg

MARINATED GOAT CHEESE

This savory appetizer originates in the antipasto platters of northern Italy. The fragrant wedges of marinated goat cheese can be served on a bed of lettuce and radicchio or can be spread on sourdough French bread or crisp rye crackers. Accompany with slices of garden-ripe tomatoes and garnish with sprigs of fresh basil. The green olive oil used in this recipe is made from unripe olives; it can be found in the gourmet aisle of most supermarkets.

   10 cloves garlic, thinly sliced
   ⅓ cup extravirgin olive oil
   ¼ cup green olive oil
   ¼ cup imported Niçoise or
       Greek olives
       Pinch of freshly ground pepper
    2 sprigs fresh thyme or
       1 teaspoon dried thyme
    2 sprigs fresh oregano or
       1 teaspoon dried oregano
    2 sprigs fresh tarragon or
       1 teaspoon dried tarragon
   ½ pound goat cheese
       Lettuce leaves or rye crackers,
       for lining platter
       Olives, whole, peeled garlic
       cloves, or sprigs of fresh herbs,
       for garnish

1. In a heavy skillet over medium heat, sauté garlic slices in olive oils until slightly golden. Remove skillet from heat.

2. Add olives, pepper, thyme, oregano, and tarragon to oil.

3. Cut goat cheese into 1½-inch pieces. Lay pieces in a flat-bottomed casserole. Pour oil mixture over cheese and cover with plastic wrap. Let marinate for 24 to 48 hours in the refrigerator before serving.

4. To serve, arrange cheese on lettuce. Garnish with olives, garlic, or herb sprigs.

Serves 8.

> *Preparation time:* 15 minutes
> *Marinating time:* 24 to 48 hours
> *Per serving:* calcium 125 mg,
> calories 302, carbohydrates 14 g,
> cholesterol 26 mg, fat 26 g, fiber
> .2 g, protein 3 g, sodium 209 mg

CREAM CHEESE AND GARLIC DIP WITH PITA TOASTS

This rich, creamy dip is surprisingly low-calorie and goes as well with a platter of crudités as with these crunchy pita toasts. It can be made up to six weeks ahead of time and frozen, or will keep refrigerated for up to 5 days. Serve the dip in a hollowed-out red or green bell pepper for an elegant presentation.

    8 ounces low-calorie cream
       cheese, such as Neufchâtel
    2 tablespoons low-calorie
       mayonnaise
       Juice of ½ lemon
    3 large cloves garlic, pressed
   ¼ small onion, finely minced
    1 teaspoon dried dill
    1 teaspoon herbal salt substitute
       Tabasco sauce, to taste
    1 red bell pepper

Pita Toasts

    3 large rounds whole wheat
       pita bread
    1 teaspoon garlic powder

In a small bowl, mix together cream cheese, mayonnaise, lemon juice, garlic, onion, dill, and salt substitute. Add Tabasco to taste. Cut top off bell pepper and remove seeds. Spoon dip into hollowed-out bell pepper, cover with plastic wrap, and chill while you make the pita toasts.

Serves 12.

Pita Toasts Cut each round of pita bread into 4 equal wedges. Toast until crisp, then open each wedge and dust inside lightly with garlic powder. Then arrange on a platter with dip.

Makes 12 wedges.

> *Preparation time:* 10 minutes
> (dip); 10 minutes (Pita Toasts)
> *Chilling time:* 10 minutes
> *Per serving:* calcium 22 mg,
> calories 79, carbohydrates 5 g,
> cholesterol 15 mg, fat 16 g, fiber
> .3 g, protein 3 g, sodium 126 mg

FILO CHEESE PASTRIES

These savory pastries are filled with feta and low-fat ricotta cheeses, flavored with garlic and dill, and baked until lightly browned. Made up to three days ahead of time, they can be frozen until ready to bake and serve.

> *Safflower oil, for coating muffin tins*
> ¾ *cup low-fat ricotta cheese*
> ¼ *cup low-fat small curd cottage cheese*
> ½ *cup crumbled feta cheese*
> ¼ *cup grated low-fat mozzarella cheese*
> 1 *egg*
> 2 *tablespoons dried dill*
> ¼ *cup finely minced parsley*
> ½ *teaspoon pressed garlic*
> 8 *sheets filo dough*
> 4 *tablespoons plus 1 teaspoon unsalted butter, melted*

1. Preheat oven to 375° F. Lightly oil muffin tin. In blender or food processor, purée cheeses. Add egg and blend mixture well.

2. By hand, stir dill, parsley, and garlic into cheeses. Spoon mixture into a bowl and cover with plastic wrap. Refrigerate while proceeding with next steps.

3. Stack sheets of filo dough on a clean, dry surface. Brush each sheet with 1 teaspoon melted butter, and lay buttered sheets one on top of another. Cut piled sheets into 24 squares of 2½ inches each.

4. Press squares into muffin tin cups, and spoon 1 tablespoon cheese filling into each. Fold edges of filo over filling and lightly brush top of each filo pastry with remaining butter.

5. Bake for 12 to 15 minutes, watching carefully so that pastries do not burn. Remove from tins, and let them cool slightly before serving.

Makes 2 dozen pastries, 10 servings.

> *Preparation time:* 40 minutes
> *Baking time:* 15 minutes
> *Per serving:* calcium 136 mg, calories 196, carbohydrates 14 g, cholesterol 64 mg, fat 12 g, fiber .4 g; protein 7 g, sodium 232 mg

Basics

HEALTHY SNACKING

Although many dieters and health-conscious cooks eliminate snacks from their menu plans, snacks have nutritional value. The trick to making healthy snacks is organization—stocking up on nutritious, quick-to-prepare foods for busy times. For example, the Cream Cheese and Garlic Dip With Pita Toasts (shown above) can be prepared in 20 minutes. The flexibility of snacking fits the pace of contemporary life and can provide a relaxing break during busy work schedules.

If you are following a weight-loss program, recognize how snacks can contribute to the daily or weekly caloric total. Learn to choose foods high in nutrient density (see page 11) and to plan ahead to control impulse eating of junk foods. Including just two healthy snack foods in a weekly menu plan will lessen the chances of an eating binge.

Plan snacks to complement regular meals so that your total food intake provides required nutrients and does not exceed daily caloric needs. If you know that you will miss lunch, for example, prepare snacks that will carry you through the day and yet not add weight. A good way to avoid after-work overeating is to look for foods that are high in nutrients and low in calories. Some examples:

Fresh fruits and vegetables
Spread nut butter on half a cored apple; trim a handful of raw vegetable sticks and dip into Cream Cheese and Garlic Dip (see page 18); spread low-fat ricotta cheese on half a banana and sprinkle with raisins.

Toasted rye or wheat crackers
Cover with Salmon Spread (see page 20) and sprinkle with minced parsley or red onion.

Homemade muffins Try Orange Date Muffins (see page 98) or Carrot-Ginger Breakfast Muffins (see page 99). Split in half, toast, and spread with nutmeg-seasoned cottage cheese.

Pita pizzas Top a split pita round with 1 or 2 tablespoons pizza sauce (see Basic Pizza Sauce, page 92) and top with sliced red or green bell pepper and grated low-fat mozzarella cheese. Broil until bubbly.

FILO PASTRIES WITH SMOKED TURKEY AND MUSHROOMS

Spoonfuls of the savory filling are layered on thin filo dough, which is then folded into triangles. See pages 110 and 111 for directions on handling filo and forming it into shapes. Prepare the pastries ahead and freeze for entertaining.

> 1 cup minced mushrooms
> 2 cloves garlic, minced
> ¼ cup minced onion
> ¼ cup sherry
> 1 teaspoon olive oil
> 3 tablespoons chopped parsley
> ½ cup crumbled feta cheese
> ¼ cup grated low-fat mozzarella cheese
> ¼ teaspoon dried oregano
> ¼ teaspoon dried thyme
> ¼ pound finely minced smoked turkey or ham, trimmed of fat
> 15 sheets filo dough
> ⅓ cup unsalted butter, melted

1. In a large skillet over medium high heat, sauté mushrooms, garlic, and onion in sherry and olive oil until soft. Add parsley, feta, mozzarella, oregano, thyme, and turkey. Remove from heat.

2. Preheat oven to 350° F. Lightly oil two 9- by 12-inch baking sheets.

3. Lay filo dough on a clean, dry surface. Cut each sheet in half widthwise to make 30 smaller sheets. Stack them evenly on top of each other, and cover with a piece of plastic wrap and a slightly dampened dish towel as you do the next step.

4. Butter 1 sheet and cut into 3 long strips. Lay the 3 strips on top of each other. Place about 2 tablespoons of filling in the lower right section near the edge. Fold bottom right corner of filo over filling to meet left edge, creating a small triangle. Continue folding pastry, as you would a flag, until you reach the top. You will end up with a triangle-shaped pastry.

5. Lightly butter top of filled triangle and place on prepared baking sheet. Repeat process until all the filling has been used.

6. Bake pastries until golden (20 minutes). Serve warm.

Makes 30 pastries, 15 servings.

Preparation time: 35 minutes
Baking time: 20 minutes
Per serving: calcium 60 mg, calories 144, carbohydrates 15 g, cholesterol 25 mg, fat 9 g, fiber .2 g, protein 8 g, sodium 260 mg

---

BLINI WITH SALMON SPREAD

Blini are the traditional yeasted pancakes used to break the Russian Orthodox Lenten fast. Some say a "real Russian" can eat more than 90 blini in one sitting, downed with plenty of vodka. This recipe is made with wheat flour and egg whites instead of the white flour and yolks called for in typically rich blini recipes. Cook the thin pancakes on a griddle or in a crêpe pan, then stack until ready to serve with tangy Salmon Spread. Both recipes can be made the day before a party, wrapped well, and refrigerated. To reheat blini, wrap in a slightly dampened kitchen towel, place in a casserole, cover with aluminum foil, and warm in a 250° F oven for 15 minutes.

> 1 package active dry yeast
> ¼ cup warm water (98° to 110° F)
> ½ tablespoon honey
> 1¼ cups whole wheat pastry flour
> ¾ cup sifted buckwheat flour
> 2 cups warm nonfat milk (98° F)
> ½ teaspoon herbal salt substitute
> 2 egg yolks
> 4 egg whites
> 1 cup evaporated nonfat milk
> Radishes, green onions, and cherry tomatoes, for garnish (optional)

Salmon Spread

> 1 cup finely chopped smoked salmon
> ¼ cup lemon juice
> 4 ounces low-calorie cream cheese, such as Neufchâtel
> 4 ounces low-fat ricotta cheese
> ¼ cup minced red onion
> Freshly ground pepper, to taste

1. In a small bowl combine yeast, the water, and honey, and stir well until yeast is dissolved. Let sit at room temperature until foam appears on top of the water (8 to 10 minutes).

2. Meanwhile, in a medium-sized mixing bowl, combine flours, nonfat milk, salt substitute, and egg yolks. Beat lightly with a whisk until well mixed. After yeast has foamed, add to flour mixture. Stir batter well, cover bowl with a clean dish towel, and let rise in a warm place, such as a gas oven with the pilot lit, for 1 hour.

3. Beat egg whites until stiff but not dry. Whip evaporated milk with electric beater until stiff peaks form. Add whipped milk to egg whites, and let mixture sit for 30 minutes while batter rises. After batter has risen, combine contents of two bowls.

4. To cook blini, lightly oil a crêpe pan or griddle. Pour ¼ cup batter onto pan. Cook on one side until pancake bubbles, then flip and cook on other side for 30 seconds. Place cooked pancakes on a paper towel. Continue until all batter is used.

5. Place crock of Salmon Spread on a platter, and arrange folded or rolled, warm blini around it. Garnish with radishes, green onions, and cherry tomatoes (if desired).

Makes 30 pancakes, 15 servings.

Salmon Spread   Purée all ingredients in blender or food processor. Spoon into a crock, cover with plastic wrap, and refrigerate until serving time.

Makes about 2 cups spread, 15 servings.

Preparation time: 10 minutes (Blini); 10 minutes (Salmon Spread)
Rising time: 1 hour (Blini)
Cooking time: 50 minutes
Per serving: calcium 125 mg, calories 152, carbohydrates 16 g, cholesterol 44 mg, fat 5 g, fiber 1.6 g, protein 10 g, sodium 158 mg

---

STUFFED SNOW PEAS

These delicate appetizers, very popular at parties, are made with a creamy blend of low-fat ricotta cheese, garlic, and dill. The low-fat cheese provides calcium, the shrimp is an excellent source of protein, and the fresh peas add fiber and vitamins. This is a very elegant and healthy appetizer, especially when combined on a platter with Stuffed Artichoke Bottoms (see page 18).

> 30 *large snow peas*
> 1 *cup low-fat ricotta cheese*
> 1 *tablespoon dried dill*
> 2 *cloves garlic, pressed*
> 3 *tablespoons grated Parmesan cheese*
> 30 *cooked bay shrimp*
> 30 *sprigs (1 in. long) fresh dill*

1. In a large stockpot bring 1 quart of water to a boil. Blanch snow peas by dropping in boiling water and cooking until they turn bright green (about 30 seconds), then rinsing in very cold water. Cut ends off snow peas, slit them open along one edge, and set aside.

2. In a small bowl mix together ricotta, dill, garlic, and Parmesan. Open slit side of each snow pea and fill cavity with ricotta mixture.

3. Garnish each stuffed snow pea with a bay shrimp and a tiny sprig of dill. Serve chilled or at room temperature.

Makes 30 snow peas, approximately 8 servings.

> *Preparation time:* 45 minutes
> *Chilling time (optional):* 30 minutes
> *Per serving:* calcium 187 mg, calories 119, carbohydrates 10 g, cholesterol 40 mg, fat 5 g, fiber 8.1 g, protein 10 g, sodium 127 mg

As hors d'oeuvres, Stuffed Snow Peas and Stuffed Artichoke Bottoms (see page 18) are sure to be a hit at your next party. Combining tiny bay shrimp and low-calorie cheeses, these tidbits are low in fat and cholesterol, high in fiber and flavor.

LIGHT MEALS

These sensational dishes fit into your menu planning as light meals, Sunday afternoon picnic fare, or party hors d'oeuvres. As an added bonus, most of the following recipes can be made in less than 30 minutes. If you are on the run, have some of these spreads and vegetable snacks ready to grab as you go out the door.

FRUIT KABOBS WITH SOUR CREAM SAUCE

This light meal is an elegant variation on fresh fruit salad. Use a wide assortment of fruits, including one or two kinds of melons, pineapple, strawberries, bananas, and peaches. The sour cream dip, deliciously flavored with nutmeg and honey, can be made ahead and stored in a tightly covered container in the refrigerator for up to one week.

- ¾ cup each *cantaloupe cubes, pineapple chunks, sliced bananas, peach chunks, and whole strawberries*
- ¾ cup *nonfat plain yogurt*
- ¼ cup *sour cream*
- 2 teaspoons *freshly grated nutmeg*
- 1 tablespoon *maple syrup*
- 1 tablespoon *honey*
  Fresh mint leaves, for garnish

1. Skewer chunks of fruit onto 12 bamboo or metal shish kabob skewers, alternating colors and types of fruit. Arrange on a platter or in a flat basket.

2. Mix together yogurt, sour cream, nutmeg, maple syrup, and honey, and pour into a small serving bowl. Garnish with mint leaves. Serve sauce with fruit kabobs.

Makes 1 dozen skewers, approximately 4 servings.

Preparation time: 30 minutes
Per serving: calcium 117 mg, calories 149, carbohydrates 28 g, cholesterol 8 mg, fat 1 g, fiber 2.1 g, protein 4 g, sodium 41 mg

BUFFALO CHICKEN WINGS WITH BLUE CHEESE DIP

This popular hors d'oeuvre has gained national fame in a very short time. The original recipe calls for deep-fried chicken wings, but in this healthier version they are baked. Serve hot from the oven with celery sticks and Blue Cheese Dip made with yogurt and sour cream.

- 2 tablespoons *melted butter*
- 4 tablespoons *Tabasco Sauce*
- 2 tablespoons *rice vinegar*
- 30 *chicken wings or drummettes*
  Paprika, for dusting
  Lettuce leaves, for lining platter
  Celery sticks, for accompaniment

Blue Cheese Dip

- ½ cup *soft tofu*
- 2 tablespoons *rice vinegar*
- ⅓ cup *nonfat plain yogurt*
- ¼ cup *sour cream*
- 2 cloves *garlic, pressed*
- 3 ounces *blue cheese, crumbled*

1. Preheat oven to 350° F. Mix together butter, Tabasco, and vinegar. Dip chicken into mixture, then place on a lightly oiled baking sheet. Dust with paprika.

2. Bake chicken until crisp and brown (about 30 minutes).

3. To serve, arrange chicken on a platter lined with lettuce leaves. Set a bowl of Blue Cheese Dip in the center and celery sticks on the side.

Serves 8.

Blue Cheese Dip   In a blender purée tofu, vinegar, yogurt, sour cream, and garlic until smooth. Stir in blue cheese. Spoon into a serving bowl, cover with plastic wrap, and chill until chicken is baked.

Makes about 1½ cups.

Preparation time: 15 minutes
Cooking time: 30 minutes
Per serving: calcium 109 mg, calories 224, carbohydrates 2 g, cholesterol 84 mg, fat 12 g, fiber none, protein 24 g, sodium 248 mg

SPICY CRABMEAT TACOS

Great for a quick meal, these healthy tacos are made with soft corn tortillas rather than the traditional deep-fried shells. Corn is a good source of fiber and vitamins, the crabmeat provides protein, and the vegetables contribute additional vitamins and minerals. Make the filling ahead and stuff into the warmed tortillas right before serving.

- ¼ cup *minced red onion*
- 1 teaspoon *safflower oil*
- ½ teaspoon *minced garlic*
- 1 cup *diced tomatoes*
- 2 tablespoons *minced cilantro*
- 2 cups *cooked crabmeat, shredded*
- 6 *corn tortillas*
- 2 tablespoons *lemon juice*
- ¼ cup *chopped green bell pepper*
- ¼ cup *peeled and chopped cucumber*
- 1 cup *shredded lettuce*

1. Preheat oven to 350° F. In a large skillet over medium-high heat, sauté onion in oil until soft (about 3 minutes). Add garlic, tomatoes, cilantro, and crabmeat. Cook for 5 minutes.

2. Wrap corn tortillas in aluminum foil and place in oven until heated (about 5 minutes). In a large bowl mix together lemon juice, bell pepper, cucumber, and lettuce. Place equal amounts of lettuce mixture on tortillas, then top with crab mixture. Serve immediately.

Serves 6.

Preparation time: 15 minutes
Cooking time: 15 minutes
Per serving: calcium 94 mg, calories 137, carbohydrates 18 g, cholesterol 51 mg, fat 2 g, fiber .9 g, protein 12 g, sodium 473 mg

GREEK SPINACH SALAD

Greek Spinach Salad is a refreshing dish on a hot summer day. Prepare the spinach ahead of time—wash and store in plastic bags. The cucumbers can be premarinated in the dressing, which gives them an additional zest. Feta cheese, an important ingredient in many Greek dishes, is added both to the greens and to the dressing. Pine nuts top the salad as a garnish. Serve with crusty French bread and chilled white wine.

  2 bunches spinach
  ½ cup thinly sliced red onion
  ½ cup peeled, seeded, and thinly sliced cucumbers
  ½ cup sliced radishes
  4 ounces feta cheese, crumbled
  1 teaspoon Dijon mustard
  2 tablespoons chopped parsley
  1 green onion, sliced
  1 tablespoon lemon juice
  1 teaspoon minced garlic
  2 tablespoons olive oil
  ¼ cup pine nuts, for garnish
  ¼ cup Greek olives, for garnish (optional)

1. Wash spinach, remove stems, and pat leaves dry, then tear into bite-size pieces. Place spinach in a salad bowl with red onion, cucumbers, radishes, and half of the feta.

2. In a blender purée remaining feta, mustard, parsley, green onion, lemon juice, garlic, and olive oil. Pour over salad. Garnish with pine nuts and Greek olives (if desired).

Serves 6.

Preparation time: 20 minutes
Per serving: calcium 116 mg, calories 111, carbohydrates 4 g, cholesterol 77 mg, fat 9 g, fiber .7 g, protein 4 g, sodium 236 mg

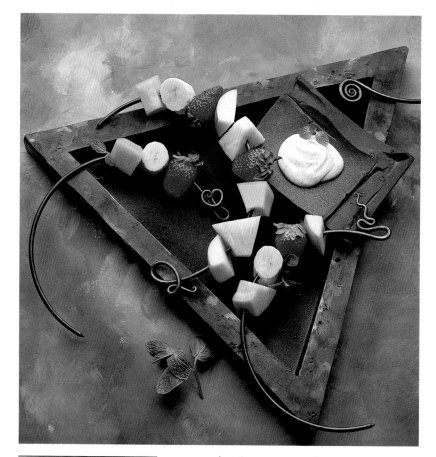

GOAT CHEESE AND SUN-DRIED TOMATO PÂTÉ

The full flavor of sun-dried tomatoes, available in gourmet stores, combines with goat cheese to make a delicious appetizer or picnic spread. For accompaniment, serve rounds of lightly toasted French bread. To reduce the calories in the spread drain the olive oil from the jarred sun-dried tomatoes.

  3 ounces jarred sun-dried tomatoes, drained and chopped
  4 ounces goat cheese
  ⅛ teaspoon dried thyme
  8 large slices fresh French bread
  2 teaspoons minced parsley

In a medium-sized bowl combine tomatoes, goat cheese, and thyme. Lightly toast French bread and spread with tomato mixture. Top with parsley and serve.

Serves 4.

Preparation time: 10 minutes
Per serving: calcium 141 mg, calories 284, carbohydrates 43 g, cholesterol 100 mg, fat 10 g, fiber 3.2 g, protein 8 g, sodium 462 mg

These tempting fruit kabobs are best made with fresh fruit in season and garnished with fresh mint leaves. The honey, nutmeg, and yogurt sauce is a sweet low-fat accompaniment.

23

DINING SOLO—HOW TO COOK HEALTHILY FOR ONE

Many single people prefer eating in busy restaurants to cooking and dining by themselves. Yet dining out may not be such a wise option if you consider the nutritional cost. Although an occasional restaurant meal may not break your bank account or your nutritional budget, eating out several times a week might make you think twice.

Dining at home can be the more reliable—and enjoyable—way to go, but it takes practice. If your meals at home are typically rushed, consumed between favorite television shows or social engagements, you can lose the nutritional benefits of home cooking.

Here are some plan-ahead tips from veteran solo diners to make your meals pleasant and health-enhancing.

☐ Buy small portions you can easily store. Many solo diners are overwhelmed by the amount of unused (and spoiling) perishables they seem to accumulate. Plan meals around fresh ingredients, such as seasonal produce and fresh fish, but give yourself a head start on menus. After shopping, store all your produce in lock-top plastic bags according to menu plans. For example, on Monday you can wash, chop, and store broccoli, carrots, and zucchini for a Thursday evening stir-fry, or you can prepare skinned chicken breasts and leave them marinating in low-sodium soy sauce and sherry, ready for baking on Tuesday.

☐ Occasionally treat yourself to something special. Consider fresh strawberries for dessert, a glass of good wine, asparagus in season, or jumbo prawns. Serve yourself as you would a favorite guest.

☐ Plan meals that take less than a half hour to make. Avoid complex recipes that will discourage you with lots of preparation and cleanup time. Plan a variety of meals, some light and easy, some more elegant and complex.

☐ Set an elegant table. Use attractive accoutrements such as tablecloths, place mats, candles, cloth napkins, and glass or china dinner plates. Play relaxing dinner music on the stereo. It does not take two to enjoy gracious dining.

☐ Recognize that on certain nights you are going to be too tired to cook. Plan ahead by making double portions of a gourmet menu and freezing half. On lazy or busy evenings, defrost the prepared meal and enjoy!

☐ Highlight some of the one-dish-meal recipes in this book. Try Stir-fry Prawns in Black Bean Sauce (see page 55) or Stewed Beef in Red Wine (see page 66). Make four servings and freeze three in individual lock-top plastic bags or containers. Plan to use these for future menus.

☐ Have salad ingredients on hand for easy, light meals. After a day spent dining with clients or at family feasts, you may want just a snack. Wash and spin-dry lettuce leaves, grate carrots and keep in lemon juice, have low-fat mozzarella cheese and sprouts ready in bags, and slice a few cherry tomatoes or radishes. A salad relaxes your digestive system, makes a convenient evening meal, and provides plenty of nutrient-rich foods with few calories.

TEMPEH OLIVE SPREAD

Tempeh comes from Javanese cuisine, where it is served in tempura and stir-fry dishes, and is skewered on shish-kabobs. It is abundant in B vitamins, low-fat protein, and calcium. Steaming the tempeh before using it neutralizes the yeasty flavor and softens it so that it absorbs spices. Tempeh looks like a thin block of textured cheese and is available in small packages in the frozen food sections of gourmet and health-food stores.

1 package (8 oz) tempeh
1 teaspoon safflower oil
2 tablespoons low-sodium tamari or soy sauce
3 tablespoons low-calorie mayonnaise
1 tablespoon minced green onion
¼ cup minced celery
2 tablespoons minced parsley
¼ cup pitted, chopped ripe olives
⅛ teaspoon cayenne pepper
⅛ teaspoon dried dill
Assorted whole wheat crackers or rice cakes

1. Cut tempeh into 1-inch squares. In a shallow pan fitted with a steamer basket, steam tempeh for 15 minutes. Drain and set aside.

2. In a medium-sized skillet heat safflower oil and lightly sauté steamed tempeh for 5 minutes, stirring frequently. Remove pan from heat and add tamari sauce, mixing with tempeh. Spoon contents of pan into a medium-sized mixing bowl.

3. Mash together tempeh, mayonnaise, green onion, celery, parsley, and olives into a thick spread. Add cayenne and dill. Serve at room temperature on whole wheat crackers.

Makes 2 cups, 8 servings.

Preparation time: 20 minutes
Cooking time: 20 minutes
Per serving: calcium 21 mg, calories 57, carbohydrates 3 g, cholesterol none, fat 5 g, fiber .5 g, protein 3 g, sodium 309 mg

HUMMUS IN PITA POCKETS

A traditional dish in Middle Eastern cuisine, Hummus is a healthy and very versatile hors d'oeuvre that combines sesame tahini and chick-peas to provide a good source of protein. Here, it is spread into whole wheat pita pockets and layered with chopped tomatoes, cucumbers, and lettuce. The pita sandwiches can be cut into wedges for snacks or appetizers or served with mugs of hot soup as a hearty lunch.

> 3 cups cooked, drained chick-peas
> 4 cloves garlic, minced
> 1 teaspoon low-sodium tamari or soy sauce
> ½ cup lemon juice
> ¾ cup tahini
> 2 tablespoons minced parsley
> 2 tablespoons minced red onion
> 2 tablespoons minced celery
> 1 cup coarsely chopped tomatoes
> 1 cup peeled, seeded, and coarsely chopped cucumber
> 2 teaspoons apple cider vinegar
> 3 teaspoons olive oil
> 2 large rounds whole wheat pita bread
> 2 cups shredded lettuce

1. In a food processor or blender, purée chick-peas, garlic, tamari sauce, lemon juice, and tahini until smooth. Set aside.

2. In a small bowl combine parsley, red onion, celery, tomatoes, cucumber, vinegar, and olive oil, and toss well. Let marinate at room temperature for 10 minutes.

3. Slice pita rounds in half. Open each half carefully and spread with hummus. Stuff with lettuce and marinated vegetables, including a small spoonful of the marinade. Serve immediately.

Serves 4.

> *Preparation time:* 25 minutes
> *Marinating time:* 10 minutes
> *Per serving:* calcium 138 mg, calories 570, carbohydrates 52 g, cholesterol 1 mg, fat 30 g, fiber 20 g, protein 24 g, sodium 460 mg

CHICKEN SATAY WITH CUCUMBER RELISH

Bite-sized chunks of marinated chicken are grilled on skewers, then served with a spicy relish made from cucumbers, garlic, and chile. The chicken, a healthy, low-fat alternative to beef kabobs, absorbs the lime juice marinade well. Both the chicken and the relish can be prepared ahead, and the meat grilled right before serving. Be sure to use rubber gloves to protect skin while preparing the fresh chile.

> 1 pound boned and skinned chicken breasts
> 1 teaspoon minced garlic
> ½ cup lime juice
> 1 tablespoon honey
> 1 tablespoon grated gingerroot
> 1 tablespoon grated lime rind

Cucumber Relish

> 1 cup peeled, seeded, and finely diced cucumber
> 1 teaspoon minced garlic
> 2 tablespoons minced cilantro
> ½ cup seeded, finely diced tomatoes
> 1 small jalapeño chile, seeded and minced
> 2 tablespoons rice vinegar

1. Cut chicken into 1-inch pieces and place in a large, shallow pan. In a small bowl mix together garlic, lime juice, honey, ginger, and rind. Pour over chicken and let marinate for 30 minutes, tossing frequently.

2. Preheat broiler or grill. Assemble chicken on short skewers. Broil or grill until browned (5 minutes). Serve immediately with Cucumber Relish.

Serves 4.

Cucumber Relish   Combine all ingredients in a bowl. Let marinate 15 minutes before serving.

Makes about 2 cups.

> *Preparation time:* 20 minutes
> *Marinating time:* 30 minutes
> *Cooking time:* 5 minutes
> *Per serving:* calcium 29 mg, calories 200, carbohydrates 10 g, cholesterol 76 mg, fat 6 g, fiber .6 g, protein 25 g, sodium 82 mg

SUPER BOWL GRAZING PARTY

Baked Artichoke Savories

Party Port and Cheddar Spread

Curried Stuffed Eggs

Hearty Beef and Barley Soup (see page 30)

Tossed Green Salad

Green Goddess Dressing (see page 41)

Apple-Apricot Pastries (see page 112)

Spiced Cider

The grazing party is ideal for a wintry Super Bowl Sunday. Various dishes are introduced at intervals throughout the game; by the end of the party, guests have eaten almost a full meal, but in stages. Start the pregame show with a platter of appetizers. At halftime, bring out the Hearty Beef and Barley Soup and a tossed green salad with Green Goddess Dressing. For postgame celebration (or condolences), pass around a plate of Apple-Apricot Pastries and mugs of hot cider spiked with cinnamon and vanilla. Menu serves 12.

BAKED ARTICHOKE SAVORIES

Guests will devour these rich-tasting, melt-in-your-mouth pastries, so make plenty. Use marinated artichokes for the best flavor, and low-fat cheeses for the best nutritional value. This recipe can be made up to three weeks ahead of time and frozen until ready to bake and serve.

> 2 tablespoons chopped onion
> 1 teaspoon pressed garlic
> ⅓ cup dry sherry
> 3 egg whites
> 1 whole egg
> ¼ cup whole wheat bread crumbs
> 3 tablespoons minced parsley
> ¼ teaspoon dried dill
> ⅛ teaspoon cayenne pepper
> 1 cup grated low-fat mozzarella cheese
> ½ cup low-fat ricotta cheese
> 10 ounces marinated artichoke hearts, drained and chopped

1. Preheat oven to 350° F. Lightly oil an 8-inch square baking pan.

2. In a heavy skillet over medium-high heat, sauté onion and garlic in sherry until soft but not browned. Lightly beat egg whites until soft peaks form. Spoon into a bowl and mix with whole egg, bread crumbs, parsley, dill, cayenne, cheeses, and artichokes. Add sautéed onion and garlic. Pour into oiled baking pan.

3. Bake until set (about 30 minutes). Let cool, then cut into about 25 squares. Serve warm or cold.

Serves 12.

> *Preparation time:* 20 minutes
> *Baking time:* 30 minutes
> *Per serving:* calcium 83 mg, calories 82, carbohydrates 5 g, cholesterol 34 mg, fat 4 g, fiber .35 g, protein 6 g, sodium 87 mg

PARTY PORT AND CHEDDAR SPREAD

This wine-rich cheese spread can be served in a variety of ways: Spread it on celery or cucumber boats; roll it into a large ball, cover with crushed pecans, and chill in wax paper until ready to serve; pack it into raw mushroom caps; or layer on rye crackers. The spread will keep for up to two weeks if refrigerated, and the wine flavor will deepen.

> ½ pound low-fat Cheddar cheese, grated
> ⅓ cup port wine
> 1 round loaf French bread

1. Place cheese and port into a food processor or large bowl, and blend together until smooth.

2. Cut the top third off the round of French bread. Scoop out interior of bread and pack cheese into hollow loaf. Smooth top with a spatula.

3. Cover loaf with plastic wrap and refrigerate for 1 hour. Serve with crackers or chunks of French bread.

Serves 12.

> *Preparation time:* 15 minutes
> *Chilling time:* 1 hour
> *Per serving:* calcium 113 mg, calories 94, carbohydrates 13 g, cholesterol 4 mg, fat 2 g, fiber 1.2 g, protein 6 g, sodium 345 mg

CURRIED STUFFED EGGS

For a healthier version of deviled eggs, use less mayonnaise and other high-fat ingredients and more seasonings. The filling for this recipe is a mixture of chopped spinach and parsley seasoned with curry. The stuffed eggs can be made up to three hours ahead of time if tightly covered with plastic wrap and refrigerated. Garnish with paprika and minced chives for a colorful presentation.

> 12 hard-cooked eggs
> Lettuce leaves, for lining platter
> 2 tablespoons curry powder
> ¾ cup low-calorie mayonnaise
> 2 tablespoons minced parsley
> 2 tablespoons minced spinach
> 1 tablespoon Dijon mustard
> Dill sprigs or chives, and paprika, for garnish

1. Peel eggs and halve lengthwise, remove yolks from whites, and place halved egg whites on bed of lettuce arranged on a platter. In a mixing bowl mash egg yolks with curry powder, mayonnaise, parsley, spinach, and mustard until smooth.

2. Spoon or pipe this filling into egg-white halves. Garnish with dill sprigs and paprika. Cover carefully with plastic wrap and chill for 15 minutes before serving.

Serves 12.

> *Preparation time:* 15 minutes
> *Cooking time:* 15 minutes
> *Per serving:* calcium 37 mg, calories 135, carbohydrates 1 g, cholesterol 253 mg, fat 11 g, fiber .2 g, protein 6 g, sodium 177 mg

A hearty, yet healthy menu for Super Bowl Sunday features a variety of appetizers, a satisfying beef and barley soup, and zesty apricot pastries.

For Avocado and Pine Nut Salad (see page 39), chicken and small chunks of avocado marinate with grapefruit in a ginger-tamari dressing.

Soups & Salads

Most health experts recommend eating plenty of homemade soups and fresh salads. In addition to several unusual, nutritious soup recipes, this chapter contains recipes for homemade stocks and soup bases that you can make ahead. Many of the soups are hearty enough for a full meal (see Minnesota Chicken and Wild Rice Soup, page 31); others are ideal for entertaining (see Summer Curried Pea Soup, page 33). Eye-catching salads include Jamaican Papaya Salad (see page 35) and an unusual Caesar salad with homemade croutons (see Tom's Caesar Salad, page 39). Many healthy salad dressings to mix and match with the salads complete the chapter.

FULL-MEAL SOUPS

These soups can be hearty dinners when paired with crusty bread and a green salad. All of these soups can be made ahead and, in fact, taste better after a night in the refrigerator.

CANADIAN CHEESE SOUP

Perfect for cold weather, this rich soup combines minced fresh vegetables with a stock flavored with wine and cheese.

- ¼ cup minced onion
- 1 teaspoon unsalted butter or safflower oil
- 2 tablespoons white wine
- ¼ cup minced celery
- ¼ cup minced carrot
- ¼ cup whole wheat pastry or white unbleached flour
- 2 cups nonfat milk
- 1½ cups defatted Chicken Stock (see page 31)
- ½ cup grated farmer's cheese
  Paprika and minced green onions, for garnish

1. In a heavy stockpot over medium-high heat, sauté onion in butter and wine until soft (about 3 minutes). Add celery and carrot and continue to cook for 5 minutes.

2. Stir in flour. Lower heat to medium and continue to cook, stirring frequently, for 2 more minutes. Pour in milk and stock, and bring soup to a boil.

3. Simmer soup, uncovered, on medium-high heat for 10 minutes. Right before serving, stir in cheese.

4. Ladle soup into prewarmed bowls and garnish with a dusting of paprika and a sprinkling of green onions.

Makes 6 cups, 6 servings.

Preparation time: 15 minutes
Cooking time: 20 minutes
Per serving: calcium 174 mg, calories 86, carbohydrates 10 g, cholesterol 3 mg, fat 2 g, fiber 3 g, protein 7 g, sodium 313 mg

HEARTY BEEF AND BARLEY SOUP

This thick soup can feed an army of hungry friends and family. Its rich aroma will entice even the finicky eater. Chunks of lean stew meat are seared in olive oil and cooked slowly with vegetables and potassium-rich barley, seasoned with garlic, bay leaf, and basil. A meal in itself, this soup can easily become your favorite Sunday night supper. It freezes well, so make a double batch and save half.

- ⅓ cup whole wheat flour
- 1 teaspoon herbal salt substitute
- 1 pound lean stew meat, cut into 1-inch chunks
- 2 tablespoons olive oil
- 1 cup chopped onion
- 1 tablespoon minced garlic
- ½ cup grated carrots
- ½ cup chopped celery
- 1 cup diced tomato
- 1 cup barley
- 5 cups defatted Chicken Stock or Veal Stock (see page 31)
- 2 tablespoons basil
- 1 bay leaf
  Herbal salt substitute and freshly ground pepper, to taste

1. In a shallow bowl combine flour and salt substitute. Dredge chunks of meat in flour mixture.

2. In a large stockpot over medium-high heat, quickly brown chunks of meat in hot oil. Add onions and garlic and cook until soft (3 to 5 minutes). Add carrots, celery, and tomato and continue cooking for 5 minutes.

3. Add barley, stock, and basil, and bring to a boil. Crush bay leaf and wrap in piece of cheesecloth or place into a tea ball. Add to soup. Lower heat to simmer and cook until barley is soft (20 to 25 minutes). Season to taste with salt substitute and pepper. Remove bay leaf before serving.

Makes 8 cups, 8 servings.

Preparation time: 15 minutes
Cooking time: 35 minutes
Per serving: calcium 52 mg, calories 281, carbohydrates 27 g, cholesterol 30 mg, fat 10 g, fiber 1 g, protein 19 g, sodium 173 mg

SWISS LENTIL SOUP

In this soup, the rich miso broth combines beautifully with the lentils, chopped tomatoes, and Swiss cheese. It has an aroma and dark flavor that work well in a European menu—perhaps with a caraway-studded rye bread, Balkan Cold Cucumber Salad (see page 36), and a frosty mug of German beer. Because the flavors need time to blend, let this soup sit overnight, if possible, before serving.

- 1½ cups chopped onions
- 1 teaspoon safflower oil
- ⅓ cup dry white wine
- 1 cup julienned carrots
- 2 cups chopped tomatoes
- ½ teaspoon dried thyme
- ½ teaspoon dried marjoram
- 1 cup washed, uncooked lentils
- 3 cups defatted Chicken Stock or Veal Stock (see page 31)
- 3 tablespoons miso, dissolved in ⅓ cup hot water
- ½ cup grated Swiss cheese
  Grated carrots and chopped green onions, for garnish

1. In a large stockpot over medium-high heat, sauté onions in oil and wine until soft but not browned. Add carrots, tomatoes, thyme, and marjoram, and continue to cook, stirring frequently, for 10 minutes.

2. Add lentils and cook for 2 more minutes. Add stock and bring to a boil. Lower heat to simmer and cook, covered, until lentils are soft (about 30 minutes).

3. Before serving, remove pot from heat and stir in miso. To serve, add about 2 tablespoons grated cheese to the bottom of each bowl and ladle soup on top. Garnish with grated carrots and chopped green onions.

Makes 6 cups, 6 servings.

Preparation time: 20 minutes
Cooking time: 45 minutes
Per serving: calcium 137 mg, calories 147, carbohydrates 18 g, cholesterol 11 mg, fat 3 g, fiber 2.11 g, protein 10 g, sodium 455 mg

MINNESOTA CHICKEN AND WILD RICE SOUP

Living in a state famous for blue lakes and blue skies, Minnesotans enjoy yearly harvests of vitamin-rich wild rice--the meaty, chewy grain that grows in the northern lake country. This rich soup combines a hearty chicken broth studded with vegetables, chunks of white-meat chicken, and rice. Accompany each serving with French bread and a green salad for a delicious luncheon.

½ cup chopped onion
2 teaspoons olive oil
¼ cup dry sherry
½ cup chopped celery
½ cup chopped carrot
½ cup chopped spinach
2 cups diced, cooked chicken, skin removed
1 cup wild rice
5 cups defatted Chicken Stock (see page 31)
½ teaspoon dried thyme
½ teaspoon dried marjoram
Pinch of ground ginger
⅛ teaspoon cumin
Herbal salt substitute and pepper, to taste
2 tablespoons low-sodium soy or tamari sauce

1. In a large stockpot over medium-high heat, sauté onion in oil and sherry until soft but not browned. Add celery, carrots, and spinach, and continue cooking for 5 minutes, stirring frequently.

2. Add chicken, wild rice, stock, thyme, marjoram, ginger, and cumin, and bring to a boil. Lower heat, cover, and simmer until rice is tender (30 to 35 minutes). Before serving add salt substitute and pepper to taste, and soy sauce.

Makes 11 cups, 8 servings.

Preparation time: 15 minutes
Cooking time: 40 to 45 minutes
Per serving: calcium 45 mg, calories 203, carbohydrates 22 g, cholesterol 32 mg, fat 4 g, fiber .8 g, protein 17 g, sodium 404 mg

Basics

HOMEMADE STOCKS AND INSTANT SOUP BASES

Regardless of the base—beef, veal, fish, vegetable, or chicken—do not boil the stock. Instead, simmer slowly. Boiling stock brings out acids and may also increase bitter tastes in vegetables and other bases.

BEEF OR VEAL STOCK

This hearty stock can be refrigerated, covered, for up to four days, and frozen for up to three months.

3 pounds beef or veal bones
1 teaspoon safflower oil
Water, to cover
1 stalk celery
1 onion, quartered
1 bay leaf
1 carrot

In a stockpot brown the bones in 1 teaspoon safflower oil. Then add remaining ingredients, simmer 3 hours, and strain.

Makes 4 cups.

FISH STOCK

Fish stock can be refrigerated, covered, for up to five days, and frozen for up to two months.

2 pounds fishtails, fish heads, shells from shrimp, or fish bones
Water, to cover
1 stalk celery
1 onion, quartered
1 bay leaf
1 carrot

In a large stockpot combine all ingredients; simmer 1½ hours and then strain.

Makes 4 to 6 cups.

VEGETARIAN STOCK

Vegetarian stock can be refrigerated, covered, for up to 10 days, or frozen for up to five months. The best vegetables to use are the ones with the richest flavors, such as tomatoes, mushrooms, onions, potatoes, and winter squash. Avoid using cucumbers, lettuce, spinach, bell peppers, and beet or carrot greens; they will give the stock an unpleasant flavor. For extra nutrition and stronger stock, replace the water with leftover liquid from steamed vegetables or cooked beans.

1 cup vegetable of choice
4 cups water
Herbal salt substitute and pepper, to taste

In a stockpot combine ingredients; simmer over low heat for 2 hours, then strain. Season with herbal salt substitute and pepper.

Makes 4 cups.

CHICKEN STOCK

This healthy chicken stock, even better than Momma used to make, can be refrigerated, covered, for up to six days and frozen for up to two months (see Note).

2 pounds chicken bones, back, and neck
Water, to cover
1 stalk celery
1 onion, quartered
1 bay leaf
1 carrot

In a large stockpot combine chicken bones, back, and neck and the water. Add celery, onion, bay leaf, and carrot. Simmer over low heat 1½ hours. Strain.

Makes 4 to 6 cups.

Note To remove fat: Allow stock to chill for 2 hours. Fat will separate and rise to the top. Scoop fat off with spoon and discard. Remaining stock may be used in recipes calling for defatted chicken stock.

Artfully combining the pungency of capers with savory sautéed vegetables and chunks of white cod, this hearty fish soup makes an easy meal for a Sunday night supper.

FISH SOUP WITH CAPERS AND ONIONS

Sometimes called by its Russian name, *solyanka,* this soup uses a fresh or thawed, frozen whitefish, such as halibut, cod, or flounder, for the base. Serve with a dark bread, such as rye or pumpernickel.

    2   cups minced onion
    2   tablespoons unsalted butter
        or safflower oil
    ⅔   cup minced celery
    ⅔   cup minced carrots
    2   large tomatoes, seeded and
        cut into thin strips
    1   cup dry white wine
    1½ pounds whitefish, bones
        removed
    1   cup peeled, seeded, and
        sliced cucumber
    4   cups water
    2   tablespoons capers, drained
    2   tablespoons minced sour
        gherkin pickles
    1   to 2 tablespoons lemon juice,
        to taste
        Herbal salt substitute and
        pepper, to taste
        Minced parsley, for garnish

1. In a large stockpot over medium-high heat, sauté onion in butter until soft but not browned. Add celery, carrots, tomatoes, and wine. Continue to cook for 5 minutes.

2. Add fish and cucumber. Cook for 3 to 4 minutes, then add the water. Bring to a boil. Lower heat and simmer until fish flakes (about 15 minutes). Add capers, pickles, lemon juice, and salt substitute and pepper to taste. Serve garnished with minced parsley.

Makes 11 cups, 8 servings.

Preparation time: 20 minutes
Cooking time: 30 minutes
Per serving: calcium 44 mg, calories 177, carbohydrates 10 g, cholesterol 27 mg, fat 6 g, fiber 1 g, protein 16 g, sodium 184 mg

SEASONAL SOUPS

Using fresh ingredients in soups is always a healthy idea. This is easy in summer, when produce is abundant. In winter, soups can be made with hearty cold-weather vegetables, beans, and grains.

SUMMER CURRIED PEA SOUP

Of Indian origin, Summer Curried Pea Soup is a brightly colored mixture of yellow and green, an ideal prelude to spicy entrées such as Indonesian Tempura (see page 52).

> 1 cup chopped onion
> 2 teaspoons dark sesame oil
> ¼ cup dry sherry
> 1 tablespoon minced garlic
> 1 tablespoon curry powder
> ½ cup chopped carrots
> 3 cups peas, fresh or frozen
> 2 tablespoons whole wheat pastry or unbleached white flour
> 3 cups defatted Chicken Stock (see page 31)
> Herbal salt substitute and ground pepper, to taste
> Minced green onion and plain nonfat yogurt, for garnish

1. In a heavy stockpot over medium-high heat, sauté onion in oil and sherry until soft (8 to 10 minutes). Add garlic, curry powder, carrot, and peas, and continue to cook, stirring frequently, for 5 minutes.

2. Add flour and cook for 2 minutes, stirring constantly. Do not let flour brown. Add stock and bring to a boil.

3. Lower heat and simmer soup, uncovered, for 10 to 12 minutes. Purée half the soup at a time, and then return to pot. Heat through. Adjust seasonings if needed, and serve hot, garnished with green onions and nonfat yogurt.

Makes 6 cups, 6 servings.

> *Preparation time:* 25 minutes
> *Cooking time:* 30 minutes
> *Per serving:* calcium 42 mg,
> calories 122, carbohydrates 17 g,
> cholesterol none, fat 2 g, fiber
> 3.7 g, protein 7 g, sodium 200 mg

FRENCH SPRING GARDEN POTAGE

A delicate and simple soup, French Spring Garden Potage reflects the harvests of the spring garden—fresh herbs, tomatoes, green onions, and peas. For the best flavor, make the soup early in the day and let it sit for several hours before serving.

> 1 cup minced green onions, including green tops
> 1 teaspoon olive oil
> ½ cup diced carrots
> ½ cup diced turnips
> ½ cup string beans, sliced diagonally into ½-inch lengths
> ½ cup chopped tomatoes
> ½ cup shelled peas
> 3 tablespoons minced parsley
> 1 teaspoon chopped fresh mint
> 1 teaspoon light honey
> ¼ teaspoon ground cloves
> 6 cups defatted Chicken Stock or Vegetarian Stock (see page 31)
> Herbal salt substitute and pepper, to taste
> Nonfat plain yogurt, for garnish

1. In a heavy stockpot over medium-high heat, sauté green onions in olive oil until bright colored and soft (4 to 5 minutes). Add carrots, turnips, beans, and tomatoes, and continue to cook for 8 minutes.

2. Add peas, parsley, mint, honey, cloves, and stock, and bring to a boil. Lower heat to simmer and cook for 15 more minutes. Taste for seasoning and add salt substitute and pepper to taste. Serve hot or chilled, garnished with a dollop of yogurt.

Makes 10 cups, 8 servings.

> *Preparation time:* 25 minutes
> *Cooking time:* 30 minutes
> *Per serving:* calcium 38 mg,
> calories 44, carbohydrates 5 g,
> cholesterol none, fat 1 g, fiber
> 1.4 g, protein 4 g, sodium 171 mg

UKRAINIAN SUMMER CUCUMBER AND LEMON BORSCHT

In the Ukraine, the bread basket of the Soviet Union, borscht is considered a great way to utilize abundant summer garden crops—even in this unusual beetless version. The yogurt provides calcium and, when combined with the cucumber, gives the soup a pleasant sweet-and-sour flavor. Try to use bottled water (tap water may flavor this uncooked soup too heavily). Serve the soup as an elegant first course before a fish entrée or a light veal dish such as Veal and Apple Scaloppine (see page 69).

> 4 cups peeled, seeded, and coarsely chopped cucumbers
> Juice of 2 small lemons
> 1 teaspoon herbal salt substitute or sea salt
> 1 tablespoon honey
> 1 cup nonfat plain yogurt
> 1 cup spring water or water that has been boiled and cooled
> 1 cup minced turkey ham
> 1 large tomato, chopped
> Herbal salt substitute and white pepper, to taste
> Fresh dill sprigs and sour cream, for garnish

1. Place cucumbers, lemon juice, salt substitute, honey, yogurt, and the water into a blender and purée until very smooth. Add minced ham. Pour soup into a large bowl, cover with plastic wrap, and refrigerate overnight (8 to 12 hours).

2. In the morning, purée tomato and add to soup. Taste for seasonings and add more salt substitute and pepper if needed. Serve soup in chilled bowls with a garnish of fresh dill and a dollop of sour cream.

Makes 6 cups, 6 servings.

> *Preparation time:* 20 minutes
> *Chilling time:* 8 to 12 hours
> *Per serving:* calcium 95 mg,
> calories 83, carbohydrates 11 g,
> cholesterol none, fat 1 g, fiber
> .5 g, protein 7 g, sodium 618 mg

MIDWESTERN CORN CHOWDER

Corn chowder is ideal for late summer or early fall parties in the backyard, especially in the Midwest corn belt. To lower the calories in the soup, nonfat milk and potato purée replace the rich cream base used in traditional recipes. This soup freezes beautifully, so make a double batch, especially when corn is at its peak.

      ¾ cup chopped onion
      1 teaspoon unsalted butter
      ¼ cup dry sherry
      1 cup chopped celery
      2 cups diced red potatoes
      1 bay leaf
      2 cups defatted Chicken Stock
         or Vegetarian Stock
         (see page 31)
      2 cups chopped tomatoes
    1½ cups corn kernels
    1½ cups nonfat milk
      ½ cup chopped parsley
         Ground pepper (optional)

1. In a large stockpot over medium-high heat, sauté onion in butter and sherry until soft but not browned. Add celery and potatoes and sauté for 2 minutes. Crush bay leaf and wrap in cheesecloth or place in a tea ball. Add stock and bay leaf to soup, and bring to a boil.

2. Lower heat to simmer and cook, covered, until potatoes are tender (20 minutes). Remove bay leaf and discard. Place 2 cups of the soup in a blender and purée. Return to pot. Add tomatoes, corn, and milk, and bring to a boil again. Lower heat and simmer for 5 minutes. Add parsley, taste for seasoning, and add pepper (if desired.)

Makes 10 cups, 8 servings.

> *Preparation time:* 15 to 20 minutes
> *Cooking time:* 35 to 40 minutes
> *Per serving:* calcium 87 mg, calories 111, carbohydrates 19 g, cholesterol 3 mg, fat 1 g, fiber 2.1 g, protein 6 g, sodium 96 mg

DOROTHY'S HEARTY HAM AND LIMA BEAN SOUP

Inspired by a recipe in *Gourmet* magazine, this winter soup combines the salty flavor of turkey ham with sautéed carrots, baby lima beans, and green onions. Make the soup the day before serving and keep it overnight in the refrigerator—the flavors blend and deepen as the soup sits. Serve with toasted halves of pita bread and a tossed green salad.

    1½ cups chopped onion
      1 cup thinly sliced carrots
      4 tablespoons unsalted butter
      1 tablespoon garlic powder
      1 teaspoon herbal salt substitute
      2 tablespoons lemon juice
      2 cups diced turkey ham
      1 package (10 oz) frozen baby
         lima beans
      1 tablespoon dried marjoram
      ½ cup chopped parsley
      4 cups water
         Croutons, for garnish
         (optional)

1. In a heavy stockpot over medium-high heat, sauté onion and carrots in butter for 5 minutes. Add garlic powder, salt substitute, and lemon juice. Cook until onions are soft (about 5 minutes). Add turkey ham, lima beans, marjoram, parsley, and water.

2. Bring soup to a boil, then lower heat to simmer and cook for 20 minutes, covered, stirring occasionally. Serve hot, garnished with croutons (if desired).

Makes 8 cups, 8 servings.

> *Preparation time:* 30 minutes
> *Cooking time:* 30 minutes
> *Per serving:* calcium 50 mg, calories 164, carbohydrates 13 g, cholesterol 19 mg, fat 8 g, fiber 2.5 g, protein 10 g, sodium 360 mg

LIGHT AND EASY SALADS

Many health professionals recommend eating one or two vegetable or fruit salads a day for a good source of fiber, enzymes, vitamins, and minerals. This suggestion is easy to follow with the tempting array of international salads in this section.

TUNA, POTATO, AND GREEN BEAN SALAD NIÇOISE

The Mediterranean coast is the birthplace of many simple and healthy salads. This version of the traditional favorite from Nice combines chunks of low-fat, water-packed tuna, cooked marinated red potatoes, and blanched green beans. Strips of red bell pepper or a few Greek olives make a good garnish.

      2 cups diced red potatoes,
         skins intact
      ⅓ cup Greek olives, pitted
      3 tablespoons olive oil
    1½ tablespoons apple cider
         vinegar
      1 teaspoon herbal salt substitute
      ¼ teaspoon ground pepper
      1 head lettuce
      4 ounces water-packed tuna,
         drained
      1 cup diagonally cut
         green beans
      1 cup sliced red bell pepper

1. In a large pot steam potatoes until tender. Place olives, olive oil, cider vinegar, salt substitute, and pepper in a blender and purée. Pour over potatoes and let marinate 40 minutes.

2. Wash and dry lettuce and arrange on a platter. Toss tuna, beans, and bell pepper with potatoes and marinade, then spoon over lettuce. Serve at room temperature.

Serves 4.

> *Preparation time:* 20 minutes
> *Cooking time:* 40 minutes
> *Per serving:* calcium 91 mg, calories 286, carbohydrates 26 g, cholesterol 18 mg, fat 18 g, fiber 7.7 g, protein 11 g, sodium 361 mg

JAMAICAN PAPAYA SALAD

This salad features fresh papaya, watercress, and hearts of palm and is topped with chopped cilantro, lime juice, and a few slices of avocado—used sparingly due to its high fat content. A slightly sweet white wine, such as a Riesling, complements the salad.

    1 cup watercress
    2 cups peeled, seeded, and thinly
       sliced papaya
  ¼ cup thinly sliced avocado
    1 cup canned hearts of palm,
       drained and sliced
    1 cup thinly sliced tomato
    2 tablespoons lime juice
    2 tablespoons chopped cilantro
  ¼ teaspoon herbal salt substitute
  ⅛ teaspoon ground coriander
  ⅛ teaspoon allspice

1. Arrange watercress on 4 small salad plates. Layer slices of papaya, avocado, hearts of palm, and tomato on top.

2. Stir together lime juice, cilantro, salt substitute, coriander, and allspice. Drizzle over papaya salads. Cover with plastic wrap and chill 30 minutes before serving.

Serves 4.

Preparation time: 20 minutes
Chilling time: 30 minutes
Per serving: calcium 41 mg, calories 87, carbohydrates 19 g, cholesterol none, fat 2 g, fiber 2 g, protein 2 g, sodium 148 mg

You can almost hear the steel drums and the beat of the Caribbean in this savory Jamaican salad. As a bonus, the dish contains only 87 calories per serving and no cholesterol.

MINTED BULGUR SALAD

A lively variation on tabbouleh—the Middle Eastern salad made of fiber-rich cracked wheat, lemon juice, and parsley—this bulgur salad adds fresh mint, cucumber, and carrot, creating an excellent picnic or casual supper dish. It can be made the day before; cover tightly with plastic wrap and refrigerate after tossing the dressing with the vegetables and wheat. This salad is a good accompaniment to Grilled Lamb and Vegetable Medley (see page 70).

    1 cup bulgur
    1½ cups boiling water
    2 cups shredded green cabbage
    ½ cup grated carrot
    ½ cup peeled and diced cucumber
    ⅓ cup diced celery
    1 cup chopped parsley
    ½ cup chopped fresh mint
    2 cups chopped tomatoes
    ¾ cup chopped green onions
    ¼ cup lemon juice
    2 tablespoons olive oil

1. Place bulgur in a medium-sized bowl. Pour the boiling water over bulgur and cover with plastic wrap. Let sit until all water has been absorbed (about 15 minutes).

2. In a large salad bowl, combine cabbage, carrot, cucumber, celery, and parsley. Add cooked bulgur.

3. Blend mint, tomatoes, green onions, lemon juice, and olive oil until smooth, then toss with salad. Let marinate for 30 minutes before serving.

Serves 4.

Preparation time: 30 minutes
Cooking time: 30 minutes
Per serving: calcium 102 mg, calories 277, carbohydrates 45 g, cholesterol none, fat 8 g, fiber 4 g, protein 9 g, sodium 549 mg

---

SPICY CHINESE POTATO SALAD

Here is a potato salad that will certainly wake up your taste buds. It combines cooked chunks of red potatoes, red bell pepper, and celery with a spicy Chinese dressing of rice vinegar, sesame oil, and gingerroot. The dressing can be made up to five days ahead of time and refrigerated until needed. Plan enough time to chill the potatoes after cooking. Spicy Chinese Potato Salad is a good choice for a picnic potluck, or it can be served with a light beef entrée such as Stir-fried Beef With Asparagus and Snow Peas (see page 67).

    3 cups cubed red potatoes, skin intact
    ¾ cup minced red bell pepper
    ½ cup minced celery
    ¼ cup finely chopped green onions
    ¼ cup rice wine vinegar
    2 tablespoons dark sesame oil
    1 teaspoon grated gingerroot
    1 teaspoon honey
    1 tablespoon lemon juice
    1 tablespoon hoisin sauce
    ¼ teaspoon cayenne pepper or more, to taste

1. In a large pot over medium-high heat, cook potatoes until tender (about 20 minutes). Drain and chill for 20 minutes.

2. In a salad bowl combine red bell pepper, celery, green onions, vinegar, oil, gingerroot, honey, lemon juice, hoisin sauce, and cayenne. Add chilled potatoes and toss well. Cover with plastic wrap and set aside to marinate at room temperature for 20 minutes more. Serve at room temperature.

Serves 4.

Preparation time: 25 minutes
Cooking time: 20 minutes
Chilling time: 20 minutes
Marinating time: 20 minutes
Per serving: calcium 46 mg, calories 208, carbohydrates 30 g, cholesterol none, fat 10 g, fiber 5.7 g, protein 4 g, sodium 356 mg

---

BALKAN COLD CUCUMBER SALAD

Most often served on spinach leaves, Balkan Cold Cucumber Salad is an ideal first course to a fish or chicken dinner. It can also be made ahead, and will keep three to four days in the refrigerator. Paired with a slice or two of pumpernickel bread and Salmon Spread (see page 20), it makes a quick and healthy lunch.

    3 cups peeled, seeded, and thinly sliced cucumbers
    2 teaspoons sea salt
    3 hard-cooked eggs
    1 teaspoon Dijon mustard
    ½ cup nonfat plain yogurt
    1 teaspoon honey
    1 tablespoon apple cider vinegar
    1 bunch spinach
    Fresh dill sprigs for garnish

1. Cut cucumber slices into half-moon shapes. Place cucumbers in a large bowl with sea salt. Toss well. Let marinate at room temperature for 30 minutes. Rinse well to remove salt.

2. Slice eggs in half. Separate yolks and whites. Chop whites and set aside. Mash egg yolks with mustard, yogurt, honey, and vinegar.

3. Toss together cucumbers, egg whites, and egg-yolk mixture. Wash spinach and remove stems. Arrange on 4 salad plates. Spoon cucumber salad on top. Garnish with dill sprigs. Serve at room temperature.

Serves 4.

Preparation time: 25 minutes
Cooking time: 30 minutes
Per serving: calcium 109 mg, calories 96, carbohydrates 7 g, cholesterol 187 mg, fat 4 g, fiber .6 g, protein 7 g, sodium 94 mg

---

CURRIED PRAWN AND PASTA SALAD

Cooked prawns are tossed with *rotelle* (spiral) pasta and a curried low-calorie mayonnaise dressing and garnished with chopped, toasted almonds. This seafood salad keeps well for three days and is best served chilled on a bed of lettuce leaves or spinach.

   1 *pound medium prawns, peeled and deveined*
  ⅔ *cup white wine*
  2 *cups rotelle pasta*
  ¼ *teaspoon pepper*
  ½ *cup minced celery*
  ½ *cup low-calorie mayonnaise*
  1 *teaspoon lemon juice*
  2 *teaspoons curry powder*
     Lettuce leaves, for lining platter or salad plates
  1 *tablespoon chopped, toasted almonds*

1. In a small saucepan over medium-high heat, place prawns and wine, and cook until prawns turn pink (about 2 minutes). Remove prawns and cut in half. Discard wine.

2. Cook pasta until al dente (about 8 minutes). Drain and refresh under cold water. In a large bowl mix pasta with cooked prawns, pepper, celery, mayonnaise, lemon juice, and curry powder. Chill 20 minutes. Arrange on a bed of lettuce and garnish with almonds.

Serves 4.

Preparation time: 20 minutes
Chilling time: 20 minutes
Per serving: calcium 92 mg, calories 308, carbohydrates 23 g, cholesterol 81 mg, fat 12 g, fiber .4 g, protein 18 g, sodium 389 mg

When tossed with the low-calorie curry dressing, the spirals of pasta form a bright yellow background for the pink prawns.

Grated beets, carrots, and turnips are sprinkled with a delicate dressing flavored with Dijon mustard.

SPICY TOMATO ASPIC

A family favorite in the South, this molded aspic is standard on many dinner tables in the summer when tomatoes are at their peak. Besides being a good source of vitamin C, juice from vine-ripened tomatoes is rich in minerals. Serve this salad with a chicken or beef entrée for a delicious luncheon. Allow plenty of chilling time—the salad must be refrigerated for at least two hours to completely set.

> 3 cups tomato juice or
>   tomato-vegetable juice
> 2 teaspoons Worcestershire sauce
> 1 package unflavored gelatin
>   or ¼ cup agar flakes
> ½ cup minced celery
> ½ cup corn kernels
> ½ cup low-calorie mayonnaise
>   Lettuce leaves, for lining
>   platter

1. In a large pot, place tomato juice, Worcestershire sauce, gelatin, celery, corn, and mayonnaise. Whisk to blend mayonnaise into tomato juice. Bring to a boil and cook over medium heat for 3 minutes, whisking constantly.

2. Remove from heat and pour into a 5-cup decorative mold or bowl. Let chill for 2 hours or until set. Line a platter with lettuce leaves.

3. To unmold, dip mold or bowl into warm water to loosen aspic and invert it over platter.

Serves 6.

Preparation time: 20 minutes
Cooking time: 2 hours
Per serving: calcium 48 mg, calories 116, carbohydrates 10 g, cholesterol 1 mg, fat 7 g, fiber 1.2 g, protein 2 g, sodium 497 mg

GRATED VEGETABLE SALAD WITH MUSTARD VINAIGRETTE

In this visually stimulating dish, a trio of grated raw vegetables—carrots, turnips, and beets—is arranged on a bed of greens. The vinaigrette balances the sweetness of the vegetables, combining Dijon mustard with lemon juice and garlic. You can make the salad and the dressing ahead of time, but be sure to toss the vegetables with lemon juice to prevent browning.

- *1 large carrot*
- *1 small turnip*
- *1 Jerusalem artichoke*
- *1 large beet*
- *1 head lettuce*
- *Juice of ½ small lemon*
- *2 teaspoons Dijon mustard*
- *1 teaspoon lime juice*
- *2 teaspoons minced garlic*
- *1 tablespoon apple cider vinegar*
- *½ teaspoon pepper*
- *2 teaspoons herbal salt substitute*
- *2 teaspoons safflower oil*
- *2 tablespoons olive oil*

1. Grate carrot, turnip, Jerusalem artichoke, and beet, keeping them separated. Wash lettuce and arrange on 4 small salad plates. Spoon grated vegetables on top of lettuce. Sprinkle with fresh lemon juice.

2. Mix together mustard, lime juice, garlic, vinegar, pepper, salt substitute, and oils. Drizzle over grated vegetables. Serve extra dressing in a sauceboat or cruet.

Serves 4.

Preparation time: 25 minutes
Per serving: calcium 26 mg, calories 133, carbohydrates 11 g, cholesterol none, fat 10 g, fiber 1.4 g, protein 1 g, sodium 100 mg

AVOCADO AND PINE NUT SALAD

Adapted from the version served in a famous Los Angeles restaurant, this recipe alters the dressing ingredients to decrease fat and salt. Avocados, normally a high-fat addition to any salad, are used here in light quantity. Cook the chicken well in advance and, if possible, allow it to marinate in the dressing. The interesting contrast of flavors—the piquant pink grapefruit sections and the savory sesame oil–gingerroot dressing—will make this dish a favorite in your entertaining repertoire.

- *1 head lettuce*
- *½ cup diced avocado*
- *1 large pink grapefruit, peeled and sectioned*
- *¼ cup toasted pine nuts*
- *1 cup cooked white-meat chicken*
- *½ cup rice vinegar*
- *⅓ cup honey*
- *1 tablespoon low-sodium tamari or soy sauce*
- *1 tablespoon grated gingerroot*
- *1 tablespoon dark sesame oil*
- *1 teaspoon herbal salt substitute*

1. Wash and dry lettuce, then tear into bite-sized pieces. Place in a large salad bowl. Add avocado, grapefruit sections, pine nuts, and chicken.

2. Toss together vinegar, honey, tamari sauce, gingerroot, oil, and salt substitute. Pour over salad and mix well. Serve immediately.

Serves 6.

Preparation time: 25 minutes
Per serving: calcium 16 mg, calories 181, carbohydrates 21 g, cholesterol 21 mg, fat 9 g, fiber 1.4 g, protein 9 g, sodium 174 mg

TOM'S CAESAR SALAD

This easy Caesar salad was adapted from the recipe of a San Francisco chef. Anchovies, traditional in Caesar salads, are optional here, but they do add a nice salty flavor to the dressing. Make the croutons ahead of time—they keep and are ideal for garnishing soups as well—and toss into the salad at the last minute.

- *1 cup cubed French bread*
- *¾ cup plus 2 teaspoons olive oil*
- *4 cups washed and torn romaine lettuce leaves*
- *3 cloves minced garlic*
- *1 tablespoon Worcestershire sauce*
- *1 teaspoon dry mustard*
- *¼ teaspoon herbal salt substitute*
- *¼ teaspoon pepper*
- *1 tablespoon mashed anchovy fillets (optional)*
- *2 tablespoons grated Parmesan cheese*
- *½ teaspoon lemon juice*
- *1 egg*

1. Toss cubed bread with the 2 teaspoons olive oil. Place cubes on a baking sheet and bake for 20 minutes at 250° F.

2. Place lettuce in a large salad bowl. In smaller bowl combine the ¾ cup oil, garlic, Worcestershire sauce, mustard, salt substitute, pepper, anchovies (if used), cheese, lemon juice, and egg. Toss with lettuce leaves. Add croutons and serve.

Serves 4.

Preparation time: 20 minutes
Baking time (croutons): 20 minutes
Per serving: calcium 111 mg, calories 614, carbohydrates 32 g, cholesterol 66 mg, fat 52 g, fiber 2.8 g, protein 8 g, sodium 507 mg

Special Note

THE BENEFITS OF FIBER

What is fiber? Scientists have found it difficult to define this essential food component. In general, nutritionists agree that fiber is basically a complex carbohydrate, the fibrous component of plant foods that is not broken down by human digestion.

Dietary fiber comes in several varieties. Some of the common types are cellulose (abundant in oat bran), lignin (in grains), pectin (in fruit and vegetables), gums (in legumes), and mucilages (in seeds). Some fibers absorb water, some lower blood cholesterol, some increase fat excretion, and some maintain blood sugar levels. Consuming a good selection of these fibers daily is recommended, since they perform different functions in the body.

For those interested in weight loss, fiber has been shown to increase the metabolism of fats. In addition, high-carbohydrate meals containing plenty of fiber satisfy the eater sooner than equal amounts of protein or fat. Low blood cholesterol and low incidences of cardiovascular disease have been reported in populations where a large amount of fiber-rich pectin (from fresh fruit) and bran (from oats or wheat) is consumed.

People on high-fiber diets rarely are troubled by constipation. Fiber promotes healthy elimination by acting like a broom that sweeps the colon as it passes out of the system. Fiber can absorb many times its weight in water, which aids regularity. Studies show that it also seems to increase elimination of fats, such as bile acids and sterols.

The typical diet in the United States, filled with refined and processed foods, contains little fiber. For example, white bread, made from bleached and refined wheat flour, contains only half the fiber of its unrefined, unprocessed cousin, whole wheat bread.

The National Cancer Institute recommends that the average intake of fiber (10 to 15 grams per day) be doubled as a preventative measure against colon and rectal cancer. Studies also show that fiber plays a role in preventing diverticulitis, gallstones, and varicose veins.

A high-fiber diet is composed of plenty of fresh fruits and vegetables, whole grains, and legumes. Look for recipes using these foods: oat bran, wheat bran, cornmeal or polenta, apples or bananas, potatoes, broccoli, carrots, kidney beans, lentils, and almonds. Try such fiber-rich recipes in this book as Ukranian Sauerkraut Bread (see page 97) or Brian's Best Bran Muffins (page 57).

HEALTHY SALAD DRESSINGS

These healthy salad dressings will make your next salad a culinary work of art. The secret to a tasty salad lies in the dressings, and these dressings, light in fat and salt, will delight your waistline as well as your palate.

LIME-MINT DRESSING

Light and refreshing, great with grapefruit and avocado.

> 6 tablespoons olive oil
> 2 tablespoons lime juice
> ½ teaspoon herbal salt substitute
> ⅛ teaspoon white pepper
> ½ teaspoon minced parsley
> ½ teaspoon minced fresh mint leaves
> ½ teaspoon chopped chives
> ½ teaspoon Dijon mustard

Combine all ingredients.

Makes about ½ cup, serves 6.

Preparation time: 15 minutes
Per serving: calcium 1 mg, calories 135, carbohydrates none, cholesterol none, fat 15 g, fiber none, protein none, sodium 6 mg

TAHINI DRESSING

A fine party dip with raw vegetables.

> ½ cup tahini
> ⅓ cup low-calorie mayonnaise
>   Juice from 1 lemon
> 1 teaspoon minced garlic
> ½ cup water
> ¼ cup freshly squeezed orange juice
> 1½ tablespoons apple cider vinegar
> 1 tablespoon low-sodium tamari or soy sauce
>   Pinch of cayenne pepper

Combine all ingredients.

Makes about 2 cups, serves 8.

Preparation time: 15 minutes
Per serving: calcium 14 mg, calories 138, carbohydrates 5 g, cholesterol 1 mg, fat 11 g, fiber 1.1 g, protein 4 g, sodium 274 mg

JAPANESE MISO DRESSING

Dress up pasta salads with this flavorful dressing.

- ½ cup safflower oil
- 2 tablespoons light miso
- 3 tablespoons nutritional yeast flakes
- 1 teaspoon cayenne pepper

Combine all ingredients.

Makes about 1 cup, serves 4.

Preparation time: 15 minutes
Per serving: calcium 45 mg, calories 558, carbohydrates 10 g, cholesterol none, fat 55 g, fiber .6 g, protein 8 g, sodium 645 mg

GREEN GODDESS DRESSING

Snappy and low in calories, this dressing is good on coleslaw.

- ½ cup low-calorie mayonnaise
- ¼ cup plain nonfat yogurt
- ¼ cup chopped parsley
- 1 teaspoon chopped chives
- 2 tablespoons apple cider vinegar
- ¼ teaspoon herbal salt substitute Dash of pepper
- ½ teaspoon dried basil

Blend all ingredients until smooth.

Makes about 1¼ cups, serves 6.

Preparation time: 15 minutes
Per serving: calcium 23 mg, calories 75, carbohydrates 1 g, cholesterol 2 mg, fat 7 g, fiber .2 g, protein 1 g, sodium 141 mg

PAPAYA SEED DRESSING

Try this one over greens or citrus.

- 1 teaspoon grated gingerroot
- 1 tablespoon minced onion
- 1 tablespoon papaya seeds, scooped from fresh papaya
- 1 teaspoon dried tarragon
- 1 teaspoon Dijon mustard
- 1 teaspoon minced garlic
- ¼ cup olive oil
- ¼ cup water
- 2 tablespoons lemon juice
- 1 tablespoon lime juice

Place all ingredients in a blender and purée.

Makes about ¾ cup, serves 4.

Preparation time: 15 minutes
Per serving: calcium 6 mg, calories 143, carbohydrates 2 g, cholesterol none, fat 15 g, fiber .1 g, protein none, sodium 18 mg

MARINADE FOR BEAN SALADS

Marinate beans for at least 2 hours in this dressing.

- 1 teaspoon dry mustard
- 2 tablespoons minced garlic
- ¼ cup rice vinegar
- ⅛ cup lemon juice
- ¼ teaspoon herbal salt substitute Dash pepper
- ¼ cup olive oil

Combine all ingredients.

Makes about ¾ cup, serves 6.

Preparation time: 15 minutes
Per serving: calcium 4 mg, calories 102, carbohydrates 3 g, cholesterol none, fat 10 g, fiber none, protein 1 g, sodium 2 mg

RUE DAUPHINE DRESSING

A heartier form of oil-and-vinegar.

- ½ cup low-calorie mayonnaise
- ¼ cup olive oil
- ⅛ cup red wine vinegar
- 1 tablespoon honey Pinch of powdered kelp (optional)
- 1 teaspoon celery seed
- 1 teaspoon herbal salt substitute Dash of pepper
- 2 tablespoons sesame seed
- ¼ teaspoon dried basil
- ¼ teaspoon dried tarragon
- ¼ teaspoon dried oregano

Combine all ingredients.

Makes about 1¼ cups, serves 6.

Preparation time: 15 minutes
Per serving: calcium 12 mg, calories 187, carbohydrates 4 g, cholesterol 1 mg, fat 18 g, fiber .1 g, protein 1 g, sodium 134 mg

COUNTRY PICNIC

Mushroom Pâté en Baguette

Cream of Sorrel Soup

Texas Blue Cheese Slaw

Poached Chicken Breasts With Lemon-and-Herb Mayonnaise (see page 62)

Baked Pear Gratin (see page 121)

California Chardonnay and Sparkling Waters

Invite friends for a day in the country. Find a shady spot by a quiet stream, open your picnic basket, and pull out this healthy and tasty picnic lunch. You might try stuffing the Mushroom Pâté into its hollowed baguette and wrapping it tightly in plastic the night before. The Cream of Sorrel Soup can be packed into a prewarmed thermos. The delicate Poached Chicken Breasts can be precooked and served either warm (from a heated thermos box) or cool. Finish with slightly decadent Baked Pear Gratin and a glass of California Chardonnay. Menu serves 6.

All the dishes in this elegant and easily prepared Country Picnic can be made ahead, wrapped and ready to go before the first rays of sunshine.

MUSHROOM PÂTÉ EN BAGUETTE

Mushrooms and herbs are blended into a savory pâté, stuffed into a hollowed-out loaf of French bread, wrapped, and refrigerated. While the loaf chills, the pâté subtly flavors it. To serve, unwrap and slice into thin rounds, revealing a circle of bread surrounding each slice of pâté.

- ½ cup chopped onion
- 1 tablespoon olive oil
- ¼ cup sake or dry sherry
- ½ cup chopped green onions, including green tops
- 2 teaspoons minced garlic
- 1½ cups sliced mushrooms
- ½ cup minced celery
- ½ cup almonds or walnuts, minced
- ½ cup minced parsley
- 1 cup rye bread crumbs
- 1 teaspoon ground rosemary
- ½ teaspoon dried thyme
- 1 tablespoon low-sodium soy or tamari sauce
- 1 teaspoon herbal salt substitute
- ½ teaspoon dried basil
- ¼ teaspoon dried oregano
- 1 baguette French bread

1. In a large skillet over medium-high heat, sauté onion in the olive oil and sherry until soft but not browned. Add green onions, garlic, and mushrooms, and continue to cook for 5 minutes.

2. When mushrooms begin to exude moisture, add celery, walnuts, and parsley, and cook 3 minutes longer.

3. Spoon sautéed vegetables into a large bowl. Add rye bread crumbs, rosemary, thyme, soy sauce, salt substitute, basil, and oregano. Purée half of mixture in a blender and mix well with pâté remaining in bowl until a pastelike consistency is achieved.

4. Cut baguette in half and slice off each end. With your fingers, remove the soft center of the loaf, hollowing out both sections. Stuff pâté into the cavity, wrap in plastic wrap, and chill for 2 hours or more.

5. To serve, unwrap baguette and slice into rounds.

Serves 6.

Preparation time: 20 minutes
Cooking time: 15 minutes
Chilling time: 2 hours
Per serving: calcium 90 mg, calories 310, carbohydrates 45 g, cholesterol none, fat 10 g, fiber 3.9 g, protein 10 g, sodium 569 mg

CREAM OF SORREL SOUP

If sorrel, a sour grass, is unavailable in a local gourmet store, substitute watercress or increase the spinach in this recipe. The soup cooks into a delicate, light green color and can be garnished with minced red bell pepper for an extremely attractive first course.

- ½ cup finely minced onion
- 1 teaspoon unsalted butter
- ¼ cup white wine
- ½ cup minced celery
- 1 cup chopped sorrel leaves
- 1 cup chopped spinach leaves
- 6 tablespoons whole wheat pastry or unbleached white flour
- 3 cups defatted Chicken Stock (see page 31)
- ¼ cup half-and-half
- 1 cup nonfat milk
- 1 teaspoon lemon juice
- 1 teaspoon honey
  Herbal salt substitute and pepper, to taste

1. In a large stockpot over medium-high heat, sauté onion in butter and wine until soft but not browned (about 3 minutes). Add celery, sorrel, and spinach, and continue to cook for 5 minutes more.

2. Add flour and cook, stirring, for 2 minutes. Add chicken stock and bring to a boil.

3. In batches, purée soup in a blender until smooth. Return to pot and add half-and-half, milk, lemon juice, and honey. Heat through, but do not let soup boil. Season to taste with salt substitute and pepper. Serve soup hot or cold.

Serves 6.

Preparation time: 20 minutes
Cooking time: 15 minutes
Chilling time (optional): 2 hours
Per serving: calcium 95 mg, calories 89, carbohydrates 7 g, cholesterol 12 mg, fat 2 g, fiber .7 g, protein 5 g, sodium 154 mg

TEXAS BLUE CHEESE SLAW

Savoy cabbage is combined with nonfat yogurt, minced green onions, and chunks of blue cheese to make this hearty—and healthy—slaw. It keeps for 24 hours, so you can make it the night before a picnic.

- 4 cups finely shredded savoy cabbage
- ½ cup minced green onions
- ½ cup minced green bell pepper
- 2 tablespoons minced fresh dill
- 1 cup nonfat plain yogurt
- 2 tablespoons sour cream
- 3 tablespoons white wine vinegar
- 1 tablespoon honey
- 3 ounces blue cheese
  Herbal salt substitute and pepper, to taste

1. In a large bowl combine cabbage, onions, bell pepper, and dill.

2. Blend together yogurt, sour cream, vinegar, honey, and blue cheese. Toss dressing with cabbage mixture. Add salt substitute and pepper to taste.

Serves 6.

Preparation time: 20 minutes
Per serving: calcium 184 mg, calories 108, carbohydrates 14 g, cholesterol 12 mg, fat 5 g, fiber 1 g, protein 6 g, sodium 236 mg

Rich in flavor and nutrients, shellfish are a healthy entrée choice. Serve them Cantonese style in an easy black bean sauce (see page 55).

Fish & Shellfish

Because fish contains certain trace minerals and other precious nutrients and very little fat, many health professionals recommend that people eat two or three fish dishes a week. If you think you are too busy to fuss with fish, take a second look at the recipes in this chapter—most of them can be prepared in less than 30 minutes. Fish is also a great choice for entertaining. Sauces and marinades can be made ahead of time (see Grilled Sweet-and-Sour Tuna Steaks, page 46), and many fish and shellfish are at their peak in flavor when prepared quickly right before serving (see Sole aux Amandes, page 47). The chapter also gives instructions for cooking in parchment (see page 50) and seasoning fish (see page 49).

EASY FISH ENTRÉES

Imagine coming home from a busy day and eating an elegant seafood dinner 20 minutes later. Many of the following recipes can be made in two stages: sauces and marinades the night before, and baking, poaching, or grilling right before you serve. These recipes can successfully be prepared with either fresh or fresh-frozen seafood.

SALMON WITH MUSTARD SAUCE

A favorite French bistro recipe, Salmon With Mustard Sauce can be served cool or hot and makes a light and elegant luncheon dish. The salmon is poached lightly in wine to retain its tender texture. The flavor of the wine combines well with the piquant mustard and dill of the sauce. The sauce can be prepared ahead of time and kept for one week in the refrigerator—it's great on sandwiches, too.

- 4 large salmon steaks
- 1 cup dry white wine
- ¼ cup minced shallots
- 3 tablespoons minced fresh dill
- ¼ cup nonfat plain yogurt
- ¼ cup Dijon mustard
- 1 tablespoon light honey
- ¼ cup lemon juice

1. Preheat oven to 400° F. Place salmon steaks in a large, deep baking pan and cover with wine. Sprinkle with shallots. Bake for 12 to 15 minutes, basting often with wine.

2. While salmon is baking, in a small bowl mix together dill, yogurt, mustard, honey, and lemon juice until smooth. Serve over salmon.

Serves 4.

Preparation time: 20 minutes
Baking time: 12 to 15 minutes
Per serving: calcium 307 mg, calories 274, carbohydrates 11 g, cholesterol 48 mg, fat 8.4 g, fiber .1 g, protein 29 g, sodium 731 mg

GRILLED SWEET-AND-SOUR TUNA STEAKS

A Hawaiian specialty, Grilled Sweet-and-Sour Tuna Steaks is perfect for outdoor grilling or indoor broiling. Make the sauce ahead of time and let the tuna steaks marinate for 30 to 60 minutes before grilling so that they really absorb the tangy flavor. If you use mesquite charcoal on the grill, the tuna takes on a teriyaki taste from the smoke as it cooks. Grill the tuna only until it turns a dull pink color inside and browns nicely on the outside.

- ½ cup dry sherry
- 2 tablespoons grated gingerroot
- 2 tablespoons low-sodium soy or tamari sauce
- 1 teaspoon light honey
- 1 teaspoon maple syrup
- 1 tablespoon minced garlic
- 2 teaspoons dark sesame oil
- 2 tablespoons minced cilantro
- 4 medium tuna steaks

1. Preheat broiler or start grill. In a small bowl combine sherry, ginger, soy sauce, honey, maple syrup, garlic, sesame oil, and cilantro. Set aside.

2. Wash and pat dry tuna steaks. Place in a shallow baking dish. Pour sauce over steaks. Let marinate 10 minutes.

3. Remove steaks from marinade and broil or grill. Cook 5 to 8 minutes on each side, turning once, and basting with marinade. Serve hot.

Serves 4.

Preparation time: 10 minutes
Marinating time: 10 minutes
Grilling time: 15 minutes
Per serving: calcium 45 mg, calories 271, carbohydrates 9 g, cholesterol 60 mg, fat 11 g, fiber .3 g, protein 26 g, sodium 510 mg

BROILED FLOUNDER WITH RED BELL-PEPPER BUTTER

Flame-roasted red bell peppers are puréed and mixed with shallots and unsalted butter to spread over this tasty entrée. You can use a variety of fish—from salmon or swordfish steaks to thin fillets such as sole or flounder. The cooking time will vary according to the thickness of the fish. Steam fresh asparagus or broccoli to accompany this easy entrée.

- 4 large fillets of flounder or sole or 4 swordfish or salmon steaks
- ½ teaspoon safflower oil, for coating pan
- 1 red bell pepper
- 4 tablespoons unsalted butter, softened
- 2 teaspoons minced shallots
- 1 teaspoon lemon juice
- ¼ teaspoon Tabasco Sauce

1. Wash fillets and pat dry. Lightly oil a large baking sheet. Preheat broiler.

2. Cut pepper in half, seed, and place, cut side down, on baking sheet. Broil until skin blackens (1 to 2 minutes). Place pepper halves in a paper bag for 1 minute to steam, then rinse and peel off blackened skin. Place in food processor or blender with butter, shallots, lemon juice, and Tabasco. Purée until thick spread is formed. Remove from blender, spoon into a small bowl, and refrigerate.

3. Broil fish on the same baking sheet. Cook 3 minutes per side for fillets, 5 to 8 minutes per side for steaks. Turn once. Test for doneness by flaking with a fork.

4. To serve, place a generous spoonful of red pepper butter on top of each piece of broiled fish.

Serves 4.

Preparation time: 25 minutes
Broiling time: 6 to 15 minutes
Per serving: calcium 69 mg, calories 213, carbohydrates 1 g, cholesterol 75 mg, fat 14 g, fiber .1 g, protein 21 g, sodium 245 mg

SOLE AUX AMANDES

Found on the menu of many fine French restaurants, sole with almonds is a traditional favorite. This version halves the calories of the traditional recipe by reducing the calories in the buttery sauce. The sauce for Sole aux Amandes can be prepared early in the day, but cook the fish right before serving for best flavor and texture.

    4 large fillets of sole
    ¼ cup nonfat milk
    ½ cup whole wheat pastry or
        unbleached white flour
    1 teaspoon unsalted butter
    1 teaspoon safflower oil
    ¾ cup chopped mushrooms
    ¼ cup slivered almonds
    1 teaspoon chopped chives
    1 teaspoon minced parsley
      Juice of 1 medium lemon

1. Preheat oven to 200° F. Dredge sole in milk and then in flour. In a large skillet over medium-high heat, melt butter with oil and lightly sauté flour-coated fish until browned. Transfer to a platter and keep warm in oven.

2. In the same pan, using drippings from sautéing fish, sauté mushrooms until soft. Add a small amount of water, if needed, to prevent sticking. Add almonds, chives, parsley, and lemon juice. Heat through, then pour over sole and serve immediately.

Serves 4.

Preparation time: 15 to 20 minutes
Cooking time: 15 to 20 minutes
Per serving: calcium 93 mg, calories 213, carbohydrates 16 g, cholesterol 32 mg, fat 7 g, fiber .9 g, protein 21 g, sodium 167 mg

Flounder's meaty texture is enhanced by quick-flame broiling and a topping of roasted red-pepper butter.

Baking in parchment seals in the delicate flavors of the spinach-stuffed trout, keeping it tender, delicious, and moist.

SALMON AND JULIENNED VEGETABLE SAUTÉ

This easy recipe is ideal for a busy cook; you can even cut the vegetables ahead of time. Use a wok or large skillet to sauté the vegetables only until they are slightly tender and bright in color. The salmon steaks are then blanketed with the sautéed vegetables and baked. Be ready to serve this entrée right away, perhaps accompanied by a dry white wine and steamed rice.

    2   teaspoons olive oil
    1   cup dry vermouth
    1½ cup sliced onions
    2   cups julienned carrots
    1   tablespoon minced garlic
    ½   cup julienned celery
    1   cup chopped lettuce or endive
    1   teaspoon ground fennel seed
    4   medium salmon steaks

1. Preheat oven to 450° F. Lightly oil a 9- by 12-inch baking dish. In a large skillet or wok over medium-high heat, heat together oil and dry vermouth. Cook onions, carrots, garlic, celery, and lettuce until soft (10 minutes). Place the vegetables in bottom of baking dish and sprinkle with fennel seed.

2. Wash and pat dry salmon steaks. Place on top of vegetables. Pour any remaining cooking liquid over fish. Cover with aluminum foil and bake for 10 minutes. Lower oven to 350° F and bake for 30 minutes. Serve hot.

Serves 4.

Preparation time: 25 minutes
Baking time: 40 minutes
Per serving: calcium 471 mg, calories 311, carbohydrates 17 g, cholesterol 47 mg, fat 10 g, fiber 2 g, protein 30 g, sodium 178 mg

BAKED SALMON PROVENÇALE

In this hearty dish from Provence, salmon steaks are sautéed in a savory sauce of tomatoes, herbs, and olives that combines the best flavors of the Côte d'Azur. The dish pairs well with a simple green salad of endive and lettuce dressed with Rue Dauphine Dressing (see page 41).

4 *salmon steaks (¾ in. thick)*
1 *teaspoon unsalted butter*
1 *teaspoon olive oil*
1 *gram (2 teaspoons) saffron threads*
1 *tablespoon minced garlic*
½ *teaspoon tarragon*
¼ *teaspoon thyme*
  Pinch of sage
2 *bay leaves, crushed*
1 *cup coarsely chopped plum tomatoes*
8 *to 10 Greek olives, pitted and chopped*
1¼ *cup white wine*
1 *cup Fish Stock (see page 31)*
1 *teaspoon herbal salt substitute*

1. Preheat oven to 400° F. Wash and pat dry salmon steaks.

2. In a large, deep, ovenproof skillet or stovetop casserole over medium-high heat, sauté salmon briefly on each side in butter and oil (about 1 minute). Remove to a platter. Add saffron, garlic, tarragon, thyme, sage, bay leaves, tomatoes, olives, wine, fish stock, and salt substitute. Bring to a boil. Lower heat and simmer for 10 minutes, uncovered.

3. Add salmon steaks. Remove pan from heat and place in oven. Bake until salmon is lightly pink and done to taste (10 minutes).

4. To serve, place salmon steaks on platter and spoon sauce over them.

Serves 4.

Preparation time: 20 minutes
Baking time: 10 minutes
Per serving: calcium 483 mg, calories 362, carbohydrates 9 g, cholesterol 50 mg, fat 19 g, fiber 1.6 g, protein 29 g, sodium 500 mg

FRESH TROUT FLORENTINE

Dishes prepared Florentine-style feature spinach—a source of vitamin A and calcium. Here, fresh trout is split and stuffed with a savory pine nut and spinach mixture. The trout is wrapped in parchment and baked.

1 *teaspoon safflower oil*
¼ *cup minced green onions, including green tops*
1 *teaspoon olive oil*
¼ *cup dry sherry*
2 *cups chopped spinach*
¼ *cup pine nuts*
1¼ *cups whole wheat bread crumbs*
4 *tablespoons nonfat milk*
¼ *teaspoon lemon juice*
4 *large fresh trout, cleaned*
1 *cup white wine*
¼ *teaspoon pepper*
2 *teaspoons unsalted butter*

1. Preheat oven to 350° F. Lightly coat a 9- by 12-inch baking pan with safflower oil.

2. In a medium skillet over medium-high heat, sauté green onion in olive oil and sherry until soft. Add chopped spinach and pine nuts, and cook until spinach has wilted (2 minutes). Remove from heat. Add bread crumbs, milk, and lemon juice and mix well.

3. Wash and pat trout dry, inside and out. Stuff cavity of each trout with one fourth of the spinach mixture. Following instructions on page 50, cut 4 sheets of parchment and place 1 trout on each. Set aside.

4. In the same skillet combine wine, pepper, and butter. Bring to a boil over high heat, and cook until alcohol has evaporated (2 minutes). Pour equal amounts of wine mixture over trout and seal parchment packets as directed on page 50. Place packets on prepared baking sheets and bake for 12 minutes. Serve hot.

Serves 4.

Preparation time: 20 minutes
Baking time: 12 minutes
Per serving: calcium 102 mg, calories 419, carbohydrates 26 g, cholesterol 61 mg, fat 10 g, fiber 1.3 g, protein 28 g, sodium 293 mg

...ON SPECIAL SEASONINGS FOR FISH

Try these easy seasoning mixtures. They work best with strong-flavored fish, such as tuna, swordfish, shark, and salmon.

Cajun Combine 2 teaspoons ground black pepper, 1 teaspoon cayenne pepper, ½ teaspoon apple cider vinegar, ½ teaspoon honey, ¼ teaspoon cumin, ¼ teaspoon ground coriander. Brush over grilling, broiling, or baking fish.

Provençal Combine 2 tablespoons white wine, 1 teaspoon chopped fresh tarragon, 1 teaspoon chopped parsley, ½ teaspoon chopped chives, ½ teaspoon dried thyme. Brush over grilling, broiling, or baking fish.

Lemon and herb Combine 2 tablespoons lemon juice, 1 tablespoon lime juice, ½ teaspoon light honey, 1 tablespoon minced parsley, ½ teaspoon minced garlic or shallot. Brush over grilling, broiling, or baking fish, or add to a poaching liquid such as white wine.

Pepper Combine 1 tablespoon white wine, 2 teaspoons minced lemon peel, 2 teaspoons ground black pepper, 1 teaspoon white pepper, 1 teaspoon herbal salt substitute. Brush over grilling, broiling, or baking fish.

Sweet honey and ginger Combine 2 tablespoons light honey, 1 teaspoon grated gingerroot, 1 clove minced garlic, 1 teaspoon lemon juice. Brush over grilling, broiling, or baking fish.

HEALTHY IDEAS WITH PARCHMENT COOKING

Many people shy away from cooking fish after one or two experiences of overcooking it. Fish that is overcooked or dried out is simply a disaster. Cooking in parchment is an excellent way to retain the moisture, flavor, and nutrients of fish as it cooks and to prevent it from drying out. Follow these easy steps to make parchment packets for cooking all types of fish from sole to salmon.

1. *Cut a piece of parchment about four times the size of the fillet or steak you are cooking. Fold parchment in half. Starting on the folded side, cut out a half-heart shape.*

2. *Open the heart and place the fish, with all seasonings and flavorings added, in the center. Starting at the fold, fold in the edge of the parchment to form an envelope around the fish, overlapping the fold as you go along.*

3. *Fold the tip of the paper several times to secure.*

4. *To serve, cut away browned parchment and lift out fish.*

5. *Spoon cooking liquid over fish. Garnish and serve right away for best flavor.*

BAKED FISH IN LETTUCE PACKETS

Wrapping fish in lettuce packets is a novel cooking technique that holds the flavor and juiciness of the fillets as they cook. Tender fillets of fish are spread with a savory herb filling, then wrapped with blanched lettuce leaves and baked. The surprise is a sweet-pungent vinegar, shallot, and garlic mixture that flavors the fish as it bakes. If you are in a hurry, preassemble the fish packets, cover with plastic wrap, and store in the refrigerator until baking.

>   2 tablespoons tarragon vinegar
>   1 cup minced shallots
>   2 tablespoons minced garlic
>   1 teaspoon safflower oil
>   6 leaves Boston lettuce
>   6 small fillets snapper
>   or flounder
>   2 teaspoons dried thyme
>   1 teaspoon dried tarragon
>   2 tablespoons green olive oil

1. In a small saucepan over medium heat, place vinegar, shallots, and garlic and cook until soft (almost 5 minutes).

2. Preheat oven to 350° F. Lightly oil a large baking sheet with safflower oil. Place lettuce leaves on baking sheet; do not overlap.

3. Wash and pat dry fish fillets. Sprinkle with thyme, tarragon, and half the olive oil. Spread with shallot mixture.

4. Starting with small end of each fillet, roll it around shallot spread and place the roll on top of a lettuce leaf. Fold lettuce around fish and place packet seam side down on baking sheet. Brush packets with remaining oil.

5. Cover baking sheet with aluminum foil and bake for 20 to 30 minutes. Remove foil and serve hot.

Serves 6.

Preparation time: 25 minutes
Cooking time: 20 to 30 minutes
Per serving: calcium 49 mg, calories 259, carbohydrates 9 g, cholesterol 43 mg, fat 13 g, fiber .8 g, protein 27 g, sodium 212 mg

MONKFISH IN PARCHMENT WITH WINE, LEMON, AND HERBS

Monkfish, a very rich-tasting white fish that has the texture of shellfish, is sometimes called "poor man's lobster." Ask the fish market to cut it into thin fillets for this recipe. It will cook quickly in the parchment wrapper and stay moist and flavorful from the wine, fresh lemon juice, and herbs (see Healthy Ideas With Parchment Cooking, opposite page). If you buy extra monkfish, try grilling it with the sweet-and-sour marinade from Grilled Sweet-and-Sour Tuna Steaks (see page 46).

  Safflower oil, for coating pan
1 *large (about 1¾ lb) monkfish fillet*
⅓ *cup low-sodium soy or tamari sauce*
⅓ *cup minced green onions, including green tops*
  Juice from 2 lemons
2 *teaspoons minced chives*
2 *teaspoons minced parsley*
¼ *cup dry white wine*

1. Preheat oven to 400° F. Lightly oil a 9- by 12-inch baking dish.

2. Lay out 4 large sheets of parchment paper. Cut monkfish into 4 equal parts and lay each on a sheet of parchment. Sprinkle with soy sauce, green onions, lemon juice, chives, parsley, and wine. Bring edges of parchment together and roll to seal on all sides (see Healthy Ideas With Parchment Cooking, opposite page). Place packets seam side down on baking sheet.

3. Bake for 20 minutes. To serve, unroll parchment packets and place fish on platter. Spoon cooking liquid and herbs over top.

Serves 4.

Preparation time: 15 minutes
Baking time: 20 minutes
Per serving: calcium 65 mg, calories 253, carbohydrates 7 g, cholesterol 65 mg, fat 7 g, fiber .2 g, protein 37 g, sodium 1320 mg

---

SHELLFISH ENTRÉES

An excellent source of low-fat protein, shellfish are easy to integrate into a menu plan. They are often easier to cook than fish fillets or steaks because of their greater tolerance of overcooking (with some exceptions—prawns and scallops become unpleasantly rubbery when cooked too long). One way to ensure plenty of shellfish in your diet is to assemble recipes, such as Prawns and Scallops on the Half Shell (see page 54) or Stir-fry Prawns in Black Bean Sauce (see page 55), and freeze in 4-ounce portions accompanied by partially steamed broccoli or asparagus. An elegant, healthy dinner is yours for the defrosting.

DRUNKEN PRAWNS

In this recipe, adapted from a popular happy-hour dish served in New York pubs, medium or jumbo prawns are poached in beer until plump and pink. Serve them steaming hot and let guests peel and eat their own. Serve the hot poaching liquid as a dipping sauce for the prawns.

1 *pound medium to large prawns*
2 *cups dark beer*
2 *teaspoons coarsely chopped garlic*
1 *tablespoon Tabasco Sauce*
1 *tablespoon minced parsley*

1. Peel and devein prawns (or omit this step and let guests peel their own when prawns are served). Place in a large pot along with beer, garlic, Tabasco, and parsley.

2. Bring to a boil and cook for 5 minutes or until prawns turn pink. Do not overcook. Serve hot.

Serves 4.

Preparation time: 10 minutes
Cooking time: 5 to 10 minutes
Per serving: calcium 75 mg, calories 121, carbohydrates 6 g, cholesterol 79 mg, fat 1 g, fiber .1 g, protein 14 g, sodium 177 mg

---

PRAWNS WITH PEANUT SAUCE

A spicy Indonesian recipe, Prawns With Peanut Sauce blends the aromatic flavors of peanuts, coriander, cumin, and cayenne pepper in a rich-tasting sauce. This dish can be prepared ahead if you follow one rule of thumb: Undercook prawns slightly, then freeze in their poaching liquid. When the prawns are reheated, they will not have the rubbery texture of overcooked fish. Since this entrée is rich in taste and appearance, plain steamed rice and a light spinach or endive salad make suitable accompaniments.

1 *pound medium prawns*
1 *cup white wine*
1½ *tablespoons smooth peanut butter*
2 *tablespoons safflower oil*
1½ *tablespoons light honey*
2 *tablespoons low-sodium soy or tamari sauce*
2 *teaspoons rice vinegar*
½ *teaspoon dark sesame oil*
½ *teaspoon cayenne pepper*
1 *tablespoon minced green onion*
1½ *teaspoons ground coriander*
½ *teaspoon ground cumin*
4 *cups steamed rice (optional)*

1. Wash prawns, peel, and devein. Place in a large saucepan with wine. Cook over medium-high heat until they turn bright pink. Set aside.

2. In a small bowl mix together peanut butter and safflower oil until smooth. Add honey, soy sauce, vinegar, sesame oil, cayenne, green onion, coriander, and cumin. Mix well, then add prawns. Place prawns and sauce in saucepan and reheat. Serve over steamed rice (if desired).

Serves 4.

Preparation time: 25 minutes
Per serving: calcium 84 mg, calories 242, carbohydrates 11 g, cholesterol 79 mg, fat 11 g, fiber .6 g, protein 16 g, sodium 657 mg

HEALTH BENEFITS OF EATING FISH

As a low-fat, high-protein source, fish is an excellent substitution for meat entrées. Believe it or not, 3 ounces of flounder contain the same amount of protein as an equal portion of roast beef.

Fish also has a caloric advantage over meat. Equal servings of broiled cod and broiled sirloin, for example, have about the same amount of protein, but cod has only about one-third the calories. Other fish particularly low in fat include flounder, haddock, monkfish, sea bass, and sole.

Fish also has less cholesterol than meat. Although this has been known for many years, people at risk for heart disease were once advised to avoid all shellfish, due to their high cholesterol levels. Recent research indicates, however, that methods used to measure the cholesterol levels of shellfish may have been inaccurate because they included other sterols (chemicals similar to cholesterol) in the count. Certain shellfish, such as shrimp, crab, and lobster, have more cholesterol than mollusks (clams, scallops, oysters), but still less than half the cholesterol in egg yolk.

In recent years, research has indicated that certain fish oils—called omega-3 fatty acids—may even lower levels of cholesterol in the blood. Studies of Greenland Eskimos in the early 1970s first noted an absence of coronary artery disease and traced this phenomenon to the fish diet of the Eskimos, which is abundant in these polyunsaturated oils. Later studies showed that omega-3 fatty acids appear to help prevent atherosclerosis and heart disease by decreasing the levels of blood triglycerides (LDLs) and cholesterol.

If you are interested in increasing your intake of omega-3 fatty acids, good fish choices are salmon, mackerel, trout, sardines, and herring.

INDONESIAN TEMPURA

The best tempura is dipped lightly in batter and fried for only 30 seconds in very hot peanut oil. As opposed to other oils, peanut oil does not leave a taste on food and is recommended by Asian cooks for deep frying. There are two secrets to successful tempura—very hot oil and very cold batter—so set the container of batter in a bowl of ice during the dipping and cooking process.

> Peanut oil, for deep-frying
> 2½ cups rice flour or whole wheat pastry flour
> 3 eggs
> 1½ cups ice water
> ½ cup coconut milk
> ¼ teaspoon ground coriander
> 1 large red bell pepper
> 1 pound large prawns
> ½ pound large scallops
> 1 cup diagonally sliced sweet potato
> 1 cup large pieces of broccoli tops

1. In a wok or large, deep skillet over medium-high heat, warm peanut oil to the 350° F mark on a fat thermometer. There should be about 4 inches of oil in the wok or 2 to 3 inches in the deep skillet.

2. In a blender at high speed, mix together flour, eggs, the ice water, coconut milk, and coriander until very smooth. Pour this batter into a bowl set inside a larger bowl filled with crushed ice.

3. Seed bell pepper and cut into eighths. Peel and devein prawns. To cook tempura, dip seafood and vegetables into batter, turning to coat lightly. Place immediately into hot oil. Tempura should brown in 30 seconds; if it takes longer, oil is not hot enough. Drain cooked tempura on paper towels. Serve immediately.

Serves 8.

> *Preparation time:* 20 minutes
> *Cooking time:* 10 minutes
> *Per serving:* calcium 109 mg, calories 295, carbohydrates 38 g, cholesterol 148 mg, fat 7 g, fiber 2.6 g, protein 20 g, sodium 193 mg

GWEN'S SEAFOOD CHOWDER

Rich-tasting but surprisingly low in calories, this seafood chowder combines carrots, onions, and chunks of potatoes with an assortment of shrimp, scallops, and whitefish. It is then seasoned and served as a creamy soup. It can be a main dish when accompanied by green salad and a loaf of dark bread. Make up to four days ahead of time and freeze.

> 2 cups minced onion
> 2 teaspoons olive oil or butter
> ⅔ cup dry sherry
> ½ cup chopped carrots
> ½ cup minced celery
> 1 cup diced red potato, skins intact
> 1 cup clam juice or Fish Stock (see page 31)
> 2 tablespoons tomato paste
>   Pinch of cayenne pepper
> 1½ cups nonfat milk
> 1 cup half-and-half
> ½ pound cooked shrimp meat
> ½ pound bay scallops
> 1 fillet red snapper, cut into ½-inch pieces
>   Herbal salt substitute and pepper (optional)

1. In a large stockpot over medium-high heat, sauté onion in oil and sherry until soft. Add carrots, celery, and potato and sauté 2 minutes.

2. Add clam juice and cover. Simmer until potatoes are soft (about 15 minutes). Purée half of the mixture in a blender until smooth, then return to pot.

3. Add tomato paste, cayenne, nonfat milk, half-and-half, shrimp, scallops, and snapper. Bring to a boil, lower heat to simmer, and cook 5 minutes. Taste for seasoning and add salt substitute and pepper (if desired).

Serves 6.

> *Preparation time:* 30 minutes
> *Cooking time:* 25 minutes
> *Per serving:* calcium 175 mg, calories 422, carbohydrates 52 g, cholesterol 78 mg, fat 7 g, fiber 2.7 g, protein 21 g, sodium 629 mg

HOT HUNAN NOODLE AND SEAFOOD SALAD

If you like spicy foods, you'll make this salad time and again. It features lightly poached scallops, prawns, and mussels, combined with boiled *soba* or rice noodles (available in Asian markets) and a marinade of hot peppers, dark sesame oil, and rice vinegar. Serve it on a chiffonade of chopped lettuce, endive, and spinach, garnished with slices of cucumber and red bell pepper. For extra flavor, marinate the seafood and noodles in the spicy sauce for an hour, then toss with greens before serving warm or chilled.

> 1 *cup white wine*
> ¼ *pound peeled medium prawns*
> ¼ *pound scallops*
> 6 *mussels in shell, scrubbed well*
> 10 *ounces uncooked rice or soba noodles*
> 4 *teaspoons finely minced garlic*
> ½ *cup minced green onions, including green tops*
> 2 *teaspoons cayenne or hot-pepper flakes*
> 4 *teaspoons tahini*
> 1 *teaspoon dark sesame oil*
> 2 *tablespoons low-sodium soy or tamari sauce*
> ½ *teaspoon honey*
> 1 *teaspoon grated gingerroot*
>   *Endive or leaf lettuce, for lining platter*
> ½ *cup peeled, halved, and sliced cucumbers*
> ½ *cup julienned red bell pepper*

1. In a saucepan over medium-high heat, bring wine to boil. Add prawns, scallops, and mussels in shell, cover, and cook 2 minutes. Drain and rinse under cold water. Remove mussels from shell and set seafood aside.

2. In a large pot over medium-high heat, bring 2 quarts water to a boil. Add noodles and cook until al dente (5 to 8 minutes). Drain and refresh under cold water. Set aside.

3. In large bowl mix together garlic, green onions, cayenne, tahini, sesame oil, soy sauce, honey, and gingerroot. Add noodles and seafood and mix well. Let chill for 30 minutes, if desired.

4. To serve, line a large platter with lettuce or endive. Pile noodles in center. Arrange cucumbers and red bell pepper around noodles.

Serves 6.

Preparation time: 25 minutes
Chilling time (optional): 30 minutes
Per serving: calcium 29 mg, calories 288, carbohydrates 47 g, cholesterol none, fat 5 g, fiber 2.6 g, protein 6 g, sodium 329 mg

For an Asian entrée, try noodles cooked al dente and then tossed with seafood and a spicy sesame oil dressing.

Prawns and Scallops on the Half Shell, a healthy variation of coquilles Saint-Jacques, contains only 145 calories per serving.

PRAWNS AND SCALLOPS ON THE HALF SHELL

For this elegant dish, wine-poached scallops and prawns are mixed with a light, low-fat cheese sauce, dusted with bread crumbs, and broiled in scallop shells until brown and bubbly. Equally appropriate as a first course or light luncheon, it has great nutritional benefits: plenty of calcium and good-quality protein are contained in both the shellfish and the sauce. A special bonus of this recipe is that it can be made ahead and frozen for several weeks. Broil right before serving.

> 6 *scallop shells*
> ¾ *pound medium prawns*
> ¾ *pound bay scallops*
> ⅓ *cup white wine or dry sherry*
> 1 *teaspoon unsalted butter*
> ½ *cup thinly sliced small mushrooms*
> 2 *tablespoons whole wheat pastry flour*
> ½ *cup nonfat or low-fat milk*
> ⅓ *cup grated Parmesan cheese*
> ⅓ *cup whole wheat bread crumbs, finely ground*

1. Wash scallop shells and place on a cookie sheet. Preheat broiler.

2. Peel and devein prawns, then coarsely chop. Quarter bay scallops. In a medium saucepan over medium-high heat, combine shellfish and wine and heat until bubbling. Cook until scallops are opaque (about 1 minute), stirring constantly. Drain and reserve cooking wine. Set scallops and prawns aside.

3. In the same pan, heat butter over medium heat and sauté mushrooms until they begin to exude moisture. If mixture gets too dry and begins to stick, add a small amount of reserved cooking wine. Stir in flour and cook for 2 minutes.

4. Add milk in a thin stream, stirring constantly with a whisk. Sauce should thicken immediately. If it doesn't, continue to cook over medium heat, stirring, until it is the consistency of heavy cream. Add Parmesan, scallops, and prawns, and remove from heat.

5. Spoon an equal amount of seafood mixture into each scallop shell. Top with bread crumbs and broil until lightly browned and bubbling (3 to 5 minutes). Serve hot (see Note).

Serves 6.

Note For easier service, fold a linen napkin under scallop shells to keep them from tipping on the plate.

Preparation time: 25 minutes
Cooking time: 15 minutes
Per serving: calcium 174 mg, calories 145, carbohydrates 9 g, cholesterol 63 mg, fat 4 g, fiber .3 g, protein 17 g, sodium 252 mg

STIR-FRY PRAWNS IN BLACK BEAN SAUCE

This Cantonese dish features fermented black beans (available in Asian markets) mashed with garlic and ginger to make savory black bean paste. When you combine this sauce with a sauté of red bell pepper and snow peas, prawns, and crunchy bok choy, you have a delicious dinner in no time.

    2 tablespoons fermented black
        beans, rinsed well
    2 teaspoons minced garlic
    1 tablespoon grated gingerroot
    1 pound large prawns
    1 cup sliced onion
    2 teaspoons peanut oil
    1 cup chopped bok choy
    ½ cup julienned red bell pepper
    ¼ cup sliced shiitake or other
        Asian mushrooms
    ½ cup chopped Chinese cabbage
    1 cup whole snow peas,
        ends trimmed
    1 teaspoon light miso
    ¾ cup defatted chicken or
        fish stock (see page 31)
    1 teaspoon honey
    1 teaspoon low-sodium soy
        or tamari sauce
    1 tablespoon arrowroot powder
        or cornstarch
    2 tablespoons cold water
        Cilantro, chopped, for garnish

1. In a small bowl mash together black beans, half the garlic, and ginger until mixture forms a paste. This can also be done in an electric minichopper or small food processor. Set aside. Peel and devein prawns.

2. In a wok or large skillet over medium-high heat, sauté onion in peanut oil until soft but not brown, stirring constantly. Add remaining garlic, bok choy, bell pepper, and mushrooms. Stir-fry for 5 minutes. Add cabbage, snow peas, and black bean mixture. Cover and let cook for 2 to 3 minutes.

3. In a small bowl mix together miso and broth. Add to stir-fry with honey, soy sauce, and prawns. Stir-fry until prawns turn pink. In a small bowl mix together arrowroot and the water and add to stir-fry. Cook until slightly thickened (3 minutes). Serve at once. Pass around chopped cilantro for garnish.

Serves 6.

Preparation time: 25 minutes
Cooking time: 12 to 15 minutes
Per serving: calcium 125 mg, calories 135, carbohydrates 15 g, cholesterol 53 mg, fat 3 g, fiber 3.0 g, protein 13 g, sodium 239 mg

SUNDAY BUFFET ON THE TERRACE

*Chinese Crab Salad
in Tomato Baskets*

*Balkan Cold Cucumber Salad
(see page 36)*

Tom's Caesar Salad (see page 39)

Brian's Best Bran Muffins

Sparkling Wine Coolers

Raspberry-Pear Crisp

Here is a menu to enjoy in the sun and warm breezes of a Sunday afternoon on your terrace or under the backyard trees. Most of the dishes are served chilled, so make them early in the day, or even the night before, and serve them right out of the refrigerator. The platters and bowls of salads should be well garnished; line them with crisp spinach, curly endive, or leaf lettuce before layering with salads. Attractive garnishes include strips of red or yellow bell pepper, cucumber slices cut in half-moons, scalloped lemon halves, minced green onions or cilantro, and grated zucchini. Menu serves 10.

Chilled salads and light desserts line the buffet table, tempting your guests to enjoy a healthy Sunday dinner on the terrace or patio.

CHINESE CRAB SALAD IN TOMATO BASKETS

Shimmering with the flavors of lemon and dark sesame oil, this salad is an upbeat version of the famous Chinese chicken salads that are so popular in California. Cut the tomatoes about an hour before serving. Lace the crabmeat with the irresistible combination of roasted macadamia nuts, cilantro, and a dressing of rice vinegar and sesame oil. Marinate the salad ahead of time, even overnight, but add the nuts and chow mein noodles (if used) right before serving.

- 4 cups fresh crabmeat
- 2 cups peeled, halved, seeded, and thinly sliced cucumbers
- 2 cups shredded green cabbage
- 2 tablespoons grated red onion
- 2 tablespoons toasted sesame seed
- ¼ cup minced cilantro
- 1 cup rice vinegar
- ⅔ cup light honey
- 2 tablespoons low-sodium tamari or soy sauce
- 2 tablespoons grated gingerroot
- 2 tablespoons dark sesame oil
- 2 teaspoons herbal salt substitute
- ½ cup chopped roasted macadamia nuts
- 1 cup chow mein noodles (optional)
  Lettuce leaves, for lining platter
- 5 large, ripe tomatoes

1. In a large bowl combine crabmeat, cucumbers, cabbage, onion, sesame seed, and cilantro. Toss well.

2. In another bowl whisk together vinegar, honey, tamari, gingerroot, oil, and salt substitute. Pour over crabmeat mixture and toss well. Add nuts and noodles (if used).

3. Line a platter with lettuce leaves. Cut each tomato in half width-wise. With a sharp knife, score interior and scoop out pulp to form a shell. Fill with a generous portion of crab salad and place on lettuce-lined platter.

Serves 10.

Preparation time: 45 minutes
Per serving: calcium 64 mg, calories 245, carbohydrates 30 g, cholesterol 62 mg, fat 9 g, fiber 1.2 g, protein 14 g, sodium 749 mg

BRIAN'S BEST BRAN MUFFINS

The secret of these muffins is in the buttermilk, which makes them rise light and fluffy. Make an extra batch and freeze for a brunch treat the following weekend.

- 2 cups wheat or oat bran
- 2 cups whole wheat pastry or unbleached white flour
- ¾ cup raisins
- 1½ teaspoons baking soda
- ⅓ cup molasses
- ⅓ cup honey
- 2 cups buttermilk
  Safflower oil, for coating muffin tin

1. In a large bowl, combine bran, flour, raisins, and baking soda. Stir together molasses, honey, and buttermilk, then pour over bran mixture. Let stand for 20 minutes.

2. Lightly oil a 12-hole muffin tin. Preheat oven to 350° F. Fill muffin cups two thirds full of batter and bake until muffins spring back slightly when pressed in the center (30 minutes). Remove from pan and serve warm.

Makes 12 muffins, 10 servings.

Preparation time: 25 minutes
Baking time: 30 minutes
Per 1 muffin: calcium 86 mg, calories 182, carbohydrates 43 g, cholesterol 1 mg, fat 1 g, fiber 6 g, protein 5 g, sodium 161 mg

RASPBERRY-PEAR CRISP

This is a surprisingly elegant dessert, and a colorful one. The sweetness of the pears combines beautifully with the tartness of the berries. This dessert is easy on the cook, since it can be made up to a week before a party, covered well, and frozen. Thaw in the refrigerator overnight and warm up slightly to serve.

- 1 teaspoon safflower oil
- 1½ cups sliced pears, such as Bosc or d'Anjou
- 2 cups fresh or unsweetened frozen raspberries
- ¼ cup dried currants
- ⅓ cup maple syrup
- 2 tablespoons arrowroot powder or cornstarch
- 1 tablespoon lemon juice
- 1 tablespoon grated lemon rind
- 1 cup uncooked rolled oats
- 3 tablespoons melted unsalted butter
- 2 tablespoons light honey
- ½ teaspoon nutmeg
- ½ teaspoon cinnamon
- ¼ teaspoon cardamom

1. Lightly oil a 9- by 12-inch baking pan and arrange pear slices in bottom of pan. Cover with raspberries, then currants. Mix together maple syrup, arrowroot, lemon juice, and rind, and drizzle over pear mixture. Preheat oven to 375° F.

2. In a large bowl combine oats, butter, honey, nutmeg, cinnamon, and cardamom. Crumble over pear mixture. Bake crisp until pears are tender and oats are lightly browned (30 to 40 minutes). Serve warm.

Serves 10.

Preparation time: 25 minutes
Baking time: 40 minutes
Per serving: calcium 32 mg, calories 161, carbohydrates 28 g, cholesterol 12 mg, fat 4 g, fiber 2.2 g, protein 1 g, sodium 39 mg

Sautéed in sherry, Chicken Breasts With Green Peppercorn Sauce (see page 60) makes a delicate, healthy variation on rich French cooking.

Light Poultry & Meat Entrées

By combining poultry and meats with vegetables, whole grains, and legumes, you can get the nutrients found in meat without eating too much fat and cholesterol. Stir-fries, such as Stir-fried Beef With Asparagus and Snow Peas (see page 67), are a good way to use small amounts of meat and still create a satisfying meal. Easy Beef Fajitas (see page 68) also uses less meat than the average recipe by combining lean strips of beef with sautéed onions and mushrooms in a sherry sauce. Poultry is often a good choice for family and entertaining menus. Turkey Chili Burritos (see page 65) and Roasted Chicken With Rosemary and Garlic (see page 62) replace high-fat meat entrées, yet satisfy the hearty meat eater.

POULTRY ENTRÉES

A welcome addition to any menu, poultry is easy to prepare, even ahead of time, yet is also a relatively low-fat, low-cholesterol source of protein. Here is a variety of recipes, including some unusual dishes for entertaining.

CHICKEN BREASTS WITH GREEN PEPPERCORN SAUCE

This rich dish should be saved for special occasions. The unripe (green) peppercorns, sold in most gourmet stores, have a slightly less acidic taste than white or black pepper. They are used whole in this recipe, enhanced by a sweet wine and cream sauce.

    4 chicken half breasts, boned
       and skinned
    1 teaspoon safflower oil
    ¼ cup dry sherry
    2 tablespoons minced onion
    ¼ cup white wine
    ½ cup half-and-half
    1 tablespoon green peppercorns
    ¼ teaspoon dried tarragon

1. Preheat oven to 400° F. In a large skillet over medium-high heat, sauté chicken breasts in safflower oil and sherry until lightly browned on both sides. Transfer to a baking dish. Bake for 15 minutes.

2. While chicken is baking, in the same skillet over medium heat, sauté onion in pan drippings until soft. Add wine, half-and-half, peppercorns, and tarragon. Heat until sauce coats the back of a spoon. Serve over baked chicken.

Serves 4.

Preparation time: 10 minutes
Baking time: 15 minutes
Per serving: calcium 60 mg, calories 302, carbohydrates 5 g, cholesterol 113 mg, fat 13 g, fiber .3 g, protein 34 g, sodium 113 mg

MOROCCAN FILO TART WITH CURRIED CHICKEN AND ALMONDS

Curried chicken filo tart, or *bastilla*, is a popular recipe served on special occasions in Morocco. Thin filo pastry is filled with seasoned chicken and an almond-gingerroot mixture, then baked until brown and crisp. The filling can also be used for small appetizers—follow directions given for Filo Pastries With Smoked Turkey and Mushrooms (see page 20). Since this dish takes a bit longer to assemble than other entrées, make the filling ahead of time and assemble the dish right before baking.

     16 sheets filo dough
      1 teaspoon safflower oil,
         for coating pan
    2½ cups cubed, cooked chicken,
         boned and skinned
      2 cups defatted Chicken Stock
         (see page 31)
      ½ teaspoon turmeric
      ½ teaspoon cardamom
      ⅛ teaspoon cayenne pepper
      ⅛ teaspoon ground ginger
      ½ cup minced onion
      3 tablespoons minced garlic
      4 whole eggs
      5 egg whites
      3 tablespoons minced parsley
      2 teaspoons herbal salt
         substitute
      ½ teaspoon ground black pepper
      ½ cup slivered almonds
      1 teaspoon grated gingerroot
      6 tablespoons plus 1 teaspoon
         unsalted butter, melted
      6 tablespoons date sugar
      2 teaspoons cinnamon
      ¼ teaspoon nutmeg

1. Lay sheets of filo dough on a clean surface. Cover with plastic wrap. Dampen and wring out a dish towel and lay over plastic-covered filo. Preheat oven to 350° F. Lightly oil a deep 9-inch-diameter baking pan.

2. In a medium saucepan over medium-high heat, simmer chicken in stock, turmeric, cardamom, cayenne, and ginger for 5 minutes. Drain, set chicken aside, and return spice broth to saucepan.

3. Add onion to spice broth and simmer until soft (8 to 10 minutes). Drain and reserve onion.

4. In large bowl mix together onion, garlic, eggs, egg whites, parsley, salt substitute, and pepper. Set aside. In a saucepan over medium-high heat, sauté almonds and gingerroot in 1 teaspoon of the butter until lightly browned. Add date sugar, cinnamon, and nutmeg. Set aside.

5. Unwrap filo. Using a wide pastry brush, brush approximately 1 teaspoon melted butter on a sheet of filo. Place buttered filo into bottom of prepared pan, letting edges hang over sides. Continue until 8 sheets are piled into bottom of pan. Place drained chicken into pan, then egg mixture, then three fourths of the almond mixture. Fold overhanging filo into center of pan on top of filling.

6. Butter remaining 8 sheets of filo, layering on top of filling, tucking edges down into interior of pan. Butter top of completed tart, sprinkle with reserved almond mixture, and bake until golden brown (about 25 minutes).

Serves 8.

Preparation time: 40 minutes
Baking time: 25 minutes
Per serving: calcium 74 mg, calories 484, carbohydrates 18 g, cholesterol 197 mg, fat 23 g, fiber .6 g, protein 24 g, sodium 594 mg

MEDITERRANEAN CHICKEN

Mediterranean Chicken, which can be prepared well in advance, delights guests with its unusual flavor combination of herbs, Greek olives, and heady balsamic vinegar. If possible, let the roasting chicken marinate for several hours, basting frequently with the sauce, and then roast right before serving. It is also great served cold for supper the next day, with a glass of white wine and a green salad.

> Oil, for greasing pan
> 1 roasting chicken (3 lb)
> 2 large cloves garlic
> 2 tablespoons green olive oil
> 1 tablespoon minced fresh tarragon
> 1 teaspoon crushed sage
> 6 tablespoons balsamic vinegar
> 6 small new potatoes
> ¼ cup pitted Greek olives

1. Preheat oven to 375° F. Lightly oil a large roasting pan or deep casserole.

2. Remove skin from chicken. Place chicken in roasting pan, breast side up. Peel and halve garlic cloves, rub surface of chicken with cut garlic, then place cloves inside chicken.

3. Mix together olive oil, tarragon, sage, and vinegar. Pour over surface of chicken and inside cavity. Cut potatoes in quarters and place olives and potatoes around chicken. Cover pan and place in oven.

4. Roast until juice runs clear when a sharp knife is inserted in thigh of bird (45 minutes to 1 hour). Slice or cut into serving pieces and serve with olives, potatoes, and cooking liquid.

Serves 6.

> *Preparation time:* 20 minutes
> *Roasting time:* 45 minutes to
> 1 hour
> *Per serving:* calcium 42 mg,
> calories 358, carbohydrates 20 g,
> cholesterol 101 mg, fat 15 g, fiber
> 1.3 g, protein 35 g, sodium
> 151 mg

Fresh tarragon leaves, garlic cloves, and crushed sage lend the sun-drenched flavor of southern European cuisine to an easy chicken dish.

POACHED CHICKEN BREASTS WITH LEMON-AND-HERB MAYONNAISE

Chicken takes well to poaching, as long as it is not overcooked. In this recipe the soy sauce and lemon permeate the chicken breasts, and the resulting flavor melds with the tart mayonnaise. Use low-calorie mayonnaise, available in most supermarkets, to reduce the calories, fat, and cholesterol in this dish.

    3 cups defatted Chicken Stock
      (see page 31)
    2 tablespoons grated
      lemon rind
    1 tablespoon low-sodium soy
      or tamari sauce
    4 chicken half breasts, boned
      and skinned
    1 cup low-calorie mayonnaise
    1 tablespoon lemon juice
    1 tablespoon minced chives
      or green onions
    1 teaspoon Dijon mustard
    ½ teaspoon minced fresh
      tarragon
      Minced chives and lemon
      slices, for garnish (optional)

1. In a large, shallow skillet over medium-high heat, bring to a boil chicken stock, half the lemon rind, and soy sauce. Lower heat to simmer. Add chicken breasts, cover, and poach for 10 minutes. Remove from poaching liquid and chill if desired.

2. In a small bowl combine mayonnaise, lemon juice, remaining lemon rind, chives, mustard, and tarragon. Chill until ready to serve.

3. Serve each half breast with a generous dollop of lemon mayonnaise on top. Garnish with minced chives and a slice of lemon.

Serves 4.

Preparation time: 20 minutes
Poaching time: 10 minutes
Chilling time (optional): 20 minutes
Per serving: calcium 24 mg, calories 434, carbohydrates 1 g, cholesterol 105 mg, fat 29 g, fiber none, protein 36 g, sodium 900 mg

---

ROASTED CHICKEN WITH ROSEMARY AND GARLIC

To preserve its moistness, the chicken is roasted in a light sauce, which is then reduced and served over the bird. The pungent flavorings, rosemary and garlic, are commonly used in the cuisines of Greece and southern France.

    4 cloves garlic
    1 teaspoon unsalted butter
    1 tablespoon olive oil
    1 roasting chicken (3 lb),
      skinned
    2 tablespoons minced fresh
      rosemary
    ½ cup dry white wine

1. Preheat oven to 350° F. Peel and halve garlic cloves. In a large ovenproof skillet over medium-high heat, heat butter and oil and sauté garlic cloves for 2 minutes. Quarter chicken. Add to pan and brown lightly on both sides. Add rosemary to pan.

2. Cover skillet and place in oven. Bake until juice runs clear when a sharp knife is inserted into thigh of bird (about 40 minutes). Remove bird from pan and keep warm on a platter in oven.

3. In the same skillet over medium-high heat, pour in wine. Cook rapidly for 2 to 3 minutes, scraping pan to loosen browned bits. Pour sauce over chicken and serve.

Serves 6.

Preparation time: 20 minutes
Roasting time: 40 minutes
Per serving: calcium 35 mg, calories 264, carbohydrates 2 g, cholesterol 103 mg, fat 12 g, fiber .2 g, protein 33 g, sodium 99 mg

---

CURRIED TURKEY BREAST

Curried Turkey Breast is a simple but delicious entrée and is great with Avocado and Pine Nut Salad (see page 39) or Jamaican Papaya Salad (see page 35). Buy large turkey breasts from the butcher, then skin and cover them with a spicy mixture of cumin, coriander, cinnamon, and turmeric. Let the meat marinate for several hours in the spice mixture, then bake until crisp on the outside and juicy in the middle.

    2 large turkey breasts, skinned
    ½ teaspoon ground coriander
    ½ teaspoon paprika
    ¼ teaspoon turmeric
    ½ teaspoon cumin
    ¼ teaspoon cayenne pepper
    ¼ teaspoon cinnamon
    2 tablespoons grated gingerroot
    1 tablespoon olive oil
    2 tablespoons lemon juice
    ½ cup nonfat plain yogurt
      Minced green onions,
      for garnish

1. Place turkey breasts in a large baking pan. In a small bowl combine coriander, paprika, turmeric, cumin, cayenne, cinnamon, gingerroot, olive oil, lemon juice, and yogurt. Spread over top of turkey breasts. Cover pan with plastic wrap and refrigerate for 2 hours.

2. Preheat oven to 350° F. Unwrap pan and place in oven; bake for 40 minutes, basting occasionally with pan juices. To serve, slice turkey, drizzle with pan juices, and garnish with green onions.

Serves 4.

Preparation time: 10 minutes
Baking time: 40 minutes
Marinating time: 2 hours
Per serving: calcium 47 mg, calories 255, carbohydrates 2 g, cholesterol 89 mg, fat 9 g, fiber .36 g, protein 38 g, sodium 107 mg

---

REDUCING CHOLESTEROL IN YOUR DIET

Dietary cholesterol is invisible, but it exists in all the animal foods you eat. Although the American Heart Association recommends consuming a maximum of 300 milligrams of cholesterol daily, most people ingest closer to 500 milligrams.

A constant companion to fat, cholesterol is a steroid alcohol that is found in many fatty foods such as cheese, red meats, and eggs. Consuming too much cholesterol and fat is the worst nutritional failing—research shows that the average American diet contains 40 to 45 percent saturated fat compared to the 30 percent recommended by the American Heart Association. This quantity of fat is difficult for the human body to process and remove. The sad results can be heart disease, obesity, and other health problems related to eating excess fat and cholesterol.

Cholesterol is sometimes labeled as an evil, but humans and animals need a certain amount of cholesterol to live. The body actually produces several different kinds of cholesterol, called lipoproteins, some of which perform important functions. The amount that the body manufactures by itself, however, is usually sufficient without having to assimilate and remove excess amounts from the diet.

The three main types of cholesterol are high-density lipoproteins (HDLs), low-density lipoproteins (LDLs), and very low-density lipoproteins (VLDLs). HDLs are considered beneficial since they are responsible for extracting cholesterol from the body cells and transporting it to the liver for processing or removal. LDLs and VLDLs, on the other hand, are responsible for depositing cholesterol on the walls of arteries.

Many studies have shown the connection between diet and levels of harmful blood cholesterols. A person with a diet high in saturated fats and cholesterol often has a higher level of LDLs and VLDLs. When you receive the results of a blood test to measure cholesterol, you should look not only at the total cholesterol count, but also at the HDL level—in most cases, the higher the HDL count, the better.

Although scientific evidence points to genetic predisposition to cholesterol levels, higher levels of HDLs and lower levels of LDLs are often found in people who exercise regularly, do not smoke, maintain normal weight, and, most importantly, follow a healthy diet that emphasizes nutritious, low-fat foods.

Desirable total cholesterol levels are counts of 200 milligram percent or below; some physicians prefer a count of 180 milligram percent or lower. Those who maintain low cholesterol levels and have few risk factors (smoking, obesity, diabetes, hypertension, stress, family history of high cholesterol or heart disease) are still advised to monitor their daily intake of fat and cholesterol and measure blood cholesterol levels as recommended by their physician.

High blood cholesterol measurements of 240 and above, or 200 and above for people with risk factors, are considered dangerous. If you fall into either of these categories, you may wish to consult with a physician and adopt a more stringent low-fat, low-cholesterol diet.

If you want to lower dietary cholesterol, but are not sure how to do it, here are some tips.

☐ Make changes gradually. Try decreasing cholesterol intake one meal at a time, perhaps starting with breakfast, which is often the most cholesterol-rich meal of the day. Instead of bacon and eggs, eat a whole-grain cereal topped with low-fat milk and fresh fruit. Whereas one egg contains 274 milligrams of cholesterol, a serving of whole-grain cereal with 1 cup of whole milk contains only 33 milligrams. Twice a week, replace red-meat dinners with fish. A 3-ounce fish fillet has only 33 milligrams of cholesterol, compared to 85 in 3 ounces of beef.

☐ Increase the amount of fresh fruits and vegetables in your diet. Begin to regard meat and dairy products more as a condiment than a centerpiece in your menu planning. Add extra vegetables to stir-fries, chili, and baked pasta dishes, and cut back on such high-cholesterol items as high-fat red meat and Cheddar, American, Swiss, and other high-fat cheeses.

☐ Avoid egg yolks. Substitute two egg whites for every other egg yolk called for in recipes for baked goods, such as muffins or pancakes. Each egg yolk contains 270 milligrams of cholesterol; an egg white contains an insignificant 4 milligrams.

☐ Use nonfat dairy products. Substitute lowfat or nonfat milk for whole milk and nonfat yogurt for sour cream.

☐ Try whipped milk instead of whipped cream. Chill a can of evaporated nonfat milk in the freezer until icy, then whip with an egg beater to make an excellent substitute for whipped cream.

☐ Sauté with polyunsaturated oils, such as safflower oil or corn oil, rather than butter, lard, or bacon grease. Polyunsaturated oils reduce cholesterol.

☐ Trim off all visible fat from meat before cooking. Select the leanest meat, use a rack to allow fat to drip off during baking or broiling, and baste with wine, stock, or tomato juice instead of drippings.

☐ Be conscious of cholesterol when eating out. Ask for sauces and gravies made without cream, and request that butter not be spread on broiled fish or baked potatoes. Avoid high-fat cheeses, sour cream, and creamy salad dressings. Choose fresh fruit desserts or sherbets rather than ice creams and puddings.

Quick browning and then basting in a sweet apple brandy sauce before baking assures a tender, delicious Braised Pheasant every time. If pheasant is unavailable in your area, Rock Cornish game hens (shown above) turn out just as tender and tasty.

GRILLED TURKEY BREAST WITH RASPBERRY AND SHALLOT MARINADE

Adapted from a California restaurant recipe, this dish features a quartered turkey breast marinated in a raspberry vinegar sauce, then grilled over hot coals. Serve Grilled Turkey Breast with Spicy Tomato Aspic (see page 38) or Minted Bulgur Salad (see page 36) for a healthy meal.

- 1 large turkey breast, skinned and quartered
- ½ cup raspberry vinegar
- 2 tablespoons minced shallots
- ½ cup nonfat plain yogurt
- 1 teaspoon curry powder

1. Place turkey breast quarters into a large, shallow pan. Mix together vinegar and shallots and pour over turkey. Cover with plastic wrap and marinate for 8 to 10 hours in the refrigerator.

2. Combine yogurt and curry powder. Set aside.

3. Prepare coals for grilling. Wrap turkey breasts in aluminum foil and place on grill. Cook over coals for 20 minutes, then unwrap and grill for 5 minutes more, turning once to brown lightly. Spoon marinade over turkey frequently during last 5 minutes of grilling.

4. Serve with curried yogurt as a spicy sauce.

Serves 4.

Preparation time: 10 minutes
Marinating time: 8 to 10 hours
Grilling time: 25 minutes
Per serving: calcium 68 mg, calories 228, carbohydrates 5 g, cholesterol 87 mg, fat 5 g, fiber .1 g, protein 39 g, sodium 114 mg

TURKEY CHILI BURRITOS

This chili made with small chunks of turkey is seasoned perfectly and wrapped in warm flour tortillas. Serve this fast and easy entrée with salsa and chopped cilantro.

1 cup minced onion
1 teaspoon safflower oil
½ cup defatted Chicken Stock (see page 31)
1 tablespoon minced garlic
4 cups diced turkey meat, skinned
½ cup diced celery
½ cup chopped carrot
¼ cup minced parsley
1 cup water
1 cup diced tomatoes
½ teaspoon ground cloves
2 tablespoons chili powder or to taste
½ teaspoon Tabasco Sauce
4 ounces canned green chiles, chopped
   Herbal salt substitute and pepper, to taste
12 flour tortillas
½ cup grated low-fat Cheddar cheese

1. In a Dutch oven over medium-high heat, sauté onion in oil and stock until soft. Add garlic, turkey, celery, carrot, parsley, and tomatoes and sauté, stirring frequently, for 10 minutes.

2. Add the water, cloves, chili powder, Tabasco, and green chiles. Lower heat, cover, and cook for 25 minutes. Taste for seasoning and add salt substitute and pepper, if necessary.

3. Warm tortillas by placing in a toaster oven or conventional oven for 5 minutes at 200° F.

4. To serve, spoon approximately ⅓ cup chili into each tortilla, cover with grated cheese, and roll.

Serves 6.

Preparation time: 25 minutes
Cooking time: 40 minutes
Per serving: calcium 200 mg, calories 436, carbohydrates 50 g, cholesterol 72 mg, fat 8 g, fiber 2.4 g, protein 41 g, sodium 710 mg

ROAST DUCKLING WITH SHERRY

The rich flavor and elegance of duckling makes it a good alternate to turkey for special occasions. In this recipe, whole duckling is rubbed with a savory herb mixture, stuffed with braised vegetables, and roasted until crisp. Serve with a simple accompaniment of wok-cooked vegetables, a green salad, roasted potatoes, and French bread.

2 small ducklings (2 to 3 lb each)
½ teaspoon celery salt
½ teaspoon onion salt
½ teaspoon celery seed
¼ teaspoon curry powder
1 teaspoon herbal salt substitute
¼ teaspoon pepper
¼ cup minced celery
½ cup minced onion
½ cup sherry

1. Place ducklings in a large Dutch oven, breasts up. In a small bowl mix together celery salt, onion salt, celery seed, curry powder, salt substitute, and pepper. Rub into skin of ducklings. Let marinate 1 hour.

2. Preheat oven to 300° F. Add celery and onion to Dutch oven. Pour in the ½ cup sherry. Place Dutch oven over medium-high heat and brown ducklings on both sides (about 20 minutes per side). Cover Dutch oven and bake for 1 hour. Slice and serve.

Serves 4.

Preparation time: 10 minutes
Marinating time: 1 hour
Browning time: 40 minutes
Cooking time: 1 hour
Per serving: calcium 30 mg, calories 493, carbohydrates 2 g, cholesterol 120 mg, fat 41 g, fiber .3 g, protein 28 g, sodium 457 mg

BRAISED PHEASANT

Rock Cornish game hens work well in this recipe if pheasant is unavailable. The birds are browned quickly and then roasted slowly to bring out the flavor, while you baste them in an apple brandy sauce. Serve with a green salad dressed with Lime Mint Dressing (see page 40) and steamed asparagus or broccoli.

3 large pheasants, cleaned and rinsed well
¼ cup safflower oil
3 cups peeled and thinly sliced green apples
1 cup thinly sliced onions
½ cup applejack or Calvados
1 teaspoon nutmeg
½ cup half-and-half
   Herbal salt substitute and pepper, to taste

1. Preheat oven to 350° F. In a large Dutch oven over medium-high heat, quickly brown pheasants in oil on all sides. Place apples and onions around pheasant. Pour applejack on top and let it heat for 1 minute, then ignite. Shake pan until flames subside.

2. Dust top of pheasant with nutmeg. Place pan in oven and bake until juice runs clear when tip of knife is inserted in thigh of bird (about 1 hour). Remove pheasant, cooked apples, and onions to a platter and keep warm in oven.

3. Transfer pan juices to a saucepan. Heat over medium-high heat until simmering, then stir in half-and-half. Let mixture cook 5 minutes, stirring frequently, then season to taste with salt substitute and pepper. Pour over pheasant and serve.

Serves 8.

Preparation time: 20 minutes
Baking time: 1 hour
Per serving: calcium 46 mg, calories 345, carbohydrates 10 g, cholesterol 6 mg, fat 14 g, fiber 1.4 g, protein 36 g, sodium 62 mg

...ON PREPARING MEAT AND CHICKEN FOR ROASTING

To retain flavor and moistness when roasting or grilling meat, you should follow some easy guidelines.

☐ For poultry, wash and dry the bird thoroughly. Remove any giblets from cavity. For meats, trim excess fat, which contributes heavily to calories and saturated fat.

☐ Season according to recipe. Be liberal with most seasonings— more flavor is lost in slow-cooking methods than in quick-cooking methods such as frying. Prepare any marinade right in the roasting pan. Pour in prepared marinade, wine, or citrus juice. Let marinate at room temperature if possible—more flavor will be absorbed. Baste often during marinating process, and turn meat or poultry every 15 minutes so all sides are covered with the sauce.

☐ Roast in a low (300° F) oven. To retain moisture, wrap meat or poultry in aluminum foil or place in a covered clay pot that has been presoaked in water for 20 minutes. You can also try the *en sac* technique: Lightly oil the inside of a large unprinted grocery bag and place turkey or chicken inside (if desired, line bottom of bag with aluminim foil or insert a rack to keep bird off bag's surface). Roll end of bag to seal.

☐ Sear thin pieces of beef, veal, or chicken before roasting. In a large, heavy ovenproof pan, quickly sauté the meat or poultry until the surfaces turn slightly opaque. Then add marinade or seasonings, cover, and place in the oven to continue roasting. After the surface of the meat has been sealed in the searing process, the interior will retain more moisture and stay tender.

LIGHT MEAT ENTRÉES

Decreasing the amount of heavy, fat-laden meats in your diet is a healthier approach to eating. This section offers intriguing ways to use cuts of veal, beef, and lamb that are chosen for their lower fat content and good flavor. Selecting lean cuts is easy. In beef, look for sirloin tip, eye of round, round steak, flank steak, tenderloin, lean stew meat, or lean ground beef. The leanest cuts of lamb are the leg and sirloin chop. Veal is inherently lean, with the exception of the breast. Trim all visible fat from meat before using it. Although fat helps to retain the juiciness of the meat as it cooks, these low-fat entrées all use sauces or special cooking techniques to hold moisture. Broiling and poaching are recommended instead of frying.

STEWED BEEF IN RED WINE

A lighter version of the traditional wine-braised beef dishes from France, this savory entrée is an elegant stew that is equally appropriate for a family supper or a party. An excellent buffet dish, it keeps well and can be prepared ahead of time and frozen for up to four weeks. Serve with plenty of crusty French bread and a large tossed salad. The same kind of wine that is used in the sauce is an appropriate table wine to accompany the stew.

> 2 *pounds stew meat, fat trimmed*
> 2 *teaspoons safflower oil*
> ¼ *cup brandy*
> 3 *cups dry red wine*
> 1 *cup defatted Beef Stock (see page 31)*
> 1 *tablespoon tomato paste*
> 2 *cloves garlic, mashed*
> ¼ *teaspoon thyme*
> 1 *bay leaf, crushed*
> 12 *small white boiling onions*
> 3 *tablespoons olive oil*
> 1 *cup water*
> ½ *pound mushrooms*
> 3 *tablespoons whole wheat pastry or unbleached white flour*
> 4 *cups cooked basmati rice or egg noodles*

1. Cut meat into .1-inch cubes. In a large Dutch oven over medium-high heat, sear beef in 1 teaspoon of the safflower oil until lightly browned on all sides. Pour in brandy and ignite, shaking pan until flames subside. Add wine, stock, tomato paste, garlic, thyme, and bay leaf. Bring to a boil, then lower heat to simmer. Cook, uncovered, until tender (about 20 to 30 minutes). Preheat oven to 200° F.

2. Peel onions and cut a small *X* in the top of each to prevent them from falling apart as they cook. In a small skillet over medium-high heat, sauté onions in 1 teaspoon of the olive oil. Add the water, cover, and cook for 15 minutes.

3. Drain onions and set aside. In the same pan over medium-high heat, sauté mushrooms in the remaining 1 teaspoon safflower oil for 5 minutes. Set aside.

4. Remove beef from sauce and keep warm on a platter in the oven. Bring sauce to a boil and reduce to half its volume by simmering, uncovered, for 10 minutes. Combine together remaining olive oil and flour and drop into boiling sauce by spoonfuls, stirring with a whisk until sauce thickens.

5. Return beef to sauce, and add onions and mushrooms. Heat through and serve over rice.

Serves 4.

Preparation time: 30 minutes
Cooking time: 35 minutes
Per serving: calcium 61 mg, calories 897, carbohydrates 54 g, cholesterol 198 mg, fat 51 g, fiber 2.2 g, protein 47 g, sodium 114 mg

STIR-FRIED BEEF WITH ASPARAGUS AND SNOW PEAS

Offering a light approach to beef, this Chinese recipe combines thin strips of lean sirloin with a rich-tasting sesame oil sauce, then adds asparagus slices, whole snow peas, and red bell pepper strips for texture and color, as well as nutrition. The sauce keeps the steak from drying out. A healthy and fast entrée for a party, buffet table, or potluck, Stir-fried Beef With Asparagus and Snow Peas can be accompanied by steamed rice and garnished with chopped unsalted peanuts.

> 1 pound lean sirloin steak, fat trimmed
> 3 tablespoons dry sherry
> 2 tablespoons dark sesame oil
> 1 tablespoon grated gingerroot
> 1 tablespoon minced garlic
> 1 teaspoon safflower oil
> 2 green onions
> ¾ pound asparagus
> ½ cup julienned red bell pepper
> 2 tablespoons oyster sauce
> 2 tablespoons arrowroot powder
> 1 cup trimmed whole snow peas

1. Cut steak into thin strips. Place in a large bowl with sherry, sesame oil, gingerroot, and garlic. Let marinate 15 minutes.

2. Cut green onions into ½-inch pieces, and trim asparagus and cut into 1-inch lengths. Heat wok over medium-high heat and add safflower oil. Stir-fry green onions, asparagus, and bell pepper for 2 minutes, then remove to a platter and keep warm in oven.

3. Add steak and marinade to wok and stir-fry for 3 minutes. In a small bowl combine oyster sauce and arrowroot. Add to steak and cook for 1 minute. Add vegetable mixture and cook for 1 minute, stirring constantly. Toss in snow peas, cover wok, and cook for 1 minute. Serve immediately.

Serves 6.

> *Preparation time:* 25 minutes
> *Marinating time:* 15 minutes
> *Cooking time:* 10 minutes
> *Per serving:* calcium 47 mg, calories 322, carbohydrates 13 g, cholesterol 49 mg, fat 23 g, fiber 2.8 g, protein 15 g, sodium 55 mg

The red and green of bell peppers, snow peas, and tender asparagus lightens and brightens this Chinese beef stir-fry.

ALL ABOUT PROTEIN

Protein derives from the Greek word *protos,* meaning *of first importance.* Protein is the foundation of a healthy body, the key component of living tissue. It is the basic building block of cells, antibodies, enzymes, and hormones.

Protein builds new tissues, repairs worn-out body tissue, provides heat and energy, regulates body secretions and the balance of fluids, and produces antibodies to resist disease. Proteins form the structure of the muscles, ligaments, hair, and nails. They are a component of hemoglobin, which moves oxygen through the bloodstream, and of insulin, which regulates blood sugar.

Essentially nitrogen compounds, proteins produce amino acids as they are utilized and broken down by the body. Proteins are composed of 23 amino acids, 8 of which are considered essential. Food is the only source for these essential nutrients since the human body does not manufacture or synthesize them. To ensure intake of proper protein building blocks, the body should receive these 8 essential amino acids in certain proportions. A balanced complex of these amino acids occurs in foods called complete proteins. Foods with incomplete protein must be combined with other proteins to complete the arrangement of the 8 essential amino acids.

Foods with animal proteins are considered complete proteins since the amino acids are in the required balance. The proteins in plant foods, such as grains, legumes, fruits, and vegetables, are less complete and must be carefully combined to be most useful. Many health professionals recommend eating several types of proteins in one meal, or in the meals consumed in the course of one day, to ensure a good balance and complete the amino acid chain. An example is a peanut butter sandwich on whole wheat bread with a glass of milk—three different sources of protein, that, when combined, offer a more usable protein complex than the peanut butter alone.

The U.S. Recommended Daily Allowance guidelines recommend an average of 44 grams of protein per day (or 6.5 ounces) for women and 56 grams per day (or 8 ounces) for men. That requirement can easily be satisfied with a skinned chicken half-breast chopped into a salad for lunch and a piece of broiled fish for dinner. Remember that protein is also contained in the slice of rye bread you may eat with a salad, the dollop of nonfat yogurt you may mix with breakfast cereal, and even the baked potato accompanying fish. So it is not hard to consume your daily protein requirement with a variety of healthy foods spread over three balanced meals.

Protein sources should be chosen carefully. An excess of animal proteins containing highly saturated fats and cholesterol, such as steak, bacon, cheeses, sausages, and hamburger, can contribute to increased blood cholesterol levels and lead to a higher risk of atherosclerosis and coronary heart disease. Furthermore, excess protein not used by the body can be converted to body fat. Excess protein also puts additional strain on the kidneys, which are responsible for excreting the by-products of protein digestion. High-protein diets in substantial excess of the recommended daily requirements can also contribute to improper absorption of some nutrients, such as calcium.

Most people in the United States eat about twice as much protein as needed for good health. Since the most common protein sources in the American diet are high-fat, high-cholesterol foods, a resulting problem can be weight gain. So the healthy option becomes quality of protein rather than quantity. Don't eat more, just eat better.

EASY BEEF FAJITAS

A Tex-Mex favorite, *fajitas* are made by combining strips of beef or chicken fried in a skillet with sautéed onions, mushrooms, and chiles, and rolling the mixture into warm flour tortillas. This recipe uses lean sirloin steak strips, sautéed quickly in a serrano chile sauce and garnished with nonfat yogurt and slices of avocado.

- *1 cup sliced onions*
- *1 cup sliced mushrooms*
- *1 teaspoon safflower oil*
- *⅓ cup dry sherry*
- *1 pound sirloin tips, fat trimmed*
- *2 serrano or jalapeño chiles, seeded and minced*
- *½ teaspoon cumin*
- *¼ teaspoon ground coriander*
- *1 teaspoon minced cilantro*
- *4 large flour tortillas*
- *½ cup bottled salsa*
- *½ avocado, thinly sliced*
- *1 cup nonfat plain yogurt*

1. In a large skillet over medium-high heat, sauté onions and mushrooms in oil and sherry for 10 minutes. Cut steak into 1½-inch strips and add to sauté, cooking for 2 minutes more. Add chiles, cumin, coriander, and cilantro, and cook 3 more minutes, stirring frequently.

2. Warm tortillas in toaster oven or conventional oven. Arrange bowls of salsa, sliced avocado, and yogurt on a tray. Wrap warmed tortillas in clean cloth napkin. Serve meat filling out of skillet or in prewarmed serving dish. Guests then assemble their own fajitas.

Serves 4.

Preparation time: 15 minutes
Cooking time: 15 minutes
Per serving: calcium 181 mg, calories 530, carbohydrates 36 g, cholesterol 75 mg, fat 29 g, fiber 1.7 g, protein 26 g, sodium 412 mg

VEAL AND APPLE SCALOPPINE

This recipe calls for tender scallops of veal. Ask the butcher to prepare the thin slices, then pound them between sheets of waxed paper until you can almost see through them. When cooked, they will be butter-soft and easy to cut with a fork. The slightly caramelized sauce of tart apples and applejack is a good foil for the savory veal slices. Serve with steamed green beans and red onions, and wild rice.

> 1 *pound veal scallops, thinly sliced*
> 2 *green apples*
> 1 *tablespoon safflower oil*
> ½ *cup applejack or Calvados*
> ½ *cup half-and-half*

1. Preheat oven to 350° F. Pound slices of veal between sheets of waxed paper until very thin and tender. Peel, core, and slice apples.

2. Lightly oil a medium-sized baking dish or casserole with some of the safflower oil. Spread apple slices over bottom of dish. Bake for 20 minutes, uncovered.

3. In a large skillet over medium-high heat, heat remaining oil and lightly brown each piece of veal on both sides. Place veal slices on top of apples in baking dish.

4. Pour applejack into skillet to deglaze pan, allowing brandy to heat and scraping pan as it cooks. Add cream and cook over medium heat for 5 minutes. Pour sauce over veal and apples. Bake veal until bubbling (about 20 minutes). Serve at once.

Serves 4.

> *Preparation time:* 20 minutes
> *Baking time:* 40 minutes
> *Per serving:* calcium 47 mg, calories 365, carbohydrates 20 g, cholesterol 73 mg, fat 18 g, fiber 1.5 g, protein 22 g, sodium 57 mg

A satisfying dish from grandmother's recipe box, Veal and Apple Scaloppine can also be a gourmet's delight.

GRILLED LAMB AND VEGETABLE MEDLEY

Originating in the Middle East, these marinated shish kabobs will become summer grilling favorites. Spear chunks of seasoned lamb, yellow and red bell peppers, pearl onions, and cherry tomatoes; grill until searing hot; then serve. Accompany this entrée with steamed basmati rice, Balkan Cold Cucumber Salad (see page 36), and crusty bread.

1 pound trimmed lamb shanks, cut into 1-inch cubes
½ teaspoon cayenne pepper
1 teaspoon ground coriander
1 teaspoon cumin
1 tablespoon minced garlic
2 tablespoons red wine, such as Zinfandel
4 pearl onions
1 large red bell pepper
1 large yellow bell pepper
2 teaspoons olive oil
4 large cherry tomatoes
Safflower oil, for coating grill

1. Place cubes of lamb into a large, shallow pan. Mix together cayenne, coriander, cumin, garlic, and wine, and pour over lamb. Toss well. Cover with plastic wrap and refrigerate for 8 to 10 hours.

2. Peel onions and steam until soft. Seed and quarter bell peppers. Arrange onions, bell peppers, and lamb on shish kabob skewers, leaving room for addition of cherry tomatoes later. Brush skewered items with olive oil and place on platter. Cover with plastic wrap and refrigerate for 8 to 10 hours.

3. Grill kabobs for 10 minutes, turning once, then add one cherry tomato to each skewer and grill until lightly brown (5 to 10 minutes). Serve hot for best flavor.

Serves 4.

Preparation time: 20 minutes
Marinating time: 8 to 10 hours
Grilling time: 15 to 20 minutes
Per serving: calcium 17 mg, calories 187, carbohydrates 4 g, cholesterol 52 mg, fat 8 g, fiber .7 g, protein 22 g, sodium 57 mg

THAI BEEF AND CHILES WITH ORANGE

This popular Thai appetizer can also be served as a main dish. Lean ground beef is sautéed with onions, garlic, and spicy chiles, then seasoned with Thai fish sauce (available in Asian markets), cilantro, and delicate palm sugar. (Similar to maple sugar except for the flavor, palm sugar is made from the pulp of the palm tree.) Traditionally served on orange or pineapple slices, in this recipe the mixture is tossed with chopped oranges and served on lettuce leaves.

½ cup minced onion
1 tablespoon minced garlic
1 teaspoon safflower oil
1 pound extralean ground beef
3 tablespoons Thai fish sauce
2 serrano or jalapeño chiles, seeded and minced
¼ cup Thai palm sugar
¼ cup chopped cilantro
¼ teaspoon cumin
⅓ cup finely chopped raw peanuts
½ cup peeled, chopped oranges
8 large lettuce leaves

1. In a wok or large skillet over medium-high heat, sauté onion and garlic in oil until soft (about 5 minutes). Add beef and continue cooking for 2 minutes.

2. In a small bowl mix together fish sauce, chiles, and palm sugar until smooth. Pour into wok and cook until liquid evaporates (5 to 7 minutes). Stir in cilantro, cumin, and peanuts. Cook 2 more minutes.

3. Remove from heat and stir in oranges. Place a generous helping of beef mixture on each lettuce leaf, roll lightly, and serve immediately.

Serves 4.

Preparation time: 20 minutes
Cooking time: 15 to 20 minutes
Per serving: calcium 66 mg, calories 369, carbohydrates 25 g, cholesterol 59 mg, fat 18 g, fiber 2.6 g, protein 29 g, sodium 79 mg

menu

HEALTHY THANKSGIVING DINNER

Roast Turkey With Grapes and Prunes

Miso Gravy

Cream Cheese and Garlic Dip with Pita Toasts (see page 18)

Fresh Cranberry-Orange Relish

Wild Rice Pilaf

Steamed Vegetable Medley

Gingered Sweet Potato Purée in Orange Baskets

Apple-Cranberry Gem Tarts (see page 112)

Nonalcoholic Wine and Sparkling Water

It is Thanksgiving, your turn to cook, and you want to present a tasty, yet healthy, dinner. The turkey in this menu is filled with a delicious stuffing combining grapes, prunes, and corn bread and is cooked en sac, so that it retains moisture. For your steamed vegetable medley, try broccoli, kale, julienned red bell pepper, and yellow squash. Served for desert, the Apple-Cranberry Gem Tarts are a perfect ending to a healthy Thanksgiving meal. Menu serves 12.

ROAST TURKEY WITH GRAPES AND PRUNES

In traditional French cooking, poultry is sometimes roasted inside a paper bag that has been lightly oiled (see Note). The bag holds in the moisture during the cooking process, the result is tender and juicy, and cleanup is easier—you just throw the bag away.

> Safflower oil, for coating paper bag
> 1 turkey (about 10 lb)
> 6 cups dry corn bread, crumbled
> 2 teaspoons thyme
> 2 teaspoons sage
> 2 teaspoons minced parsley
> ¼ cup port
> ½ cup pitted, chopped prunes
> ½ cup green seedless grapes
> 1 cup diced apples
> 1 cup minced onion
> 2 teaspoons safflower oil
> ¼ stick unsalted butter

1. Preheat oven to 350° F. Lightly oil inside of a large, unprinted paper grocery bag. Wash and pat turkey dry.

2. In a large bowl mix corn-bread crumbs with thyme, sage, and parsley. Set aside.

3. In a saucepan over medium heat, simmer port, prunes, grapes, and apples for 15 minutes. In a skillet over medium-high heat, sauté onion in oil until soft but not browned (8 to 10 minutes). Add fruit mixture and sautéed onion to bread crumbs and mix well.

4. Stuff cavity of turkey with bread stuffing. Lace opening shut with kitchen twine. Dot exterior of turkey with small pieces of butter. Place turkey inside prepared sack, roll opening of sack to seal tightly, and place sack in a large roasting pan. Place in oven and roast for 2½ to 3 hours. During the last 30 minutes, tear away top of bag to let exterior brown. To test for doneness, pierce a leg with the tip of a sharp knife.

The juice should spurt out a clear yellow; if it is pink, roast the bird for 10 to 15 minutes longer.

Serves 12.

Note If you are concerned about chemicals in the paper of the bag, you may want to line the bottom of the bag with aluminum foil or a rack.

> *Preparation time:* 30 minutes
> *Roasting time:* 3 hours, or according to poundage of turkey
> *Per serving:* calcium 198 mg, calories 624, carbohydrates 47 g, cholesterol 153 mg, fat 18 g, fiber 2.1 g, protein 68 g, sodium 510 mg

MISO GRAVY

A lighter version of traditional gravy, this version is flavored with miso, which replaces salt. Make the gravy ahead of time through step 3, if you wish, and add the pan drippings during the last 30 minutes of cooking the turkey.

> ½ teaspoon finely minced garlic
> 2 teaspoons safflower oil or unsalted butter
> ¼ cup port
> 2 tablespoons whole wheat pastry or unbleached white flour
> 2 cups nonfat milk
> ½ teaspoon dry mustard
> ¼ cup grated low-fat cheese, such as mozzarella
> 3 tablespoons light miso
> ⅓ cup pan drippings from roasting turkey

1. In a medium saucepan over medium-high heat, sauté garlic in oil and port for 2 minutes. Add flour and cook for 2 more minutes.

2. Slowly pour in milk, whisking constantly. Sauce should thicken slightly. Continue to cook, whisking, until it becomes the consistency of whipping cream.

3. Add mustard and cheese. Mix miso with 3 tablespoons of hot water; stir until smooth and add to sauce. Remove saucepan from heat.

4. Stir in pan drippings. Serve hot.

Makes 3 cups, 12 servings.

> *Preparation time:* 20 minutes
> *Cooking time:* 5 to 10 minutes
> *Per serving:* calcium 67 mg, calories 46, carbohydrates 4 g, cholesterol 3 mg, fat 1 g, fiber .2 g, protein 3 g, sodium 185 mg

FRESH CRANBERRY-ORANGE RELISH

The tartness of the cranberries in this sauce combines well with the sweet flavor of the oranges. Directions are given in the variation for creating a cranberry mold.

> 4 cups fresh cranberries
> 4 large oranges, peeled and chopped
> 2 tablespoons honey

Place cranberries, oranges, and honey in a food mill or grinder, and grind until pulpy but not puréed. Chill and serve.

Makes approximately 6 cups.

Variation If molded cranberry sauce is desired, add 1 package gelatin or 1 cup agar flakes to sauce and place in a small pan. Bring to a boil over medium-high heat and simmer 5 minutes. Pour into a lightly oiled decorative mold and refrigerate until set (3 to 4 hours). To unmold, dip decorative mold in hot water then invert it over a platter.

Makes 7 cups.

> *Preparation time:* 5 minutes
> *Cooking and chilling time (optional):* 3 to 4 hours
> *Per serving:* calcium 22 mg, calories 55, carbohydrates 4 g, cholesterol none, fat 9 g, fiber 1.2 g, protein 2 g, sodium 1 mg

WILD RICE PILAF

Accompany the turkey stuffing with a serving of Wild Rice Pilaf, topped with toasted pine nuts and raisins. Orzo, an Italian pasta, is cooked with the rice for added flavor.

- 5 cups uncooked wild rice
- 5 cups boiling water
- 1 cup chopped onion
- 2 teaspoons olive oil
- ¾ cup orzo
- 5 cups defatted Chicken Stock (see page 31)
- ½ cup toasted pine nuts
- ½ cup raisins
  Herbal salt substitute, to taste

1. Place rice in a large bowl and cover with the boiling water. Let stand for 10 minutes.

2. In a large, heavy pot over medium-high heat, sauté onion in olive oil until soft but not browned (about 5 minutes). Add orzo and continue to cook for 2 minutes.

3. Drain rice from soaking water. Add rice to sautéed onion and orzo and stir constantly until rice sizzles (about 10 minutes).

4. Pour in stock. Bring to a boil, then lower heat to medium and simmer, covered, until liquid is absorbed (about 45 minutes).

5. Add toasted pine nuts, raisins, and salt substitute, to taste. Remove from heat, cover, and let stand until raisins soften (about 5 minutes). Serve hot.

Serves 12.

Preparation time: 20 minutes
Cooking time: 65 minutes
Per serving: calcium 18 mg, calories 273, carbohydrates 50 g, cholesterol none, fat 4 g, fiber 1.2 g, protein 10 g, sodium 94 mg

GINGERED SWEET POTATO PURÉE IN ORANGE BASKETS

The piquant flavor of the orange peel cooks into the sweet potatoes as they bake. Serve one stuffed orange-peel basket per person.

- 6 medium oranges
- 4 large sweet potatoes
- 1 egg
- ½ teaspoon powdered ginger
- ½ teaspoon cinnamon
- ½ teaspoon nutmeg
- 1 teaspoon grated lemon peel
- 2 tablespoons chopped walnuts

1. Preheat oven to 350° F. Halve oranges and scoop pulp into a bowl. Reserve pulp for another use (such as Fresh Cranberry-Orange Relish, see page 71).

2. Peel and slice sweet potatoes. Steam until soft (about 15 minutes). Mash in a large bowl with egg, ginger, cinnamon, nutmeg, and lemon peel.

3. Spoon purée into orange baskets, dividing equally. Set on a large baking sheet and sprinkle with chopped walnuts. Bake for 25 minutes.

Serves 12.

<u>Note</u> To save time, assemble this side dish in advance and freeze before baking. There is no need to thaw the purée before baking; just add 15 minutes to baking time.

Preparation time: 30 minutes
Baking time: 25 minutes
Per serving: calcium 42 mg, calories 134, carbohydrates 26 g, cholesterol 25 mg, fat 2 g, fiber 3.5 g, protein 3 g, sodium 13 mg

Slow-roasted turkey stuffed with grapes and prunes, Miso Gravy, Wild Rice Pilaf, and spicy puréed sweet potatoes highlight this healthy Thanksgiving menu.

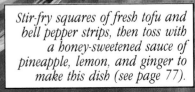

Stir-fry squares of fresh tofu and bell pepper strips, then toss with a honey-sweetened sauce of pineapple, lemon, and ginger to make this dish (see page 77).

Vegetarian Dishes

Fresh vegetables are one of the mainstays of a healthy diet, providing essential vitamins, minerals, and fiber. With the convenient and delicious recipes featured in this chapter, vegetable main dishes can be a pleasant, low-fat change from menus based on meat. The vegetable recipes here emphasize satisfying combinations of whole grains, legumes, and soy products and will become favorites for both entertaining and family suppers. For entertaining try an Asian theme with entrées such as Sweet-and-Sour Walnuts (see page 76) or Szechuan Sautéed Tofu and Vegetables (see page 76). For a family meal, try Mushroom Tart (see page 85) or Claudia's Eggplant Casserole With Tofu (see page 82).

WOK-COOKED ENTRÉES

Main dishes prepared in a wok are perfect for the busy cook—they are fast to make, and the ingredients can be chopped, sliced, and diced up to four hours before cooking. (If you don't have a wok, use a large, deep skillet.) Wok cooking is always done rapidly, over medium-high or high heat. This fast cooking method preserves the color, texture, and flavor of the ingredients, as well as the nutrient value.

SWEET-AND-SOUR WALNUTS

This low-fat variation on batter-fried pork is a winning recipe from a popular San Francisco restaurant. It combines walnut halves cooked in a light batter, pineapple chunks, red bell peppers, and broccoli in a sweet-and-sour sauce of sesame oil, honey, and rice vinegar. Serve Sweet and Sour Walnuts with steamed rice and green tea.

    1 quart (approximately) peanut
      oil, for deep-frying
    ½ cup arrowroot powder
    ½ cup whole wheat pastry or
      unbleached white flour
    2 eggs
    ½ cup plus 1½ tablespoons
      water
    2 cups walnut halves
    1 cup pineapple chunks
    1 cup julienned red bell pepper
    2 cups broccoli florets
    ½ cup rice vinegar
    ¼ cup low-sodium soy or
      tamari sauce
    ⅓ cup light honey
    2 tablespoons dark sesame oil
    1 tablespoon minced garlic
    1 tablespoon cornstarch

1. In a wok or deep skillet over medium heat, begin heating peanut oil to deep-fry temperature of about 350° F (8 to 10 minutes).

2. In a small bowl mix arrowroot, flour, eggs, and the ½ cup water to form a smooth batter. Dip walnuts in batter. When oil is hot, fry walnuts until lightly browned (30 seconds). Line a baking sheet with paper towels and drain cooked walnuts on towels.

3. Pour hot oil into a container and wipe wok clean. Return 1 teaspoon of oil to wok and place over medium-high heat. Stir-fry pineapple, red pepper, and broccoli until vegetables are bright in color.

4. In a small bowl mix rice vinegar, soy sauce, honey, sesame oil, garlic, the 1½ tablespoons water, and cornstarch. Add to vegetables and cook, stirring frequently, until mixture thickens. Add walnuts. Toss to reheat and serve immediately.

Serves 8.

> *Preparation time:* 25 minutes
> *Cooking time:* 15 minutes
> *Per serving:* calcium 90 mg, calories 513, carbohydrates 41 g, cholesterol 63 mg, fat 39 g, fiber 4.2 g, protein 10 g, sodium 475 mg

---

SZECHUAN SAUTÉED TOFU AND VEGETABLES

The Szechuan and Hunan provinces of China are famous for their hot chiles. Szechuan cuisine brought spiciness back to wok cooking in the United States. This recipe combines lightly sautéed tofu squares with an assortment of vegetables. Cooking the ingredients quickly in the wok maintains their bright color and texture.

    ⅔ cup sliced green onions
    1 tablespoon grated gingerroot
    ¼ teaspoon honey
    2 teaspoons dark sesame oil
    ⅓ cup low-sodium soy or
      tamari sauce
    ¼ teaspoon dried chile flakes
    1 pound firm tofu
    ½ cup sliced Chinese cabbage
    ½ cup sliced mushrooms
    ¼ cup sake or dry sherry
    2 tablespoons arrowroot powder
    ⅓ cup cold water
    ¼ cup whole wheat pastry or
      unbleached white flour
    2 eggs
    2 teaspoons safflower oil

1. In a large bowl combine green onions, gingerroot, honey, sesame oil, soy sauce, and dried chile flakes. Slice tofu into 2-inch squares and add to mixture. Carefully toss to mix thoroughly and set aside to marinate for 20 minutes.

2. In another large bowl combine cabbage, mushrooms, and sake. Toss well and set aside to marinate for 15 minutes.

3. In a small bowl mix together arrowroot and 3 tablespoons of the cold water. Set aside.

4. In a fourth bowl mix together flour, eggs, and the remaining water. Extract tofu from its marinade and dip slices into flour batter. In a flat-bottomed skillet, over medium-high heat, heat safflower oil and sauté tofu on both sides until lightly browned. Remove tofu and set on a platter.

5. In a wok over medium-high heat, stir-fry contents of both bowls of marinade for 5 minutes, then add arrowroot mixture and cook until mixture thickens (about 2 minutes). Add tofu, cover, and steam 1 minute. Serve immediately.

Serves 8.

> *Preparation time:* 20 minutes
> *Marinating time:* 20 minutes
> *Cooking time:* 10 minutes
> *Per serving:* calcium 114 mg, calories 127, carbohydrates 10 g, cholesterol 63 mg, fat 6 g, fiber .6 g, protein 8 g, sodium 618 mg

TOFU AND BELL PEPPERS IN SWEET-AND-SOUR SAUCE

Crunchy, brightly colored bell peppers complement the white cubes of protein-rich tofu in this entrée. The sweet-and-sour sauce is slightly spicy. The vegetables and tofu can be marinated ahead of time in sesame oil for added flavor. Cook the dish the night before and reheat for lunch the next day—it gets better as it sits and the flavors blend.

    1   cup thinly sliced red
        bell pepper
    ½   cup thinly sliced green
        bell pepper
    ⅓   cup thinly sliced yellow
        bell pepper
    2   teaspoons safflower oil
    1   tablespoon arrowroot powder
    ½   cup rice vinegar
    ½   cup pineapple juice
    ½   cup lemon juice
    ⅓   cup honey
    ½   teaspoon herbal salt substitute
    ½   teaspoon grated gingerroot
    1   pound firm tofu
    2   tablespoons low-sodium soy
        or tamari sauce
    ¼   teaspoon cayenne pepper,
        or to taste

1. In a wok over medium-high heat, sauté bell peppers in the safflower oil until shiny (about 5 minutes).

2. In a large bowl combine arrowroot, vinegar, pineapple juice, lemon juice, honey, salt substitute, and ginger. Pour over peppers and cook, stirring, until mixture thickens slightly.

3. Cut tofu into thin slices. Add to wok, cover, and steam 3 minutes. Add soy sauce and cayenne. Toss well and serve.

Serves 6.

Preparation time: 10 minutes
Cooking time: 10 minutes
Per serving: calcium 113 mg, calories 194, carbohydrates 35 g, cholesterol none, fat 5 g, fiber 6 g, protein 7 g, sodium 314 mg

Step·by·Step

WOK STIR-FRY TECHNIQUES

Stir-fry cooking should always be done at medium-high to high heat. If any ingredients need marinating or soaking, this should be done first. It is important to have all the ingredients cut and ready, since the stir-fry process is so quick.

Organization is essential. Once you start cooking a stir-fried dish, there is no time to cut up the ginger or carrots or run to the kitchen cabinet for the soy sauce. So cut, measure, marinate, and assemble all the ingredients before you turn on the heat.

Also, try to combine ingredients that will go into the wok at the same time. Assemble all the tools you will need—spatula, ladle, and serving plate—before beginning to cook.

Some stir-fry recipes call for cooking the meat first and then removing it while the vegetables cook. In others, the ingredients are simply added to the wok according to their cooking times so that they all finish at once. Each recipe will specify the appropriate technique to use.

1. *Begin by adding the oil in a thin stream around the outside of the wok. Heat the oil until ripples form on the surface. Rotate the wok to distribute the oil evenly over the surface.*

2. *Add the first ingredient. Using a wok spatula or a wooden spoon, briskly toss the food in the hot oil until it is well coated. This will preserve the color and texture, as well as help seal in vitamins and minerals as the food cooks.*

3. *Add the next ingredients in the order given in the recipe when the first ingredient looks bright in color (if a vegetable) or slightly opaque (if seafood, chicken, or lean meat).*

4. *If your wok has a long handle, tip the food into the serving platter, scraping the sauce over it with the spatula. If it does not, scoop the food into a ladle with the spatula and transfer to the serving dish.*

Sliced shiitake mushrooms absorb the flavor of the sesame oil and soy sauce and add a meaty texture to this healthy vegetarian stir-fry.

BROCCOLI, MUSHROOM, AND WATER CHESTNUT STIR-FRY WITH NOODLES

A colorful yet simple combination, this recipe is easy to make after a busy day at the office. Precut the broccoli stalks, slice the mushrooms and water chestnuts, and cook the noodles the night before; store in plastic bags. Cooking takes only 10 minutes. Be sure not to overcook the broccoli; its crispness and bright green color are essential to the success of this dish.

> 2 teaspoons minced garlic
> 2 teaspoons dark sesame oil
> 1 cup sliced shiitake or domestic mushrooms
> 4 cups broccoli florets
> ½ cup sliced water chestnuts
> 4 cups cooked linguine or rice noodles
> 2 tablespoons low-sodium soy or tamari sauce
> ¼ cup minced green onions

1. In a wok or large skillet over medium-high heat, sauté garlic in sesame oil for 1 minute. Add mushrooms and cook until they exude moisture.

2. Add broccoli and water chestnuts and stir-fry for about 3 minutes. Add noodles, soy sauce, and green onions. Toss together well. Cover and steam for 2 minutes, then serve.

Serves 6.

Preparation time: 10 minutes
Cooking time: 7 to 10 minutes
Per serving: calcium 113 mg, calories 148, carbohydrates 25 g, cholesterol none, fat 3 g, fiber 4.6 g, protein 5 g, sodium 320 mg

HEARTY MAIN DISHES

For those evenings when you want a really satisfying meal, here is a collection of hearty entrées: casseroles and pot pies that are rich in nutrition but low in fat and sodium. Most can be made ahead and frozen for quick reheating. When entertaining, try French Buckwheat Crêpes With Mushrooms and Herbs (below). Pair with French Spring Garden Potage (see page 33) for an elegant menu. Pasta With Walnut-Garlic Sauce (see page 80) is a winner for informal parties or Christmas Eve dinners.

FRENCH BUCKWHEAT CRÊPES WITH MUSHROOMS AND HERBS

The aroma of sautéing mushrooms, seasonings, and wine is hard to resist. The applejack, a sweet apple brandy, melds well with the cheese and asparagus. A crêpe pan should be used for this recipe, but if you do not have one, a large heavy skillet will do. Crêpes are quick to make; if you are in a hurry, prepare the crêpes ahead of time. They keep for 10 days in the refrigerator or up to three months frozen (simply stack between sheets of waxed paper and cover tightly in plastic wrap). Make the filling ahead of time, too, and assemble the crêpes for last-minute baking.

　½　cup buckwheat flour
　1　cup whole wheat pastry or unbleached white flour
　3　egg whites, lightly beaten
　1　whole egg
　1½　cup nonfat milk
　½　teaspoon salt
　2　teaspoons safflower oil
　4　cups sliced mushrooms
　½　cup minced green onions
　1　cup asparagus tips
　1　teaspoon nutmeg
　½　teaspoon dried thyme
　¼　cup applejack, Calvados brandy, or white wine
　1　teaspoon safflower oil, for coating baking dish
　½　cup grated low-fat jack or mozzarella cheese

1. In a blender purée flours, egg whites, whole egg, milk, and salt until the consistency of heavy cream. In a crêpe pan or skillet over medium-high heat, heat ½ teaspoon oil until a drop of water sizzles on surface of pan. Ladle ¼ cup batter onto pan. Cook crêpe until lightly browned (30 to 60 seconds on each side). Set cooked crêpes on a plate, and continue until all batter is used.

2. Preheat broiler. In a skillet over medium-high heat, warm remaining oil and sauté mushrooms and green onions for 5 minutes, stirring frequently. Add asparagus, nutmeg, thyme, and applejack. Cook for 2 minutes, stirring frequently.

3. Lightly oil a baking dish. Spoon about 2 tablespoons filling into center of each crêpe. Roll and lay, seam side down, in baking dish. Stack them if you run out of room. Sprinkle grated cheese over top and broil until lightly browned and bubbling.

Serves 8.

Preparation time: 25 minutes
Cooking time: 40 minutes
Per serving: calcium 129 mg, calories 184, carbohydrates 23 g, cholesterol 38 mg, fat 5 g, fiber 3.1 g, protein 10 g, sodium 219 mg

MINNESOTA VEGETABLE AND WILD RICE PILAF WITH CASHEW GRAVY

The Land of Lakes is also famous for its wild rice, and here is a favorite Minnesota recipe. Brown and wild rices are sautéed with onions, celery, and carrots, then mixed with pine nuts and herbs. A rich cashew gravy is poured over the rice for a satisfying side dish or whole-grain entrée. Serve it with Braised Pheasant (page 65) for a tasty autumn meal.

　1　cup minced onion
　2　teaspoons olive oil
　¼　cup dry sherry or white wine
　½　cup minced celery
　½　cup diced carrots
　1　teaspoon minced garlic
　¼　cup pine nuts or chopped almonds
　2　cups wild rice
　1　cup long-grain brown rice
　3　cups Vegetable Stock (see page 31)
　½　teaspoon thyme
　¼　teaspoon sage
　1　teaspoon low-sodium soy or tamari sauce
　1　cup toasted whole cashews
　2　cups water
　2　teaspoons safflower oil
　2　tablespoons whole wheat pastry or unbleached white flour
　2　teaspoons grated gingerroot
　2　teaspoons herbal salt substitute
　1　tablespoon minced parsley
　1　tablespoon miso

1. In a large saucepan or Dutch oven over medium-high heat, sauté onion in olive oil and sherry for 5 minutes, then add celery, carrots, and garlic. Cover and steam for 2 minutes. Add pine nuts, wild rice, and brown rice, and stir-fry for 1 minute.

2. Pour in broth. Raise heat to high and bring to a boil. Lower heat to medium and simmer, uncovered, for 15 minutes, then cover and steam until rices are soft but chewy (about 20 minutes). Add thyme, sage, and soy sauce.

3. While rice is cooking, purée cashews and the water in blender to a smooth gravy. In a saucepan over medium heat, heat safflower oil and add flour. Stirring frequently, cook for 2 minutes. Add cashew gravy, gingerroot, salt substitute, and parsley. Cook until thick, whisking frequently.

4. Remove some of the cashew gravy to a small bowl, and mix with miso until smooth. Return to saucepan and take off heat. Serve over cooked rice.

Serves 8.

Preparation time: 20 minutes
Cooking time: 45 minutes
Per serving: calcium 52 mg, calories 423, carbohydrates 58 g, cholesterol none, fat 18 g, fiber 1.6 g, protein 14 g, sodium 598 mg

PASTA WITH WALNUT-GARLIC SAUCE

A traditional favorite in southern France, this pasta dish is surprisingly simple and unusually delicious. The roasted garlic gives the sauce a sweet flavor that complements the walnuts. Decorate the top with minced fresh basil leaves and red bell pepper. It's a rich dish, so serve it with simple fare, such as a green salad with Lime Mint Dressing (see page 40) and crusty French bread.

   2 *large heads garlic*
  ⅓ *cup olive oil*
  ⅔ *cup walnuts*
  ¼ *cup boiling water*
   1 *teaspoon herbal salt substitute*
  ¼ *teaspoon cayenne pepper*
   6 *cups cooked linguine or egg noodles*
   1 *teaspoon chopped parsley*
   2 *tablespoons minced fresh basil, for garnish*
   2 *tablespoons minced red bell pepper*

1. Preheat oven to 300° F. Slice tops of garlic heads to expose cloves. Brush lightly with 1 teaspoon olive oil. Place on ungreased baking sheet and roast for 20 minutes. Let cool slightly, then squeeze heads to extract roasted cloves without peel.

2. Place garlic into a blender or food processor. Add walnuts, remaining oil, the water, salt substitute, and cayenne. Blend until smooth.

3. Toss sauce with hot pasta, then add parsley. Garnish with basil and red bell pepper.

Serves 6.

Preparation time: 10 minutes
Roasting time: 20 minutes
Per serving: calcium 55 mg, calories 426, carbohydrates 45 g, cholesterol 57 mg, fat 24 g, fiber 1.1 g, protein 10 g, sodium 9 mg

---

MARTINIQUE CASSEROLE WITH RED PEPPERS AND BLACK BEANS

Besides being an excellent source of low-fat protein, the reduced-fat cheeses and black beans in this recipe are a tasty combination. They are paired with sautéed onions, red bell peppers, and yellow squash for a colorful and delicious casserole that freezes well and makes a great impromptu meal for family or guests. Be sure to examine the black beans before cooking—wash them well under running water, removing stones and broken beans.

    1 *large acorn squash or ½ large butternut squash*
  1½ *cup sliced onion*
    1 *teaspoon safflower oil*
   ¼ *cup dry sherry*
    4 *julienned red bell peppers*
    3 *cloves garlic, minced*
    2 *teaspoons ground coriander*
    2 *teaspoons cumin*
    1 *teaspoon dry mustard*
   ½ *cup nonfat plain yogurt*
   ½ *cup sour cream or sour half-and-half, if available*
   ¼ *cup minced parsley*
    1 *cup cooked black beans*
    1 *cup cooked brown rice (short-grain, long-grain, or brown basmati)*
   ⅓ *cup grated low-fat jack cheese*
    2 *tablespoons lemon juice*
     Safflower oil, for coating casserole pan
   ¼ *cup thinly sliced red bell pepper, for garnish*

1. Preheat oven to 350° F. Line a baking sheet with aluminum foil. Split squash in half and place, cut side down, on baking sheet, leaving in seeds (moisture from seeds helps speed cooking process). Bake squash for 20 minutes.

2. While squash is baking, in a large skillet over medium-high heat, sauté onion in safflower oil and sherry until soft but not browned. Add red peppers and garlic to sauté and cook for 5 more minutes.

3. Mix sautéed vegetables with coriander, cumin, dry mustard, yogurt, sour cream, parsley, beans, brown rice, cheese, and lemon juice. When squash is baked, scoop out seeds and remove peel. Cube cooked squash and add to other ingredients.

4. Lightly oil a large casserole dish and spoon mixture into it. Garnish top with red pepper slices. Bake for 25 minutes.

Serves 8.

Preparation time: 30 minutes
Baking time: 45 minutes
Per serving: calcium 129 mg, calories 159, carbohydrates 20 g, cholesterol 6 mg, fat 4 g, fiber 2.0 g, protein 8 g, sodium 295 mg

---

POLENTA AND CURRIED VEGETABLES

It is hard to find a family in Italy that does not appreciate slices of polenta—coarsely ground baked cornmeal often served with a rich tomato sauce and cheese. Here is a new version—the polenta is baked, then combined with sautéed vegetables in a slightly spicy curry sauce. Slice the polenta into wedges and arrange on a large platter, then spoon the brightly colored vegetable curry on top.

    1 *teaspoon olive oil*
    1 *cup sliced onion*
   ½ *cup julienned carrots*
    1 *teaspoon minced garlic*
    3 *tablespoons chopped parsley*
   ½ *teaspoon cumin*
    1 *teaspoon ground coriander*
    2 *teaspoons curry powder*
   ¼ *cup apple juice*
   ½ *teaspoon cayenne pepper, or to taste*
   ¾ *cup polenta*
   ½ *cup cold water*
   ½ *teaspoon herbal salt substitute*
    2 *cups boiling water*
    1 *cup grated low-fat jack cheese*

1. In a large skillet over medium-high heat, heat oil and sauté onion for 5 minutes, stirring frequently. Add carrots, garlic, and parsley, and sauté 5 more minutes. Add cumin, coriander, curry, apple juice, and cayenne. Cover and reduce heat to low. Let vegetables continue to cook while you make polenta.

2. Preheat oven to 350° F. In a medium bowl, mix polenta, the cold water, and salt substitute into a paste. In medium saucepan place the boiling water and stir in polenta paste, whisking until smooth. Cook over medium heat, whisking frequently, until thick (5 to 10 minutes). Stir in cheese.

3. Spoon polenta into a lightly oiled 8-inch-diameter cake pan and bake 20 minutes.

4. To serve, slice polenta into wedges, then place on platter and top with curried vegetables. Serve immediately.

Serves 6.

Preparation time: 25 minutes
Cooking time: 15 to 20 minutes
Per serving: calcium 261 mg, calories 153, carbohydrates 22 g, cholesterol 5 mg, fat 4 g, fiber 1.3 g, protein 10 g, sodium 832 mg

This polenta recipe is topped with a surprise—bright curried vegetables. Low in calories and rich in protein, the dish will please health-conscious family members or dinner guests.

NUTRITIONAL BENEFITS OF TOFU

Although many people think of tofu as an unusual or strange health food, it has become quite common in the cuisine of the United States. If you have never used tofu before, you will be surprised at its taste and versatility.

Tofu is a soybean curd with a texture much like soft cheese. It is ivory in color and soft in texture and is used extensively as a protein source by Asian and Middle Eastern cultures because it is easy to make, inexpensive, and nutritious.

Like low-fat dairy products, such as cottage cheese or yogurt, tofu is an excellent source of calcium. Tofu is also a good source of iron, phosphorus, and potassium as well as B vitamins and vitamin E.

The process of making tofu is similar to that of making dairy cheese. Soaked soybeans are blended with water, then strained and heated, and a curding agent is added. The agent causes the tofu to separate into solid curds and a clear liquid whey. The solid curds are poured into a tofu press, and after about 30 minutes, the tofu hardens into a block. The tofu is ready to eat.

Tofu keeps about 10 days, refrigerated and stored in a closed container in fresh water. The water should be replaced every two days.

Two different kinds of tofu are available (usually in the produce section of the supermarket): soft and firm (or *nigari*) tofu. Use soft tofu for blending into sauces, salad dressings, cream soups, and dessert toppings. Firm tofu is best for stir-fries since it holds its shape fairly well (see Szechuan Sautéed Tofu and Vegetables, page 76).

Tofu can also be frozen. After thawing, squeeze to remove excess water and crumble into small pieces. The resulting texture is similar to that of ground beef, and the tofu can be seasoned and added to chili, lasagne, and other traditionally meat-based dishes for a low-fat protein substitute.

TOFU POTPIE

This dish has all the appeal (but half the calories) of a meat potpie.

- ¾ cup rice flour
- ½ cup plus 2 tablespoons nutritional yeast flakes
- 1½ teaspoons herbal salt substitute
- 1 teaspoon garlic powder
- 1 pound firm tofu
- 2 teaspoons safflower oil
- 1 cup thinly sliced onions
- ½ cup thinly sliced carrots
- 1 cup shelled peas
- 3 tablespoons low-sodium soy or tamari sauce
- 1 tablespoon olive oil
- 1½ cup water

1. In a small paper bag, place ½ cup of the rice flour, the 2 tablespoons yeast, salt substitute, and garlic powder. Cut tofu into 1-inch cubes. Add to bag and shake to coat thoroughly with flour mixture.

2. In a large skillet over medium-high heat, heat 1 teaspoon of the safflower oil. Sauté tofu until lightly browned. Place in a large casserole. Heat remaining safflower oil in pan and sauté onion until soft, then add carrots and cook for 3 minutes. Add peas and soy sauce. Cover and steam 2 minutes, then take off heat and place into casserole.

3. Preheat oven to 350° F. In a clean saucepan over medium heat, cook remaining flour and yeast until fragrant (about 3 minutes). Do not allow to brown. Add olive oil and, whisking, pour in the water. Cook until mixture is as thick as gravy. Pour over tofu and vegetables.

4. Bake casserole until bubbling (about 10 minutes). Serve hot.

Serves 8.

> *Preparation time:* 20 minutes
> *Cooking and baking time:* 25 minutes
> *Per serving:* calcium 194 mg, calories 238, carbohydrates 29 g, cholesterol none, fat 7 g, fiber 2.0 g, protein 16 g, sodium 501 mg

CLAUDIA'S EGGPLANT CASSEROLE WITH TOFU

This casserole combines tofu and low-fat cheese to create a savory filling. The eggplant is sautéed lightly, then baked in a rich tomato-basil sauce for flavor.

- 1 large eggplant
- 2 teaspoons safflower oil, plus oil for coating pan
- 1 cup mashed firm tofu
- ½ cup grated Parmesan cheese
- ¼ cup chopped parsley
- ½ cup whole wheat or rye bread crumbs
- 1 cup thinly sliced onion
- 1 teaspoon minced garlic
- 1 teaspoon minced fresh basil
- ½ cup thinly sliced green bell pepper
- 1 cup sliced mushrooms
- 1 cup grated low-fat mozzarella cheese
- 1½ cups low-calorie spaghetti sauce

1. Preheat broiler. Cut eggplant into slices about ½ inch thick. Lay on ungreased baking sheet and brush with 1 teaspoon safflower oil. Broil until lightly browned (1 to 2 minutes). Turn slices over, brush with remaining oil, and broil. Set aside. Preheat oven to 375° F.

2. In a large bowl combine tofu, Parmesan, and parsley. Lightly oil a 9- by 12-inch baking pan and sprinkle with bread crumbs. Arrange sliced eggplant on top of crumbs.

3. Spoon tofu mixture over eggplant, then top with sliced onion, garlic, basil, bell pepper, and mushrooms. Sprinkle with any remaining bread crumbs and mozzarella. Top with spaghetti sauce.

4. Bake until well browned (45 to 55 minutes).

Serves 8.

> *Preparation time:* 20 minutes
> *Baking and broiling time:* 50 to 60 minutes
> *Per serving:* calcium 216 mg, calories 153, carbohydrates 13 g, cholesterol 17, fat 8 g, fiber 1.7 g, protein 10 g, sodium 399 mg

LIGHT AND EASY

For the occasions when you just don't have time to cook a large meal, here are some mini-meals that are great for brunch or light suppers. Try Eggs à la Suisse (see page 84), a new version of eggs Benedict, for a springtime Sunday. These dishes also make excellent accompaniments to a buffet or potluck dinner.

BROCCOLI MOUSSE WITH HORSERADISH SAUCE

This recipe is an eye-catcher: The bright green of the broccoli contrasts with the slightly pink beet and yogurt sauce. It originated in the Caribbean, where bright colors are common to many dishes. Serve on a bed of greens or shredded cabbage as a light salad entrée, or slice into wedges for an elegant side dish for a fish entrée, such as Baked Fish in Lettuce Packets (page 50).

> 3   cups chopped broccoli
> 4   teaspoons lime juice
> 1½ cup defatted chicken stock (see page 31)
> ½   cup agar flakes or 1 envelope unflavored gelatin
> ⅓   cup minced green onions
> 1   egg white, beaten
> ¼   cup low-calorie mayonnaise
> 1½ tablespoons dried dill
>   Safflower oil, for coating soufflé dish
> 1   cup nonfat plain yogurt
> ¼   cup minced cooked fresh beets or minced canned beets
> ¼   cup prepared horseradish
>   Lettuce leaves, for lining salad plates

1. In a small saucepan steam broccoli until tender. Drain and purée in blender with lime juice.

2. Heat stock to boiling. If using agar, cook in stock over medium-high heat until dissolved. If using gelatin, dissolve in hot stock. Let cool. Mix with broccoli.

3. Add green onions, egg white, mayonnaise, and dill to broccoli mixture. Lightly oil a 1½-quart soufflé dish and pour mixture into it, then chill in refrigerator for 3 hours.

4. While mousse is chilling, mix yogurt, beets, and horseradish, and chill for 1 hour. Stir well again and set aside until serving time. To serve, spoon equal amounts of broccoli mousse onto 4 salad plates lined with lettuce leaves. Garnish each with a dollop of horseradish sauce.

Serves 4.

Preparation time: 30 minutes
Chilling time: 3 hours
Per serving: calcium 228 mg, calories 152, carbohydrates 29 g, cholesterol 5 mg, fat 7 g, fiber 5 g, protein 11 g, sodium 286 mg

Almost a work of art, Broccoli Mousse With Horseradish Sauce is a healthy gourmet addition to any entertaining menu.

Rather than using a heavy cream-based sauce, as in eggs Benedict, this poached egg dish is served Swiss style: a low-fat cheese mixture is spread on the English muffins beforehand.

EGGS À LA SUISSE

This easy-to-make brunch item can replace eggs Benedict because it is lower in calories. Lightly poached eggs are nestled on English muffin halves spread with low-calorie cream cheese, then sprinkled with green onions, Parmesan cheese, and nutmeg. Serve with mimosas made from champagne or nonalcoholic sparkling wine and fresh orange juice, and accompany with Carrot-Ginger Breakfast Muffins (see page 99).

> 4 ounces low-calorie cream cheese, such as Neufchâtel
> 1 tablespoon plus 1 teaspoon low-calorie mayonnaise
> 2 cups water
> 8 large eggs
> 4 whole wheat English muffins, split in half
> ½ cup minced green onions
> 1 teaspoon freshly grated nutmeg
> ¼ cup grated Parmesan cheese

1. In a small bowl mix together cream cheese and mayonnaise. Set aside while poaching eggs.

2. In a large skillet over medium-high heat, bring the water to a boil. Lower heat to keep water at an even simmer. Break each egg one at a time into a small bowl and gently slide egg into the simmering water. Repeat until all eggs are in water. Poach for 3 minutes.

3. While eggs are poaching, toast English muffins and spread each half with cream cheese mixture. Place a poached egg on each half. Sprinkle each half with green onions, nutmeg, and Parmesan. Serve immediately.

Serves 4.

Preparation time: 10 minutes
Cooking time: 8 to 10 minutes
Per serving: calcium 324 mg, calories 424, carbohydrates 32 g, cholesterol 532 mg, fat 22 g, fiber 2.2 g, protein 23 g, sodium 521 mg

MUSHROOM TART

A light pastry crust is filled with wine-cooked mushrooms, onions, carrots, and broccoli, topped with cheeses and tofu, and baked until lightly browned and firm. This dish is equally good served hot out of the oven as an entrée or cold for a brown-bag lunch the next day.

¼ cup minced onion
1 teaspoon butter or oil
¼ cup dry white wine
1 teaspoon minced garlic
2 cups sliced mushrooms
¼ cup grated carrots
¼ cup minced broccoli
1 teaspoon dried thyme
½ teaspoon dried marjoram
½ pound soft tofu
¾ cup plain nonfat yogurt
3 tablespoons minced parsley
¼ cup grated low-fat Swiss cheese
¼ cup grated low-fat Cheddar cheese or low-fat mozzarella cheese
1 nine-inch pie shell

1. Preheat oven to 350° F. In a large skillet over medium high-heat, sauté onion and garlic in butter and wine until soft (2 to 3 minutes). Add mushrooms and cook until they exude moisture.

2. Add carrots, broccoli, thyme, and marjoram, and cook 5 minutes more. Remove pan from heat and set aside.

3. With your hands, gently squeeze block of tofu to remove excess water, then purée in blender or food processor with half-and-half until smooth. Stir into vegetable mixture.

4. Stir parsley and cheeses into vegetable mixture and spoon into pie shell. Bake until firm in the center and lightly brown (about 40 minutes). Let cool before slicing.

Serves 8.

Preparation time: 30 minutes
Baking time: 40 minutes
Per serving: calcium 140 mg, calories 213, carbohydrates 18 g, cholesterol 30 mg, fat 12 g, fiber .8 g, protein 8 g, sodium 255 mg

COUSCOUS WITH MUSHROOMS AND CURRY

Platters of couscous are often a staple in Middle Eastern households; the accompaniment varies from lamb to chicken to vegetables. Couscous, available in the gourmet section of supermarkets, is a lightly steamed wheat that tastes a little like orzo pasta—slightly nutty and sweet. In this recipe sautéed mushrooms, carrots, and onions are combined with turmeric, coriander, and a touch of cinnamon to create a spicy assortment of flavors. This is a good dish to make ahead and reheat before serving. Accompany with a large green salad and a dry white wine.

½ cup sliced onion
2 teaspoons minced garlic
1 teaspoon olive oil
1 cup sliced mushrooms
½ cup grated carrots
1 teaspoon curry powder
¼ teaspoon turmeric
½ teaspoon ground coriander
2 teaspoons cinnamon
½ cup raisins
3 cups defatted Chicken Stock (see page 31)
2 tablespoons low-sodium soy or tamari sauce
½ cup chopped parsley
2 cups uncooked couscous

1. In a large skillet over medium-high heat, sauté onions and garlic in oil for 2 minutes, stirring frequently. Add mushrooms and carrots and cook for 5 minutes.

2. Add curry powder, turmeric, coriander, cinnamon, and raisins, and cook for 3 minutes more. Add stock and bring to a boil.

3. Stir in soy sauce, parsley, and couscous. Cover pan and remove from heat. Let it sit for 15 minutes. Fluff couscous with a fork. Serve hot.

Serves 4.

Preparation time: 20 minutes
Cooking time: 25 minutes
Per serving: calcium 58 mg, calories 353, carbohydrates 75 g, cholesterol none, fat 2 g, fiber 3 g, protein 13.6 g, sodium 638 mg

WHOLE-GRAIN SIDE DISHES

Besides contributing fiber and complex carbohydrates to your diet, whole grains are a rich source of B-complex vitamins. Add a grain dish to your next chicken or fish menu for more balanced nutrition or enjoy it as a small meal in itself.

GREEN RICE

Green Rice gets its color from minced or chopped parsley, spinach, green onions, and basil. It is a low-calorie version of Chinese fried rice—only a teaspoon of oil goes into this dish. Try this colorful accompaniment to fish or chicken with Mediterranean Chicken With Balsamic Vinegar and Olives (see page 61) or Fresh Trout Florentine (see page 49).

½ cup minced green onion
2 tablespoons minced garlic
1 teaspoon olive oil
¼ cup dry sherry or white wine
½ cup chopped parsley
⅓ cup minced spinach leaves
2 tablespoons minced fresh basil
3 cups cooked long-grain brown rice
2 tablespoons pine nuts
2 tablespoons minced red bell pepper
¼ cup grated Parmesan cheese

1. In a large skillet over medium-high heat, sauté green onion and garlic in olive oil and sherry for 5 minutes, stirring frequently. Add parsley, spinach, and basil and cook for 3 more minutes.

2. Add rice and pine nuts and heat through, stirring constantly, for about 5 minutes. Remove from heat and stir in bell pepper and Parmesan cheese. Serve hot.

Serves 4.

Preparation time: 20 minutes
Cooking time: 15 minutes
Per serving: calcium 157 mg, calories 290, carbohydrates 47 g, cholesterol 6 mg, fat 6 g, fiber 1.8 g, protein 9 g, sodium 479 mg

THE FOUR MOST OVER-LOOKED NUTRIENTS

Iron, calcium, vitamin A, and vitamin C are all essential to maintaining good health, yet they are often lacking in the diets of many people in the United States. Fast food, skipped meals, and packaged instead of fresh vegetables deprive many people of adequate amounts of these nutrients.

Vitamin A

Many people grow up with memories of Mother saying, "Eat your carrots: They're good for your eyes." Well, she was right. Carrots, as well as other dark yellow, red, and leafy green vegetables, such as broccoli, collards, spinach, and carrots, contain large amounts of vitamin A. This vitamin is essential for a number of visual functions, including the formation of the photosensitive visual purple in the human retina, which helps prevent night blindness. Vitamin A also helps increase resistance to disease and infections and promotes bone and tooth development.

A diet rich in fresh fruits and vegetables provides you with more than enough vitamin A. One half cup of carrots alone contains 8,140 International Units of vitamin A, almost double the daily requirement of 4,000 to 5,000. Look for vitamin A in such foods as sweet potatoes, carrots, broccoli, spinach, chard, tomatoes, squash, apricots, cantaloupe, peaches, beef, liver, eggs, and cheeses. Some nutritionists believe that getting vitamin A from foods is a safer resource than supplements, since vitamin A is a fat-soluble vitamin and can build up in the body, possibly causing toxic levels in the process.

Iron

Iron is an essential part of hemoglobin, the part of the blood that transports oxygen. But only small amounts of iron are available in most foods. Women require about 18 milligrams of iron per day; men need less, about 10 milligrams per day. Absorption of iron is enhanced by eating foods rich in vitamin C or by using cast-iron cookware. Some iron-rich foods include prunes; dried peaches, apricots, and raisins; liver; beans and rice; clams and oysters; and spinach and beet greens. One-half cup prune juice provides 5.2 milligrams of iron, one-half cup dried peaches almost 5 milligrams.

Calcium

Calcium, a major ingredient of the skeletal structure—the bones and teeth—also retards bleeding and aids in muscle contraction and in nerve impulse transmission. The body can store excess dietary calcium in the bones: If your diet is chronically low in calcium, however, too much calcium is removed from the bones and osteoporosis may result.

The daily requirement of calcium is around 1,000 milligrams per day—the equivalent of 3 cups of kale or three glasses of milk. Milk and dairy products are good sources of calcium, but it can also be found in leafy greens, tofu, and certain fish and shellfish.

Vitamin C

Vitamin C forms the substances of the cell that hold it together, such as collagen. It aids in strengthening blood vessels and is essential in the healing process. It is a delicate vitamin that is easily destroyed by heat, light, or exposure to air. The daily vitamin C requirement is about 60 milligrams per day, or the equivalent of one-half cup fresh orange juice. Other good sources of vitamin C are green and red bell peppers, broccoli, lemons, strawberries, and tomatoes. Storing fresh fruits and vegetables in the refrigerator helps to preserve their vitamin C content for about five days.

MUSHROOM MILLET BAKE

Millet is a nutritious grain that grows in northern climates. It has a pearly white color and a nutty flavor similar to some pastas. In this simple recipe it is combined with mushrooms sautéed in a sherry sauce and freshly grated low-fat cheese, then baked until lightly browned. It makes a good side dish with Braised Pheasant (see page 65) or Roast Duck With Sherry (see page 65).

> *Safflower oil, for coating pan*
> ½ *cup minced green onion*
> 1 *teaspoon butter or safflower oil*
> ⅓ *cup dry sherry*
> 1 *cup thinly sliced mushrooms*
> ¼ *cup minced celery*
> 1 *teaspoon minced garlic*
> 2 *cups cooked millet*
> 3 *tablespoons grated low-fat Cheddar cheese*

1. Preheat oven to 350° F. Lightly oil an 8-inch-square baking pan or casserole dish.

2. In a large skillet over medium-high heat, sauté green onion in butter and sherry for 5 minutes. Add mushrooms, celery, and garlic, cover, and cook for 10 minutes.

3. Add millet and cook, stirring frequently, to heat through (about 5 more minutes). Remove from heat and stir in cheese. Spoon into baking pan. Bake until lightly browned (about 15 minutes). Serve hot.

Serves 4.

Preparation time: 15 minutes
Cooking time: 35 minutes
Per serving: calcium 105 mg, calories 413, carbohydrates 79 g, cholesterol 2 mg, fat 3 g, fiber 1.5 g, protein 15 g, sodium 247 mg

HERBED RYE-BERRY TIMBALES

Timbales are small casseroles of grains, vegetables, or fish, pressed into soufflé dishes and baked. Unmolded before serving, they make an elegant side dish. This recipe combines rye berry (available in most health-food stores; if unavailable, substitute wheat berries) with herbs, onions, garlic, and chopped tomatoes. Low in calories and rich in fiber, these timbales make a good Thanksgiving or other holiday menu item.

    ¾ cup raw rye berries
    ⅓ cup chopped celery
    2 tablespoons grated onion
    1 teaspoon minced garlic
       Safflower oil, for coating
       ramekins
    1 cup chopped tomatoes
    ½ teaspoon ground dill seed
    ¼ teaspoon dried sage
    1 teaspoon minced cilantro
    2 tablespoons low-sodium soy
       or tamari sauce
    1 egg, beaten
    ½ cup grated low-fat mozzarella
       cheese

1. In a large pot over medium-high heat, bring 2 cups of water to a boil. Add rye berries, celery, onion, and garlic. Simmer until berries are tender and all water has been absorbed (about 45 minutes).

2. Preheat oven to 350° F. Lightly oil 8 ramekins (small 4-ounce soufflé dishes) and place in a shallow baking pan. Fill pan with ½ inch of boiling water.

3. In a large bowl combine tomatoes, dill, sage, cilantro, soy sauce, egg, and cheese. Stir in cooked rye berries and vegetables. Spoon mixture into ramekins, filling to within ¼ inch of top. Bake until firm (about 45 minutes). Unmold and serve hot.

Serves 8.

Preparation time: 25 minutes
Cooking time: 1½ hours
Per serving: calcium 57 mg, calories 100, carbohydrates 15 g, cholesterol 37 mg, fat 3 g, fiber .6 g, protein 5 g, sodium 266 mg

LENTIL SPREAD WITH WHOLE-GRAIN CRACKERS

This rich-tasting, healthy pâté, an easy sandwich or canapé spread, includes lentils, sautéed carrots, onions, mushrooms, and garlic, and a variety of herbs and spices. In this recipe it is served on homemade graham crackers made with whole wheat pastry flour and molasses.

       Safflower oil, for coating pan
    ½ cup minced onion
    ½ cup minced mushrooms
    ¼ cup grated carrots
    2 tablespoons minced
       garlic
    1 teaspoon olive oil
    ⅓ cup white wine
    2 cups cooked lentils
    1 cup whole wheat or rye
       bread crumbs
    1 tablespoon minced fresh
       basil leaves
    ¼ teaspoon nutmeg
    ¼ teaspoon cumin
    ¼ teaspoon curry powder
    1 tablespoon low-sodium soy
       or tamari sauce

Whole-Grain Crackers

       Safflower oil, for coating
       baking sheet
    ¼ cup tahini
    1 tablespoon molasses
    ¼ cup nonfat milk or nonfat
       plain yogurt
    1¼ cup whole wheat
       pastry flour

1. Preheat oven to 400° F. Lightly oil a 2-quart loaf pan.

2. In a large skillet over medium-high heat, sauté onion, mushrooms, carrots, and garlic in olive oil and wine until soft (about 10 minutes). Remove from heat.

3. Stir in lentils, bread crumbs, basil, nutmeg, cumin, curry powder, and soy sauce. If mixture is too dry to form a ball, add a bit of water; if runny, add more bread crumbs. Press into prepared loaf pan. Cover with aluminum foil and bake for 45 minutes. Serve with Whole-Grain Crackers.

Serves 10.

Whole-Grain Crackers

1. Preheat oven to 400° F. Lightly oil a large baking sheet.

2. In a large bowl combine tahini, molasses, and milk, mixing until smooth and creamy. Stir in flour to form a soft dough.

3. Lightly flour a work surface and roll out dough. Cut into cracker shapes or rounds about ¹∕₁₆ inch thick. Poke each cracker several times with a fork—the holes keep it from curling as it bakes. Place on baking sheet and bake for 5 to 8 minutes. Watch carefully: They tend to brown quickly.

Makes approximately 2 dozen crackers.

Preparation time: 25 minutes
Baking time: 50 minutes
Per serving: calcium 56 mg, calories 190, carbohydrates 29 g, cholesterol none, fat 5 g, fiber 2.7 g, protein 8 g, sodium 206 mg

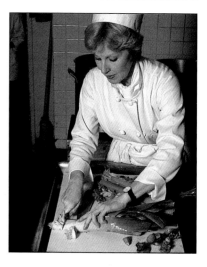

Serve a healthy new twist on pizza: thin slices of roasted new potatoes laid over a rich pesto sauce (see page 93).

Pasta, Pizza & Breads

Homemade pasta, pizza, and whole-grain breads have enjoyed increasing popularity for their health benefits and gourmet appeal. In addition, they are easy to make, great for snacks or light meals, and elegant enough for entertaining. This chapter includes a collection of versatile pasta recipes for quick dinners (see Pasta Shells With Peas and Chicken, page 90); savory pizzas for parties, lunches, or snacks (see Roasted New-Potato Pizza With Pesto, page 93); and satisfying whole-grain quick and yeast breads (see Orange-Date Muffins, page 98). A hearty Fireside Feast (see page 99) of nutritious soups, breads, and muffins completes the chapter.

EASY PASTA DISHES

Pasta can be the ideal comfort food for a chilly day. In pasta dishes the sauces are the key—they will make or break the recipe, in terms of taste and nutrition. This selection features both hot- and cold-weather pasta dishes with light and healthy toppings. Almost all the recipes can be made ahead of time, and most of the sauces can be frozen and reheated before serving for impromptu dinners.

SUNDAY NIGHT SPAGHETTI

This may become your favorite pasta recipe. It is tasty and quick to prepare, and kids love it. The lean meat sauce is a variation on Basic Pizza Sauce (see page 92), so leftovers can top your next pizza.

- ⅓ pound lean ground lamb or beef
- 2 teaspoons minced garlic
- ¼ cup dry red wine
- 1 tablespoon chopped fresh basil
- 1 cup chopped fresh tomatoes
- 1 recipe Basic Pizza Sauce (see page 92)
- 1 pound whole wheat or spinach spaghetti

1. In a large Dutch oven or deep skillet over medium-high heat, brown lamb and garlic in red wine for about 15 minutes, stirring frequently. Pour off any excess fat.

2. Add basil, tomatoes, and Basic Pizza Sauce. Bring to a boil, lower heat to medium, and simmer sauce for 25 minutes, stirring occasionally.

3. While sauce is simmering, bring 2 quarts of water to boil in a large pot. Cook spaghetti until al dente (8 minutes). Drain and toss with sauce. Serve hot.

Serves 6.

Preparation time: 10 minutes
Cooking time: 50 minutes
Per serving: calcium 113 mg, calories 455, carbohydrates 79 g, cholesterol 13 mg, fat 7 g, fiber 2.6 g, protein 18 g, sodium 23 mg

LINGUINE WITH WINTER PESTO

Pesto, a popular sauce for pasta, is usually made with fresh basil leaves, pine nuts, and Parmesan cheese. In the winter when fresh basil is scarce, try dried basil—which is hard to distinguish when the basil is mixed with the other ingredients. This dish has many fewer calories than the original version and also features parsley and spinach, which provide plenty of vitamin A. Make a double batch of the pesto and freeze half in an ice cube tray. After the pesto cubes freeze, store them in lock-top plastic bags and use for quick make-ahead meals all winter. (You will need 3 to 6 cubes per serving, depending on the size of the ice cube tray.)

- 1 pound linguine
- ½ cup minced spinach leaves
- ½ cup chopped parsley
- 1 tablespoon dried basil
- 1 tablespoon minced garlic
- ¼ cup coarsely chopped walnuts
- 3 tablespoons olive oil
- ¼ cup grated Parmesan cheese

1. In a large pot over high heat, bring to a boil 2 quarts of water and cook linguine until al dente (8 minutes).

2. While noodles are cooking, combine spinach, parsley, basil, garlic, walnuts, oil, and Parmesan in a blender or food processor until a thick paste is formed.

3. Drain noodles and toss with pesto while still warm. Serve at once.

Serves 4.

Preparation time: 15 minutes
Per serving: calcium 149 mg, calories 544, carbohydrates 72 g, cholesterol 109 mg, fat 22 g, fiber 1.6 g, protein 17 g, sodium 67 mg

PASTA SHELLS WITH PEAS AND CHICKEN

Try this colorful recipe in the summertime, when fresh peas are ripe off the vine and bursting with flavor. Small pasta shells are cooked until just slightly underdone and baked with a sauté of red bell peppers, fresh peas, and slivers of skinned chicken breasts. A low-fat recipe that can be made ahead of time, Pasta Shells With Peas and Chicken will become a warm-weather favorite with family and guests.

- 4 cups small pasta shells
- 2 cups slivered cooked chicken, skinned
- 2 teaspoons olive oil
- ½ cup shelled peas
- 1 tablespoon minced garlic
- 2 tablespoons chopped fresh basil
- 2 tablespoons chopped fresh thyme, or 1 teaspoon dried thyme
- 3 tablespoons chopped parsley
- ¼ cup minced red bell pepper
- ¼ cup grated Parmesan cheese

1. In a large pot over high heat, bring 2 quarts of water to a boil and cook pasta shells until just underdone (about 5 minutes). Drain and rinse under cold water, then set aside. Preheat oven to 400° F.

2. In a large skillet over medium-high heat, sauté chicken in olive oil for 2 minutes, then add peas, garlic, basil, thyme, parsley, and bell pepper. Cook 2 minutes more, then pour mixture into large baking dish. Add pasta shells and toss well. Add Parmesan.

3. Bake for 20 minutes. Serve hot.

Serves 4.

Preparation time: 25 minutes
Baking time: 20 minutes
Per serving: calcium 170 mg, calories 524, carbohydrates 69 g, cholesterol 69 mg, fat 12 g, fiber 3.2 g, protein 35 g, sodium 144 mg

SCAMPI FETTUCCINE WITH GARLIC AND OLIVE OIL

Shrimp is an excellent and tasty source of protein. In this fettuccine recipe, large prawns are briefly poached in sake, then cooked in a sauce that is high in garlic and low in oil. Since it keeps well on a heated tray, this fettuccine is an elegant main dish for a party buffet.

1 pound fresh fettuccine
1 pound large prawns
½ cup sake, dry sherry, or white wine
2 teaspoons olive oil
2 tablespoons minced garlic
¼ cup minced red bell pepper
¼ cup chopped parsley

1. In a large pot over high heat, bring 2 quarts of water to a boil and cook fettuccine for 3 minutes. Strain from cooking pot and refresh under cold water.

2. Peel and devein prawns. In a large skillet over medium-high heat, sauté prawns in sake until they turn bright pink (4 to 5 minutes). Remove from pan and set aside.

3. Pour off all but 2 tablespoons of sake. Add olive oil, garlic, and red bell pepper to pan, and cook over medium-high heat for 5 minutes, stirring frequently. Add parsley, cooked prawns, and fettuccine. Toss well to reheat thoroughly. Serve hot.

Serves 4.

Preparation time: 15 minutes
Cooking time: 15 minutes
Per serving: calcium 96 mg, calories 283, carbohydrates 34 g, cholesterol 120 mg, fat 6 g, fiber 2.0 g, protein 20 g, sodium 178 mg

Olive oil, garlic, and fresh basil provide a savory background for Pasta Shells with Peas and Chicken.

BAKED NOODLE RING

This rich-tasting dish substitutes low-fat yogurt and extra vegetables for the heavy cream and cheese traditionally used in the recipe.

- ¼ pound large, flat noodles
  Safflower oil, for coating pan
- 2 teaspoons unsalted butter
- ¼ cup minced green onion
- ¼ cup minced red bell pepper
- ½ cup thinly sliced mushrooms
- 2 teaspoons whole wheat pastry or unbleached white flour
- ½ teaspoon herbal salt substitute
- ½ cup nonfat milk
- ¼ cup nonfat plain yogurt
  Dash of freshly ground pepper
- 2 egg whites
- 2 whole eggs
- ¼ cup finely chopped parsley

1. In a large pot over high heat, bring to a boil 2 quarts of water. Cook noodles until barely tender (about 5 minutes). Drain and refresh under cold water, then set aside.

2. Preheat oven to 350° F. Lightly oil an 8-inch ring mold or an 8-inch-square baking pan.

3. In a large skillet over medium-high heat, heat butter and sauté green onion, bell pepper, and mushrooms for 5 minutes. Add flour and salt substitute and cook, stirring, for 2 minutes. Pour in milk and cook, stirring frequently, until thick (about 8 minutes). Stir in yogurt and pepper and remove from heat.

4. Separate eggs. In a small bowl combine all egg whites and beat until stiff. In a separate bowl beat egg yolks until foamy, then add to sautéed vegetables. Add drained noodles and fold in egg whites, then parsley. Pour mixture into prepared pan.

5. Bake until set (about 30 minutes). Unmold and serve hot.

Serves 6.

Preparation time: 30 minutes
Baking time: 30 minutes
Per serving: calcium 69 mg,
calories 124, carbohydrates 15 g,
cholesterol 104 mg, fat 4 g, fiber
.6 g, protein 7 g, sodium 59 mg

SAFFRON ORZO WITH VEGETABLES

Orzo is a tiny Italian pasta that resembles long-grain rice and has a creamy, slightly sweet taste. In this recipe it is cooked in a saffron sauce that gives it a rich yellow color and a nutty flavor. An assortment of fresh vegetables is lightly sautéed, then tossed with the orzo for an appealing side dish to a fish dinner. Try it with Sole aux Amandes (see page 47) and a tossed green salad.

- 1½ cups orzo
- $\frac{1}{16}$ gram (⅛ teaspoon) saffron threads
- 2 tablespoons chopped chives
- 2 teaspoons unsalted butter or olive oil
- ¼ cup minced green onion
- ¼ cup minced red bell pepper
- ½ cup thinly sliced mushrooms
- ¼ cup thinly sliced yellow summer squash
- 1 teaspoon herbal salt substitute
- ¼ teaspoon dried thyme

1. In a large pot over high heat, bring to a boil 1 quart of water and cook orzo until tender (10 minutes). Drain and set aside.

2. In a large skillet over medium-high heat, sauté saffron and chives in butter for 1 minute, then add green onion, bell pepper, mushrooms, and squash, and sauté for 10 minutes. Add salt substitute and thyme.

3. Stir cooked orzo into vegetable mixture; reheat briefly and serve.

Serves 4.

Preparation time: 25 minutes
Cooking time: 25 minutes
Per serving: calcium 15 mg,
calories 99, carbohydrates 14 g,
cholesterol none, fat 4 g, fiber
.56 g, protein 2 g, sodium 7 mg

PIZZA

The secret of healthy pizza lies in using a whole wheat or other whole-grain crust (see page 95), a good low-calorie tomato sauce rich in vegetables and low in oil (see Basic Pizza Sauce, below), and a colorful array of fresh vegetables, lean meat, and fish toppings with only a small amount of cheese.

BASIC PIZZA SAUCE

A good, low-fat pizza sauce is a must for the healthy cook. The secret to the flavor of this sauce, which uses very little oil, is steeping the dried basil and oregano in wine before cooking. This simple step draws out the flavor of the herbs—the sauce tastes as if it had been cooking for hours.

- ¼ cup minced fresh basil or 2 tablespoons dried basil
- 1 teaspoon dried oregano
- ¼ cup white wine
- ½ cup grated onion
- 2 teaspoons minced garlic
- 2 teaspoons olive oil
- 3 cups coarsely chopped plum tomatoes
- 1 tablespoon tomato paste

1. In a small bowl steep basil and oregano in white wine for 10 minutes.

2. In a large skillet over medium-high heat, sauté onion and garlic in olive oil for 5 minutes, stirring frequently. Add tomatoes and tomato paste, then steeped herbs and wine. Cover and cook 15 minutes.

3. Remove sauce from heat and purée in a blender or food processor. Sauce may be used on pizza or over pasta.

Makes about 3 cups, 10 servings.

Preparation time: 15 minutes
Cooking time: 20 minutes
Per serving: calcium 41 mg,
calories 39, carbohydrates 5.6 g,
cholesterol none, fat 1 g, fiber
1.1 g, protein 1.4 g, sodium 5 mg

ROASTED NEW-POTATO PIZZA WITH PESTO

A California version of traditional Italian pizza with potatoes, this recipe combines a creamy spinach-basil pesto with slices of roasted red potatoes and a light olive oil and tomato topping.

> *Safflower oil and cornmeal, for coating pizza pan*
> 1 *recipe Basic Pizza Dough (see page 95)*
> 2 *cups thinly sliced red-skinned new potatoes*
> *Herbal salt substitute and freshly ground pepper*
> 1 *teaspoon safflower oil*
> ½ *cup minced spinach leaves*
> ½ *cup chopped parsley*
> 1 *tablespoon dried basil*
> 1 *tablespoon minced garlic*
> ¼ *cup coarsely chopped walnuts*
> 3 *tablespoons olive oil*
> ¼ *cup grated Parmesan cheese*

1. Preheat oven to 450° F. Lightly oil a 14-inch-diameter pizza pan or large baking sheet and sprinkle with cornmeal. On a lightly floured surface, roll pizza dough into a circle. Place in pizza pan and press edges into a 1-inch rim.

2. Lightly oil a second baking sheet. Place sliced potatoes in a bowl and sprinkle with salt substitute, pepper, and the 1 teaspoon safflower oil. Toss well to coat evenly. Place on prepared second baking sheet and roast until browned (about 10 minutes).

3. Place spinach, parsley, basil, garlic, walnuts, olive oil, and cheese into a blender or food processor and purée to the consistency of a paste. Spread thickly on pizza dough. Place roasted potatoes on top. Bake pizza in oven until dough is lightly browned (about 15 minutes). Serve hot.

Makes 1 fourteen-inch pizza, 8 servings.

> *Preparation time:* 25 minutes
> *Cooking time:* 25 minutes
> *Per serving:* calcium 66 mg, calories 146, carbohydrates 12 g, cholesterol 3 mg, fat 10 g, fiber 1.3 g, protein 3 g, sodium 32 mg

PRISCILLA'S RICE-CRUSTED PIZZA

This pizza recipe provides an innovative way to use leftover cooked rice—mix it with herbs, cheese, and eggs, and press it into a pizza pan. The crust comes out chewy and slightly crisp on the bottom and is a real favorite of children. Make it in a large sheet pan for the next block party or children's birthday.

> *Safflower oil, for coating baking sheet*
> 2 *cups cooked short-grain brown rice*
> 2 *eggs*
> 1 *cup grated low-fat mozzarella cheese*
> 2 *cups Basic Pizza Sauce (see page 92)*
> ½ *teaspoon dried oregano*
> ½ *teaspoon dried basil*
> ½ *teaspoon minced garlic*
> ¼ *cup grated Parmesan cheese*
> ¼ *cup sliced marinated artichoke hearts*
> ¼ *cup sliced pitted black olives*

1. Preheat oven to 450° F. Lightly oil a large baking sheet.

2. In a large bowl mix together rice, eggs, and mozzarella. Press into baking sheet to form a thick crust. Bake crust until lightly browned (15 to 20 minutes).

3. In a large bowl combine pizza sauce, oregano, basil, and garlic. Spoon over baked crust. Top with Parmesan, artichoke hearts, and olives. Bake 10 more minutes, then slice and serve.

Serves 8.

> *Preparation time:* 20 minutes
> *Baking time:* 25 to 30 minutes
> *Per serving:* calcium 174 mg, calories 188, carbohydrates 19 g, cholesterol 77 mg, fat 9 g, fiber 1.4 g, protein 8 g, sodium 276 mg

THE VALUE OF COMPLEX CARBOHYDRATES

Carbohydrates function as the primary energy source for the human body. They are also converted to glycogen and stored in the liver to help regulate blood sugar levels, and they are essential for proper nerve function through their effect on glucose levels in the blood.

Carbohydrates may be categorized as either simple or complex, according to various criteria, such as absorption rate and chemical structure. Types of simple carbohydrates include maltose (in beer), fructose (a fruit sugar), and sucrose (table sugar). Complex carbohydrates—cellulose, starch, and dextrins—are abundant in such foods as pasta, pizza, vegetables, whole grains, and fruit.

Simple carbohydrates are a source of instant energy for the body. Sugar, a simple carbohydrate, has become the main source of carbohydrate in the American diet. Unfortunately, a diet high in sugar is often associated with a diet low in fiber, vitamins, minerals, and other nutrients—high-sugar foods are often high in fat. Most refined foods, such as white sugar products (candy and soft drinks), baked goods made with white flour (pastries and cakes), and so-called junk foods, are mostly just a source of calories.

Complex carbohydrates take longer to be absorbed by the body and are therefore considered a more enduring source of energy. Countless recommendations by national medical organizations urge consumers to eat fewer simple carbohydrates and more complex carbohydrates because they contain vital nutrients and fiber, and are a superior energy source. Your daily requirement of carbohydrates—50 to 55 percent of total daily calories—can easily be met with a whole-grain cereal and milk for breakfast, a few pieces of fresh fruit during the day, and a baked potato for dinner.

The polenta crust on this pizza is not only an eye-catcher but also flavorful and rich in calcium and other nutrients.

POLENTA PIZZA

A cornmeal crust gives Polenta Pizza extra nutrition. Polenta is low in calories and rich in vitamin A and minerals.

> Safflower oil, for coating baking sheet
> 2 cups polenta
> 1 cup cold water
> 1 cup boiling water
> 2 eggs
> 1 cup grated low-fat mozzarella cheese
> ¼ cup chopped green onions
> 1 teaspoon olive oil
> ¼ cup chopped red bell pepper
> 1 cup thinly sliced mushrooms
> 2 cups Basic Pizza Sauce (see page 92)
> 1 cup thickly sliced plum tomatoes
> ¼ cup chopped parsley
> 1 tablespoon minced fresh basil

1. Preheat oven to 450° F. Lightly oil a 12- by 15-inch baking sheet.

2. In a large bowl combine polenta with the cold water, then add the boiling water in a steady stream, mixing with a whisk. Stir in eggs and mozzarella. Press mixture evenly into baking sheet. Bake until lightly browned and crisp (10 to 15 minutes).

3. In a large skillet over medium-high heat, sauté green onions in olive oil for 1 minute, then add bell pepper and mushrooms. Cover and let steam for 5 minutes.

4. Spoon sauce over cornmeal crust, then top with sautéed vegetables, sliced tomatoes, parsley, and basil. Bake until bubbly (12 to 15 minutes).

Serves 8.

Preparation time: 25 minutes
Cooking time: 6 to 10 minutes
Baking time: 25 to 30 minutes
Per serving: calcium 225 mg, calories 221, carbohydrates 30 g, cholesterol 74 mg, fat 8 g, fiber 2.6 g, protein 8.5 g, sodium 484 mg

Basics

THREE EASY PIZZA CRUSTS

Substitute these easy crusts for traditional pizza dough. The cornmeal crust, which originated in Italy, has a very crunchy texture. The colorful vegetable crust is great as an appetizer—top it with sliced raw or lightly sautéed vegetables and broil until brown. Try the Basic Pizza Dough with any of your favorite pizza toppings. You can make a double batch and freeze half, already pressed into a pizza pan, ready to cook.

CORNMEAL CRUST

Fresh vegetable toppings are a good complement to the golden color and pleasing texture of this crust.

> *Safflower oil, for coating baking sheet*
> 2 *cups polenta*
> 1 *cup cold water*
> 1 *cup boiling water*
> 2 *eggs*
> 1 *cup grated low-fat mozzarella cheese*

1. Preheat oven to 450° F. Lightly oil a large baking sheet.

2. In a large bowl combine polenta with the cold water, then add the boiling water in a steady stream, mixing with a whisk. Stir in eggs and mozzarella. Press mixture evenly into baking sheet. Bake until lightly browned and crisp (10 to 15 minutes).

Makes 1 large pizza crust, 4 servings.

> *Preparation time:* 10 minutes
> *Baking time:* 10 to 15 minutes
> *Per serving:* calcium 339 mg, calories 330, carbohydrates 43 g, cholesterol 148 mg, fat 11 g, fiber .5 g, protein 13 g, sodium 949 mg

VEGETABLE CRUST

Grated zucchini and carrot give a confetti effect to this easy pizza crust. Salt is used to extract moisture from the raw vegetables, making them easier to form into dough. Be sure to rinse vegetables thoroughly to remove the salt and squeeze out excess moisture before combining with other ingredients.

> ¾ *cup grated raw zucchini*
> ½ *cup grated raw carrot*
> ½ *cup minced red or green bell pepper*
> 1 *teaspoon salt*
> 2 *eggs*
> 1 *cup grated low-fat mozzarella cheese*
> *Safflower oil, for coating baking sheet*

1. In a colander set over a large bowl, toss together zucchini, carrot, bell pepper, and salt, and allow to drain for 10 minutes. Run water through colander to rinse salt from vegetables, then squeeze to remove excess moisture. Combine in a bowl with eggs and mozzarella cheese.

2. Preheat oven to 375° F. Lightly oil 1 medium or 2 small baking sheets. Press vegetable mixture evenly onto sheets. Bake until lightly browned and crisp (12 to 15 minutes).

Makes 1 medium pizza crust, 4 servings.

> *Preparation time:* 15 to 20 minutes
> *Baking time:* 12 to 15 minutes
> *Per serving:* calcium 181 mg, calories 140, carbohydrates 5 g, cholesterol 148 mg, fat 10 g, fiber .7 g, protein 9 g, sodium 680 mg

BASIC PIZZA DOUGH

Use this easy recipe for all bread dough pizzas. Begin making it about 2 hours before you want to serve the pizza, since the dough needs time to rise.

> 1 *teaspoon light honey*
> 1 *cup lukewarm water (98° to 100° F)*
> 1 *package active dry yeast*
> 2 *cups whole wheat or unbleached white flour*
> 1 *teaspoon olive oil*
> ½ *teaspoon herbal salt substitute*
> *Flour, for dusting breadboard*
> *Safflower oil, for coating bowl*

1. In a large mixing bowl, combine honey, the warm water, and yeast, and stir until yeast dissolves. Let mixture stand, uncovered, at room temperature for 5 minutes.

2. Stir in 1 cup of the flour and mix well. Let batter rise for 20 minutes, then stir down and add remaining flour, oil, and salt substitute.

3. Lightly flour a counter or breadboard and turn dough onto it. Knead dough for 5 minutes, flouring lightly as needed to prevent stickiness. Dough should be smooth and elastic.

4. Lightly oil a large bowl and place dough into it. Cover with a dish towel and let rise for 30 minutes. Punch down, then divide into 4 balls and roll into rounds. Dough is now ready to use for pizza.

Makes 4 small pizza crusts, 8 servings.

> *Preparation time:* 20 minutes
> *Rising time:* 55 minutes
> *Per serving:* calcium 13 mg, calories 108, carbohydrates 22 g, cholesterol none, fat 1 g, fiber 2.9 g, protein 4 g, sodium 1 mg

PITA PIZZAS WITH SUN-DRIED TOMATOES

These quick little pizzas are assembled on halves of pita bread. Sun-dried tomatoes packed in olive oil, available in gourmet shops, provide a great deal of flavor as well as vitamin A and potassium. These pizzas transport easily, so pack one or two in your next bag lunch.

    2   cups well-washed and
        thinly sliced leeks
    1   teaspoon butter
    1   tablespoon dry sherry
    2   cups sliced mushrooms
    ¼   cup jarred sun-dried
        tomatoes, drained
        and chopped
    1   teaspoon olive oil
    4   large whole wheat pita
        bread rounds
    ½   cup grated low-fat
        mozzarella cheese
    ¼   cup crumbled goat cheese
        (optional)

1. In a large skillet over medium-high heat, sauté leeks in butter and sherry until soft (about 10 minutes). Add mushrooms and tomatoes and continue to sauté for 10 minutes, stirring frequently.

2. Preheat oven to 450° F. Lightly oil a large baking sheet with olive oil and place pita rounds on it. Sprinkle pita with half the mozzarella cheese, reserving half for topping.

3. Spoon sautéed vegetables onto pita rounds, top with remaining mozzarella and goat cheese (if used). Cook until browned and bubbly (about 10 minutes).

Makes 4 small pizzas, 4 servings.

> *Preparation time:* 20 minutes
> *Cooking time:* 30 minutes
> *Per serving:* calcium 126 mg,
> calories 181, carbohydrates 23 g,
> cholesterol 15 mg, fat 6 g, fiber
> 2.3 g, protein 7 g, sodium 214 mg

ZUCCHINI-CRUSTED VEGETABLE PIZZA

Vegetable crusts are a delicious and healthy way to create a pizza base. This recipe combines grated zucchini with a topping of green and red bell pepper, tomatoes, diced green chiles, and a rich tomato sauce. The pizza is a colorful and tasty addition to a buffet party and can be served in small wedges as a low-calorie appetizer.

    2   cups grated raw zucchini
    1   teaspoon salt
    2   eggs
    1   cup grated low-fat
        mozzarella cheese
        Safflower oil, for coating
        baking sheet
    2   cups Basic Pizza Sauce
        (see page 92)
    1   large red bell pepper
    1   large green bell pepper
    ½   cup thickly sliced tomatoes
    ¼   cup diced canned green chiles
    ½   cup grated Parmesan cheese

1. In a colander set over a large bowl, toss together zucchini and salt and allow to drain for 10 minutes. Run water through colander to rinse salt from zucchini, then squeeze to remove excess moisture. (Salt pulls water from zucchini and keeps crust from being too wet.) Combine in a bowl with eggs and mozzarella.

2. Preheat oven to 375° F. Lightly oil a medium baking sheet. Press zucchini mixture evenly onto sheet. Bake until lightly browned and crisp (12 to 15 minutes).

3. Spread sauce over top of zucchini crust. Slice bell peppers into rings, then lay on top of pizza along with tomatoes and chiles. Sprinkle with Parmesan. Bake for 10 minutes and serve hot.

Serves 6.

> *Preparation time:* 25 minutes
> *Baking time:* 25 minutes
> *Per serving:* calcium 284 mg,
> calories 180, carbohydrates 11 g,
> cholesterol 107 mg, fat 10 g,
> fiber 2.6 g, protein 11 g, sodium
> 524 mg

WHOLE-GRAIN BREADS AND MUFFINS

Few aromas are as pleasing as freshly baked bread—but who has the time to make homemade bread? Even if you can reserve only a few hours each week for baking, you will find some unusual additions to your repertoire in this section. If you do not have time to bake yeast bread, try the quick bread recipes. Prepared and baked in less than an hour, they are ideal for brunch with friends or a potluck party.

MOM'S CINNAMON SWIRLS

Mom's Cinnamon Swirls may become a favorite Sunday morning treat in your family, too. The dough is started a few hours before brunch, left to rise in a warm kitchen, then spread with a cinnamon-orange-walnut filling. Roll it up, cut into rounds, and bake. The swirls are best when eaten fresh out of the oven, but they can also be made up the night before and re-heated for mornings when sleeping late is a priority.

    1½ cup scalded low-fat buttermilk
    ½   cup lukewarm water
        (98° to 110° F)
    1   package active dry yeast
    ½   cup plus 2 tablespoons
        light honey
    4   eggs
    10 to 14 cups whole wheat or
        unbleached white flour
    2   tablespoons safflower oil,
        plus oil for coating pans
    ⅓   cup melted butter
    ½   cup maple syrup
    2   tablespoons cinnamon
    1   cup chopped walnuts
    ¾   cup raisins
    1   teaspoon freshly ground
        cardamom powder
    1   tablespoon grated orange peel
    1   beaten egg white

1. In a large bowl combine buttermilk, the water, yeast, and the 2 tablespoons honey. Stir until yeast dissolves. Let stand for 5 minutes.

2. In a small bowl beat eggs, then add to yeast mixture. Stir in 5 to 6 cups of flour, or enough to form a thick batter. Stir well and let stand 20 minutes.

3. Stir batter vigorously for 1 minute, then add 2 tablespoons oil and enough flour to form a thick dough. Lightly flour a counter or breadboard and turn dough onto board. Knead until smooth and elastic (5 to 10 minutes). Lightly oil a mixing bowl and put kneaded dough into it. Cover bowl with a dish towel and let rise for 40 minutes.

4. Punch down the dough, then cover again and let rise an additional 30 minutes. Preheat oven to 350° F. Lightly oil a large, deep baking pan.

5. While dough is rising the second time, in a mixing bowl combine butter, maple syrup, remaining honey, cinnamon, walnuts, raisins, cardamom, and orange peel. Roll out risen dough and spread filling thickly on surface. Roll into a jelly-roll shape and cut into 12 slices. Place slices on end, packing them into the baking pan. Lightly brush with egg white.

6. Bake until lightly browned (about 30 minutes). Let cool slightly, then remove from pan.

Makes 1 dozen rolls, 12 servings.

Preparation time: 50 minutes
Rising time: 90 minutes
Baking time: 30 minutes
Per serving: calcium 142 mg, calories 671, carbohydrates 120 g, cholesterol 102 mg, fat 17 g, fiber 13 g, protein 21 g, sodium 126 mg

---

UKRAINIAN SAUERKRAUT BREAD

An authentic recipe of Ukrainian origin, this traditional bread is made at the beginning of the week and improves as the days progress. Only the most revered family member has the privilege of eating the last piece. The secret to making this surprisingly sweet bread is cooking the sauerkraut with a little honey and grated carrots until it loses its sharpness, then packing it between two layers of egg-based dough. The bread bakes like a huge sandwich and can be served as a main course or quick snack, cut into sandwich-sized wedges.

  1½ *cup scalded low-fat buttermilk*
  ½   *cup lukewarm water (98° to 110° F)*
  1   *package active dry yeast*
  2   *tablespoons light honey*
  4   *eggs*
  10 *to 14 cups whole wheat or unbleached white flour*
  3   *tablespoons safflower oil, plus oil for coating pans and bowl*
  2   *cups drained sauerkraut*
  ½   *cup grated carrots*
  ½   *teaspoon pepper*
  ½   *teaspoon herbal salt substitute*

1. In a large bowl combine buttermilk, the water, yeast, and honey. Stir until yeast dissolves and let stand for 5 minutes.

2. In a small bowl beat eggs, then add to yeast mixture. Stir in 5 to 6 cups of flour, or enough to form a thick batter. Stir well and let stand 20 minutes.

3. Stir batter vigorously for 1 minute, then add 2 tablespoons of the oil and enough flour to form a thick dough. Lightly flour a counter or breadboard and turn dough onto board. Knead until smooth and elastic (5 to 10 minutes). Lightly oil a mixing bowl and put kneaded dough into it. Cover bowl with a dish towel and let rise for 40 minutes.

4. Punch dough down, then cover again and let rise an additional 30 minutes.

5. While dough is rising the second time, combine remaining oil, sauerkraut, carrots, pepper, and salt substitute in a small saucepan. Cook this mixture uncovered, over medium-high heat, for 10 minutes, stirring frequently. Remove from heat and pour into a colander set over the sink. Let sauerkraut drain for 10 minutes.

6. Lightly oil a 9- by 12-inch baking pan and preheat oven to 350° F. Separate dough into 2 balls and roll each into a 9- by 12-inch rectangle. Place one rectangle into the baking pan. Spoon sauerkraut mixture on top of it. Place second rectangle of dough on top of sauerkraut. Reach into pan and pinch edges of bottom and top layers of dough together, sealing tightly. Let it rise for 10 minutes.

7. Bake sauerkraut bread until browned (about 45 minutes). It should lift easily out of the pan. Let cool on a rack, and then slice into thick wedges.

Serves 15.

Preparation time: 45 minutes
Rising time: 1 hour and 45 minutes
Baking time: 45 minutes
Per serving: calcium 91 mg, calories 390, carbohydrates 73 g, cholesterol 68 mg, fat 6 g, fiber 9.8 g, protein 16 g, sodium 288 mg

---

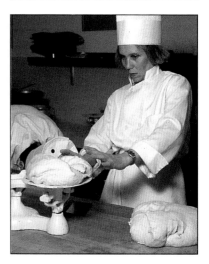

Bursting with fall flavors, rich-tasting Pumpkin Bread is a delicious treat served with a mug of hot apple cider.

ORANGE-DATE MUFFINS

Tart yet sweet, these easy muffins acquire their lightness and refreshing flavor from fresh orange juice and grated orange rind. Make plenty of muffins for Sunday brunches—they freeze well and can be reheated in a 450° F oven for 8 minutes before serving.

> *Safflower oil, for coating muffin tin*
> 1 *orange*
> ½ *cup chopped, pitted dates*
> 2 *tablespoons safflower oil*
> 1 *egg*
> 1 *egg white*
> 2 *tablespoons light honey*
> 2 *tablespoons nonfat plain yogurt*
> 1½ *cups whole wheat pastry or unbleached white flour*
> 1 *teaspoon baking powder*
> 1 *teaspoon baking soda*

1. Preheat oven to 400° F. Lightly oil a 12-hole muffin tin.

2. Grate peel from orange, then juice orange. In a large bowl combine peel and juice with dates, oil, egg, egg white, honey, and yogurt.

3. In a separate bowl combine flour, baking powder, and baking soda. Mix together contents of both bowls, stirring briefly, then spoon into prepared muffin cups, filling them three fourths full. Bake for 12 to 15 minutes. Remove from pan and let cool.

Makes 1 dozen muffins, 12 servings.

Preparation time: 15 minutes
Baking time: 12 to 15 minutes
Per serving: calcium 27 mg, calories 119, carbohydrates 21 g, cholesterol 21 mg, fat 3 g, fiber 2.0 g, protein 3 g, sodium 114 mg

PUMPKIN BREAD

Pumpkins are not only for Halloween, as this bread will show. Cooked pumpkin purée is combined with rich-smelling spices, then mixed with a whole wheat and oatmeal batter. You can easily double this one-loaf recipe and freeze the second loaf for several months. Let the freshly baked bread cool first, then wrap carefully in plastic wrap and aluminum foil.

	Safflower oil, for coating loaf pan
1½	cups whole wheat pastry or unbleached white flour
½	cup raw oats, ground in blender
2	teaspoons baking powder
2	teaspoons baking soda
2	teaspoons cinnamon
2	teaspoons nutmeg
¼	teaspoon allspice
2	teaspoons grated gingerroot
½	cup maple syrup
¼	cup molasses
¼	cup safflower oil or softened butter
2	egg whites
1	whole egg
2	tablespoons lemon juice
1	tablespoon grated orange peel
1	cup canned or cooked fresh pumpkin purée

1. Preheat oven to 350° F. Lightly oil a 2-quart loaf pan.

2. In a large mixing bowl, combine flour, oats, baking powder, baking soda, cinnamon, nutmeg, and allspice.

3. In a separate bowl combine gingerroot, maple syrup, molasses, oil, egg whites, egg, lemon juice, orange peel, and pumpkin.

4. Combine contents of both bowls, mixing very lightly. Pour into prepared loaf pan and bake for 50 to 60 minutes. Let cool before slicing.

Makes 1 large loaf, 8 servings.

Preparation time: 20 minutes
Cooking time: 50 to 60 minutes
Per serving: calcium 85 mg, calories 263, carbohydrates 43 g, cholesterol 31 mg, fat 9 g, fiber 2.7 g, protein 6 g, sodium 332 mg

CARROT-GINGER BREAKFAST MUFFINS

Once considered dessert, carrot cake now takes on many different roles in a meal. Here is a new twist: Add freshly grated gingerroot to the batter, bake it in muffin tins, and serve the sweet muffins for breakfast or as a snack. Warm them in the toaster oven or microwave and serve with Cream Cheese and Garlic Dip (see page 18).

	Safflower oil, for coating muffin tins
2	cups whole wheat pastry or unbleached white flour
1	tablespoon baking powder
1	teaspoon baking soda
½	teaspoon herbal salt substitute
½	teaspoon nutmeg
½	teaspoon cinnamon
2	teaspoons grated gingerroot
½	cup nonfat yogurt or buttermilk
¼	cup safflower oil
¼	cup maple syrup
¼	cup light honey
3	eggs
2	cups grated carrot

1. Preheat oven to 400° F. Lightly oil a 12-hole muffin tin.

2. In a large bowl combine flour, baking powder, baking soda, salt substitute, nutmeg, and cinnamon.

3. In a separate bowl combine gingerroot, yogurt, the ¼ cup safflower oil, maple syrup, honey, and eggs.

4. Stir together contents of both bowls, then stir in carrots. Spoon into muffin tins, filling about three quarters full, and bake for 15 to 18 minutes. Remove from pan; let cool.

Makes 1 dozen muffins, 12 servings.

Preparation time: 20 minutes
Baking time: 15 to 18 minutes
Per serving: calcium 64 mg, calories 186, carbohydrates 28 g, cholesterol 64 mg, fat 7 g, fiber 2.4 g, protein 5 g, sodium 205 mg

FIRESIDE FEAST

Russian Black Bread

Molasses Corn Muffins

Herb Muffins

Minnesota Chicken and Wild Rice Soup (see page 31)

Dorothy's Hearty Ham and Lima Bean Soup (see page 34)

Swiss Lentil Soup (see page 30)

When winter winds howl, prepare this hearty buffet of soups and homemade breads and muffins and serve it by the fire. Russian Black Bread can be started early in the morning—it needs about three hours of rising time before baking. Molasses Corn Muffins and Herb Muffins are rich-tasting and can be made ahead of time. They freeze well, so bake an extra batch for Sunday breakfasts. Start the soups the night before, and their flavors will improve overnight in the refrigerator. Keep them warm on the buffet table in electric slow cookers or over candle warmers. Menu serves 12.

RUSSIAN BLACK BREAD

This strong, dark bread combines caraway seed, molasses, honey, rye and wheat flours, and carob powder.

½ cups lukewarm water
1 cup low-fat buttermilk, at room temperature
2 tablespoons molasses
2 tablespoons light honey
1 package active dry yeast
3 to 4 cups whole wheat flour
1½ cups rye flour
1 tablespoon crushed caraway seed
½ teaspoon onion powder
½ teaspoon crushed fennel seed
2 tablespoons grain coffee
2 tablespoons carob powder
2 tablespoons safflower oil, plus oil for coating pans

1. In a large bowl combine the water, buttermilk, molasses, honey, and yeast. Stir until yeast dissolves. Let stand for 5 minutes. Stir in 2 cups of flour, or enough to form a thick batter. Stir well; let stand 20 minutes.

2. Stir batter down, then add rye flour, caraway seed, onion powder, fennel seed, grain coffee, carob powder, and 2 tablespoons safflower oil to form a thick dough. Lightly flour a counter or breadboard and turn dough onto board. Knead until smooth and elastic (5 to 10 minutes). Lightly oil a mixing bowl and put kneaded dough into it. Cover with a dish towel and let rise for 40 minutes.

3. Punch down dough; cover again and let rise 30 minutes. Lightly oil a 2-quart loaf pan and preheat oven to 350° F. Form dough into 1 large loaf; press into pan. Let rise 10 minutes.

4. Bake until loaf sounds hollow when tapped and comes easily out of pan (50 minutes to 1 hour). Let cool before slicing.

Makes 1 large loaf, 12 servings.

Preparation time: 55 minutes
Rising time: 1 hour, 35 minutes
Baking time: 50 minutes to 1 hour
Per serving: calcium 78 mg, calories 347, carbohydrates 69 g, cholesterol none, fat 4 g, fiber 5.1 g, protein 10 g, sodium 35 mg

MOLASSES CORN MUFFINS

Molasses—especially the blackstrap variety—is rich in iron and trace minerals. However, if you use the blackstrap, use only half the recipe amount because it has a stronger flavor than regular, unsulfured molasses. The cornmeal in this recipe gives the muffins a pleasantly crunchy texture and a slightly crisp crust that goes well with the hearty soups in this menu.

Safflower oil, for coating muffin tin
1 cup whole wheat pastry or unbleached white flour
3 teaspoons baking powder
1 teaspoon salt or herbal salt substitute
½ cup boiling water
½ cup finely ground cornmeal
2 tablespoons molasses
¼ cup light honey
3 beaten eggs
¼ cup safflower oil
½ cup grated low-fat Cheddar cheese

1. Preheat oven to 400° F. Lightly oil a 12-hole muffin tin.

2. In a large mixing bowl, combine flour, baking powder, and salt. In a separate bowl combine the boiling water and cornmeal. Mix well.

3. Add molasses, honey, eggs, oil, and cheese to cornmeal and stir well. Add to flour mixture, stirring briefly as you combine. Spoon into prepared muffin cups, filling about three fourths full.

4. Bake for 25 minutes. Let cool slightly, then remove from tins.

Makes 1 dozen muffins, 12 servings.

Preparation time: 20 minutes
Baking time: 25 minutes
Per serving: calcium 94 mg, calories 148, carbohydrates 17 g, cholesterol 65 mg, fat 7 g, fiber 1 g, protein 5 g, sodium 319 mg

HERB MUFFINS

Thyme, basil, and oregano are combined in this savory whole-grain herb muffin. It is lightly laced with Parmesan cheese, which provides a creamy texture as well as calcium. Made ahead of time, these muffins freeze well and will keep for up to two weeks. Reheat them for 10 minutes in a 450° F oven right before serving.

Safflower oil, for coating muffin tin
2 cups whole wheat pastry or unbleached white flour
1 tablespoon baking powder
1 teaspoon baking soda
½ teaspoon herbal salt substitute
2 teaspoons dried oregano
2 teaspoons dried thyme
2 teaspoons dried basil
2 eggs
1 egg white
1 cup nonfat buttermilk
2 tablespoons safflower oil
1 tablespoon light honey
¼ cup grated Parmesan cheese

1. Preheat oven to 400° F. Lightly oil a 12-hole muffin tin.

2. In a large mixing bowl, combine flour, baking powder, baking soda, herbal salt substitute, oregano, thyme, and basil.

3. In a separate bowl combine eggs, egg white, buttermilk, the 2 tablespoons safflower oil, honey, and Parmesan. Mix together the contents of both bowls, stirring briefly, then spoon into prepared muffin cups, filling two thirds full.

4. Bake for 25 minutes. Let cool slightly, then remove from tins.

Makes 1 dozen muffins, 12 servings.

Preparation time: 10 minutes
Baking time: 25 minutes
Per serving: calcium 90 mg, calories 128, carbohydrates 17 g, cholesterol 44 mg, fat 4 g, fiber 2.0 g, protein 6 g, sodium 228 mg

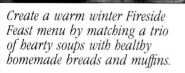

Create a warm winter Fireside Feast menu by matching a trio of hearty soups with healthy homemade breads and muffins.

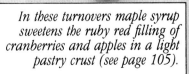

In these turnovers maple syrup sweetens the ruby red filling of cranberries and apples in a light pastry crust (see page 105).

Desserts

C an the dessert course be as nutritious as the rest of the meal? You might be surprised that these dessert recipes are loaded with nutrients and yet can satisfy the urge for sweets. None of the recipes contain white sugar; only unrefined maple syrup, honey, fruit purées, fruit concentrates, and date sugar are used. Many of the desserts, such as Cranberry Turnovers With Maple Glaze (see page 105), can be served for brunch, and other recipes, such as Chilled Banana Custard (see page 104), are light enough to serve as an after-school snack. Try Lime Soufflé From Barbados (see page 104) or Hazel's Carob Cheesecake (see page 109) as a dessert at your next party.

FRESH FRUIT DESSERTS

Fruits are a rich source of vitamins, minerals, and fiber, and many nutritionists and health experts recommend several servings a day. Desserts made from fresh fruits are also lower in calories than traditionally high-fat, high-sugar desserts.

COMPOTE OF WINTER FRUITS IN RED WINE

A simple dessert rich in flavor but low in calories, this recipe blends dried apricots and pineapple with simmered pears, apples, and spices. A good source of iron and other minerals, the compote makes a healthy and stunning finish to a holiday dinner. Serve it chilled or slightly warm with a dollop of nonfat yogurt.

> 2 cups sliced pears
> 2 cups sliced green apples
> ⅓ cup chopped dried apricots
> ¼ cup chopped dried pineapple
> 1 teaspoon vanilla extract
> 1½ cup dry red wine
> ¼ teaspoon ground ginger
> ¼ teaspoon cinnamon
> ½ teaspoon nutmeg
>   Grated rind of 1 lemon
> 2 tablespoons orange juice
> 1 cup nonfat plain yogurt

1. In a large saucepan over medium heat, combine pears, apples, apricots, pineapple, vanilla, wine, ginger, cinnamon, nutmeg, lemon rind, and orange juice. Cook, stirring frequently, until most of wine has been absorbed and fruit is very soft (about 30 minutes).

2. Serve warm or chilled, topped with nonfat yogurt.

Makes approximately 5 cups compote, 8 servings.

> *Preparation time:* 20 minutes
> *Cooking time:* 30 minutes
> *Chilling time (optional):* 2 hours.
> *Per serving:* calcium 67 mg,
> calories 107, carbohydrates 18 g,
> cholesterol 2 mg, fat 1 g, fiber
> 2.4 g, protein 2 g, sodium 24 mg

CHILLED BANANA CUSTARD

Bananas are a rich source of potassium, an essential mineral for good nerve functioning. In this light and easy dessert, puréed bananas are mixed with eggs, nonfat milk, and maple syrup, and then chilled to form a thick, creamy custard. Serve it cold as a wonderful finish to a warm-weather menu.

> 1 cup nonfat milk
> 1 whole egg
> 2 egg yolks
> 3 tablespoons maple syrup
> 3 tablespoons whole wheat
>   pastry or unbleached
>   white flour
> 1 teaspoon vanilla extract
> 1 tablespoon arrowroot
> 1 tablespoon apple juice
>   or water
> 2 large bananas

1. In a small saucepan over medium-high heat, heat milk until it steams. Remove from heat and pour into a mixing bowl.

2. In a separate bowl whisk together egg, egg yolks, and maple syrup until smooth. Add flour and vanilla. Mix arrowroot with apple juice and add to egg mixture. Add hot milk. Purée bananas in a blender, then add to egg mixture.

3. Return custard to pan and cook over medium-high heat, stirring, until thick. Pour into 8 dessert glasses and chill in the refrigerator for 4 hours before serving.

Serves 8.

> *Preparation time:* 20 minutes
> *Chilling time:* 4 hours
> *Per serving:* calcium 59 mg,
> calories 100, carbohydrates 17 g,
> cholesterol 95 mg, fat 2 g, fiber
> .7 g, protein 3 g, sodium 27 mg

LIME SOUFFLÉ FROM BARBADOS

This cloudlike soufflé is composed of vitamin-rich fresh lime juice, grated lime rind, and egg whites, sweetened with a small amount of maple syrup. The tart taste of the lime makes it a good dessert to serve after a rich-tasting entrée, such as Chicken Breasts in Green Peppercorn Sauce (see page 60). Plan to make the soufflé the night before and set it overnight in the refrigerator.

> 1 tablespoon butter, for coating
>   soufflé dish
> ½ cup agar flakes or 2 packages
>   unflavored gelatin
> 1 cup freshly squeezed lime juice
> 3 egg yolks
> 1 cup coconut milk
> ½ cup maple syrup
> 2 tablespoons arrowroot powder
> 3 tablespoons grated lime rind
> ½ cup grated fresh coconut
> 6 egg whites

1. Lightly butter a large (2-quart) soufflé dish.

2. In a small saucepan over medium-high heat, cook agar in lime juice until completely dissolved. In a small bowl combine egg yolks, coconut milk, maple syrup, and arrowroot. Add to lime juice mixture and cook, stirring constantly, until a thick custardlike sauce forms. Remove saucepan from heat.

3. Stir in lime rind and coconut. Beat egg whites until stiff peaks form, then fold into lime mixture. Pour into prepared soufflé dish and refrigerate until firm (about 8 hours). Serve chilled.

Serves 8.

> *Preparation time:* 20 minutes
> *Chilling time:* 8 hours
> *Per serving:* calcium 45 mg,
> calories 242, carbohydrates 24 g,
> cholesterol 99 mg, fat 16 g, fiber
> .8 g, protein 6 g, sodium 82 mg

CRANBERRY TURNOVERS WITH MAPLE GLAZE

Cranberries are full of natural pectin, a rich source of fiber and vitamin C. In this recipe they are simmered with apples, currants, and cinnamon, wrapped with a light pastry dough, brushed with maple glaze, then baked until crisp. Make the turnovers ahead, wrap tightly, and freeze to reheat as an easy brunch dessert.

- 1 package active dry yeast
- 1 cup lukewarm milk (98° to 110° F)
- 3 tablespoons honey
- 3 cups whole wheat pastry or unbleached white flour
  Pinch of salt
- 3 tablespoons melted butter or safflower oil
- ¾ cup cranberries
- 2 cups cored, peeled, and sliced green apples
- ½ cup water
- ¼ cup dried currants
- 1 cup maple syrup
- 3 tablespoons arrowroot powder
- 1 tablespoon lemon juice
- ½ teaspoon cinnamon
- 1 tablespoon grated lemon rind
  Safflower oil, for coating baking sheet

1. In a large bowl combine yeast, milk, and honey. Let mixture stand for 5 minutes. Stir in 1½ cups of the flour and let batter rise for 15 minutes. Add remaining flour, salt, and butter to form a dough. Knead dough for 5 minutes on a floured breadboard, then place in a clean bowl and cover with a dish towel. Let dough rise for 45 minutes.

2. In a covered saucepan over medium-high heat, simmer cranberries, apples, the water, and currants until berries pop. In a small bowl mix ⅔ cup of the maple syrup, arrowroot, lemon juice, cinnamon, and lemon rind. Uncover saucepan and add maple syrup mixture to cooking cranberries. Stir well. Heat, stirring constantly, until thick. Remove from heat and let cool 15 minutes.

3. Preheat oven to 375° F. Lightly oil a large baking sheet. Separate dough into 8 balls. Roll into 5-inch circles on a floured breadboard. Place equal amounts of cranberry filling into the center of each circle. Lightly dampen edges of circle with water and fold edges in to form a turnover, pressing to seal.

4. In a small saucepan over high heat, bring the remaining maple syrup to a boil. Cook for 3 to 4 minutes. Remove from heat and then brush tops of turnovers with syrup. Place turnovers on prepared baking sheet and bake until browned (about 20 minutes). Let cool slightly before serving.

Makes 8 turnovers, 8 servings.

Preparation time: 30 minutes
Rising time: 65 minutes
Baking time: 20 minutes
Per serving: calcium 104 mg, calories 390, carbohydrates 79 g, cholesterol 4 mg, fat 7 g, fiber 5.1 g, protein 7 g, sodium 75 mg

A splendid finale to your next elegant dinner is Compote of Winter Fruits in Red Wine, served warm or chilled with a dollop of yogurt.

PEACH STRUDEL WITH VANILLA SAUCE

In this recipe the filo sheets are lightly buttered, filled with fresh peaches, and sprinkled with almonds. The vanilla sauce is a creamy mixture of egg whites, nonfat milk, vanilla extract, and honey. Serve the strudel hot from the oven. Its elegant appearance makes it a good choice for after-theater parties.

Safflower oil, for coating baking sheet
4 cups sliced peaches
½ teaspoon cinnamon
½ teaspoon nutmeg
½ cup maple syrup
2 tablespoons arrowroot powder
6 large sheets filo
¼ cup melted butter
½ cup ground almonds
2 tablespoons date sugar
½ cup honey
2 tablespoons unsalted butter
2 egg yolks
1 cup nonfat milk
1 teaspoon vanilla extract

1. Preheat oven to 375° F. Lightly oil a large baking sheet.

2. In a large saucepan mix together peaches, cinnamon, nutmeg, maple syrup, and arrowroot. Cook over medium-high heat until peaches soften. Let cool.

3. Place filo on a clean counter. Sprinkle each sheet with 2 teaspoons melted butter, then spread butter to cover as much of filo sheet as possible (see Preparing Filo, page 110). Sprinkle equal amounts of almonds and date sugar on top of buttered sheets, reserving 1 teaspoon each for topping. Stack sheets evenly on top of each other in a pile.

4. Place cooled peach mixture along one end of filo and roll filo around peaches, forming a log. Place seam side down on prepared baking sheet. Brush top of filo with any remaining melted butter and sprinkle with remaining almonds and date sugar.

5. Bake filo roll for 20 minutes or until crisp and brown. While it is baking, in a small saucepan over medium heat combine honey, unsalted butter, egg yolks, milk, and vanilla. Cook, stirring constantly, until mixture thickens. Let cool slightly and serve over slices of strudel.

Serves 10.

Preparation time: 35 minutes
Baking time: 20 minutes
Per serving: calcium 80 mg, calories 306, carbohydrates 46 g, cholesterol 74 mg, fat 13 g, fiber 1g, protein 4 g, sodium 175 mg

ERIC'S FAMOUS CARROT-PINEAPPLE CUPCAKES

Made with plenty of vitamin A—rich carrots, these cupcakes will become a favorite dessert. The secrets to their flavor and airy texture are crushed fresh pineapple and stiffly beaten egg whites. The batter can be baked in cupcakes or in a large sheet cake pan, or in three layers. The low-calorie cream cheese frosting makes this dessert a healthy choice for birthday parties.

Safflower oil, for coating muffin tins (optional)
2 eggs
3 tablespoons pineapple juice
¼ cup low-fat buttermilk
¼ cup safflower oil
1 cup sifted whole wheat pastry or unbleached white flour
2 teaspoons baking powder
½ teaspoon salt or herbal salt substitute
1 tablespoon cinnamon
1 teaspoon nutmeg
⅓ cup chopped walnuts
½ cup raisins or dried currants
¾ cup crushed pineapple
¼ cup date sugar
1 cup grated carrots
4 ounces low-calorie cream cheese
1 tablespoon vanilla extract
2 tablespoons maple syrup

1. Preheat oven to 350° F. Lightly oil a 12-hole muffin tin or line with cupcake papers.

2. Separate eggs. Place egg yolks in a large bowl and add pineapple juice, buttermilk, and the ¼ cup safflower oil. Mix well and set aside.

3. In a separate bowl mix flour, baking powder, salt, cinnamon, and nutmeg. Set aside. Beat egg whites until stiff peaks form.

4. In another bowl combine walnuts, raisins, pineapple, date sugar, and carrots. Add egg yolk mixture and stir well. Make a well in center of dry ingredients and pour in carrot mixture. Mix until just blended. Fold in egg whites.

5. Spoon batter into prepared muffin tin, filling cups two thirds full. Bake until firm in center (about 15 minutes).

6. While cupcakes are baking, mix cream cheese, vanilla, and maple syrup until smooth and creamy. Let cupcakes cool, then frost with cream cheese mixture.

Makes 1 dozen cupcakes, 12 servings.

Preparation time: 20 minutes
Baking time: 15 minutes
Per serving: calcium 57 mg, calories 200, carbohydrates 23 g, cholesterol 52 mg, fat 11 g, fiber 2.1 g, protein 4 g, sodium 208 mg

RICE WAFFLES WITH FRUIT SAUCE

These light waffles are made with cooked rice and sweetened with cinnamon, nutmeg, and honey. Serve them with a cooked sauce made with seasonal fruit. Here, strawberries are recommended.

Safflower oil or vegetable cooking spray, for coating waffle iron
¾ *cup sifted rice flour*
2 *teaspoons baking powder*
1 *teaspoon nutmeg*
1 *teaspoon cinnamon*
Pinch of salt
1 *tablespoon honey*
2 *eggs, separated*
1 *cup nonfat milk*
¼ *cup safflower oil*
1 *cup cooked rice*
1 *cup sliced strawberries*
2 *teaspoons date sugar or maple syrup*
2 *teaspoons arrowroot powder*
½ *cup nonfat yogurt*

1. Preheat waffle iron and lightly brush with safflower oil.

2. In a medium bowl combine rice flour, baking powder, nutmeg, cinnamon, and salt. In a separate bowl combine honey, egg yolks, milk, the ¼ cup safflower oil, and rice. Beat egg whites until stiff peaks form. Combine dry and wet ingredients, then fold in egg whites.

3. Preheat oven to 200° F. Cook waffles, one at a time, keeping them warm in the oven on a heatproof platter. In a small saucepan combine strawberries, date sugar, and arrowroot. Cook over medium-high heat until thick. Let cool slightly, then mix with yogurt.

4. Pour strawberry sauce over warm waffles and serve.

Makes about 8 waffles, 8 servings.

Preparation time: 20 minutes
Cooking time: 20 minutes
Per serving: calcium 101 mg, calories 197, carbohydrates 25 g, cholesterol 64 mg, fat 9 g, fiber 1.9 g, protein 5 g, sodium 293 mg

WATERMELON SHERBET

This dessert could not be easier—fresh watermelon is combined with honey, cardamom, and lime juice; then frozen. You don't even need an ice cream maker or sorbet machine. Simply pour the mixture into ice cube trays, freeze until solid, then cut into chunks and lightly blend. Serve the sherbet in tall champagne glasses garnished with a mint leaf.

8 *cups chopped, seeded watermelon*
1½ *tablespoons lime juice*
1 *cup light honey*
½ *teaspoon ground cardamom*
½ *package unflavored gelatin*
½ *cup nonfat plain yogurt*
12 *mint leaves*

1. Place watermelon and lime juice in a blender and purée. Set a colander or sieve over a large bowl and pour puréed watermelon through sieve, separating juice from pulp. Place juice, honey, cardamom, and gelatin in a large saucepan over medium-high heat. Cook just to boiling point, then remove from heat. Let cool. Pour into a shallow pan or ice cube tray and freeze to slush point (about 1½ hours).

2. Whisk yogurt into watermelon slush, then return to freezer. Allow to freeze solid (about 2 hours). Stir every hour to break up ice crystals.

3. To serve, cut sherbet into large chunks and purée very briefly in a blender or food processor. Spoon into dessert glasses, garnish with mint leaf, and serve.

Serves 12.

Preparation time: 25 minutes
Freezing time: 3½ hours
Per serving: calcium 26 mg, calories 120, carbohydrates 30 g, cholesterol 1 mg, fat none, fiber .4 g, protein 1 g, sodium 9 mg

... ON SUBSTITUTING UNREFINED SWEETENERS

Cooking with maple syrup, honey, barley malt, fruit juice concentrates, and dried fruits instead of refined sugars is easy once you know the substitution rules.

In traditional baking, white or brown sugar is considered a dry ingredient and is balanced in a recipe by the use of liquids such as milk, cream, or eggs. Since most unrefined sweeteners are in liquid form, the ratio of dry to wet ingredients must be altered.

Maple syrup   For every 1 cup of white or brown sugar, use ½ to ¾ cup maple syrup; decrease the oil or butter by 2 tablespoons; and increase the flour by 2 tablespoons.

Molasses   For every 1 cup of white or brown sugar, use ½ cup molasses; decrease the oil or butter by 2 tablespoons; and increase the flour by 2 tablespoons.

Honey   For every 1 cup of white or brown sugar, use ½ cup honey; decrease the oil or butter by 2 tablespoons; and increase the flour by 2 tablespoons.

Barley malt   For every 1 cup of white or brown sugar, use ⅓ to ½ cup barley malt; decrease the oil or butter by 2 tablespoons; and increase the flour by 2 tablespoons.

Fruit juice concentrate   For every 1 cup of white or brown sugar, use ¼ cup apple juice concentrate; decrease the oil or butter by 4 to 6 tablespoons; and increase the flour by 4 to 6 tablespoons. Concentrates are best in cobblers and pies.

Dried fruits   For every 1 cup of white or brown sugar, use ½ cup dried fruit purée (made by blending equal amounts of fruit and water); decrease the oil or butter by 2 tablespoons; and increase the flour by 2 tablespoons.

PROTEIN-RICH DESSERTS

Add more protein to a menu and satisfy your sweet tooth at the same time with these protein-rich desserts made with low-fat dairy products. Some take a little extra time to prepare, but the creamy texture and rich taste make most of these recipes elegant enough for entertaining.

MAPLE–COTTAGE CHEESE SQUARES

Even though these small creamy bars practically melt in your mouth, they are low in fat because they contain low-calorie cottage and ricotta cheeses. Make them ahead of time and refrigerate until serving.

Safflower oil, for coating pan
2½ cups finely crushed graham cracker crumbs
1 teaspoon cinnamon
¼ cup date sugar
¼ cup safflower oil
¼ cup nonfat milk
2 cups low-fat cottage cheese
1 cup nonfat ricotta cheese
1 tablespoon melted butter
3 tablespoons maple syrup
2 tablespoons grated orange rind
1 teaspoon orange juice

1. Preheat oven to 300° F. Lightly oil an 8-inch-square baking pan.

2. In a large bowl combine graham cracker crumbs, cinammon, date sugar, the ¼ cup safflower oil, and enough milk to form a ball. Press into bottom of pan. Set aside.

3. In a blender or food processor, purée cottage cheese, ricotta, butter, maple syrup, orange rind, and orange juice. Pour into prepared pan and bake until firm (about 25 minutes). Remove from oven and let cool, then slice into squares.

Makes 16 squares, 8 servings.

Preparation time: 15 minutes
Baking time: 25 minutes
Per serving: calcium 135 mg, calories 384, carbohydrates 45 g, cholesterol 32 mg, fat 16 g, fiber .7 g, protein 14 g, sodium 572 mg

CAROB-MOCHA SOUFFLÉ

This creamy soufflé features the rich taste of carob and coffee. Grain coffee, a good substitute for coffee liqueur, is usually sold in health-food stores. Soufflés typically combine the jelling power of egg yolks with the fluffy texture of beaten egg whites. In this low-calorie recipe, arrowroot powder replaces the egg yolks. The secret of a super soufflé is to gently fold in the egg whites at the last minute so they retain their airiness.

2 tablespoons softened butter
1 tablespoon unbleached white flour
⅓ cup milk
4 tablespoons honey
2 tablespoons carob powder
1 tablespoon coffee liqueur or grain coffee
1 teaspoon vanilla extract
1 tablespoon arrowroot powder
2 tablespoons orange juice
2 egg whites

1. Preheat oven to 375° F. Using 1 tablespoon of the butter, lightly butter 4 custard cups.

2. In a small saucepan over medium heat, melt remaining butter. Stir in flour and cook for 2 minutes, stirring constantly. Pour in milk and cook until mixture thickens. Remove from heat and add in honey, carob powder, coffee liqueur, and vanilla. Mix arrowroot with orange juice and add to carob mixture.

3. Beat egg whites until stiff peaks form. Fold into carob mixture and pour into prepared custard cups. Set custard cups in a shallow baking pan and fill with hot water to one half the height of the pan. Bake soufflé until slightly puffed and springy (15 to 20 minutes). Let cool and serve.

Serves 4.

Preparation time: 20 minutes
Baking time: 15 to 20 minutes
Per serving: calcium 59 mg, calories 210, carbohydrates 32 g, cholesterol 22 mg, fat 7 g, fiber .7 g, protein 3 g, sodium 98 mg

ORANGE-PUMPKIN SPICE PUDDING

Warm pudding scented with holiday spices is a great treat for a Christmas Eve or Hanukkah party. Pumpkin is a good source of potassium and vitamin A, and this pumpkin recipe takes a relatively short time to prepare.

Safflower oil, for coating custard cups
1 cup nonfat milk
1 tablespoon arrowroot powder
2 tablespoons molasses
1 cup canned or cooked, fresh pumpkin purée
2 tablespoons cinnamon
½ teaspoon ground cloves
1 teaspoon ground cardamom
2 teaspoons grated gingerroot
1 teaspoon nutmeg
½ cup maple syrup
2 tablespoons grated orange rind
¼ cup orange juice
2 eggs
Nonfat plain yogurt, for garnish

1. Preheat oven to 350° F. Lightly oil 8 custard cups.

2. In a large bowl combine milk, arrowroot, and molasses, and whisk until well blended. Add pumpkin, cinnamon, cloves, cardamom, gingerroot, nutmeg, maple syrup, orange rind, and orange juice.

3. Separate eggs. Add yolks to pumpkin mixture. In a small bowl beat egg whites until stiff peaks form. Fold into pumpkin mixture.

4. Pour into prepared custard cups. Place in a shallow baking pan. Add hot water to one half the height of pan. Bake until firm (about 40 minutes). Let cool slightly and serve garnished with yogurt.

Serves 8.

Preparation time: 20 minutes
Baking time: 40 minutes
Per serving: calcium 130 mg, calories 130, carbohydrates 25 g, cholesterol 64 mg, fat 2 g, fiber .8 g, protein 4 g, sodium 45 mg

HAZEL'S CAROB CHEESECAKE

Layers of dark-carob and white-yogurt filling, topped with carob fudge sauce, produce a striped effect when this cheesecake is sliced. Carob should not be viewed as a substitute for chocolate; it has a delicate, rich flavor all its own.

> 2½ cups finely crushed graham cracker crumbs
> 1 teaspoon cinnamon
> ¼ cup date sugar
> ¼ cup safflower oil
> 1 cup nonfat milk
> ½ cup ground cashews
> ½ cup water
> ⅓ cup arrowroot powder
> 3 tablespoons vanilla extract
> ⅔ cup maple syrup
> ⅔ cup carob powder
> 8 ounces low-fat cream cheese
> 3 cups nonfat plain yogurt or low-fat sour cream
> 3 tablespoons unsalted butter
> 3 tablespoons honey
> 2 tablespoons finely chopped almonds

1. Preheat oven to 300° F. In a large bowl combine graham cracker crumbs, cinnamon, date sugar, oil, and enough milk to form a ball. Press into sides and bottom of a 9-inch springform pan. Set aside.

2. In a blender or food processor, purée cashews and the water. Strain through a colander, reserving cashew milk. Place cashew milk in blender or food processor and purée with ¼ cup of the arrowroot, 1 tablespoon of the vanilla, ⅓ cup of maple syrup, ⅓ cup of carob powder, and cream cheese until very smooth. Pour into prepared crust and bake 30 minutes, then cool 15 minutes in pan.

3. In blender or food processor, cream together yogurt and remaining maple syrup and vanilla. Pour carefully on top of baked cheesecake and return it to oven. Bake 10 minutes more, then cool 10 minutes in pan.

4. In blender or food processor, purée butter, honey, and remaining nonfat milk, carob powder, and arrowroot. Pour carefully over cheesecake. Sprinkle with chopped almonds. Refrigerate for 6 hours before serving.

Makes 1 nine-inch cheesecake, 15 servings.

Preparation time: 50 minutes
Baking time: 50 minutes
Chilling time: 6 hours
Per serving: calcium 221 mg, calories 526, carbohydrates 58 g, cholesterol 71 mg, fat 26 g, fiber 1.4 g, protein 13 g, sodium 485 mg

A French pastry chef would be proud to serve this rich—yet surprisingly light—cheesecake.

PREPARING FILO

Filo has less than half the calories of traditional butter pastry. The paper-thin sheets are wrapped carefully to prevent them from drying out.

1. *Count out the number of filo sheets called for in the recipe and stack on a clean counter. Place a sheet of plastic wrap and a lightly dampened dish towel over the filo to keep it from drying out.*

2. *Next, melt a small amount of butter in a saucepan. Lay one sheet of filo on the counter or table. Using a pastry brush, lightly flick dots of butter on the filo, then spread to cover most of surface. The flicking motion keeps you from using too much butter. Stack the buttered filo to the side of the work area, ready to cut into desired shapes.*

HOLIDAY TORTE WITH MAPLE GLAZE

This recipe derives its creamy texture and tangy flavor from a mixture of cooked sweet potatoes, grated orange rind, and walnuts.

> *Safflower oil and flour, for coating pan*
> 1 *cup puréed, cooked and peeled sweet potato*
> ¼ *cup safflower oil or melted butter*
> 1 *teaspoon vanilla extract*
> 4 *eggs, separated*
> ⅔ *cup light honey*
> ¼ *teaspoon nutmeg*
> ½ *cup whole wheat pastry or unbleached white flour*
> 1 *tablespoon baking powder*
> 1 *teaspoon baking soda*
> ¾ *cup ground walnuts*
> *Pinch of salt*
> *Grated rind of 1 orange*
> ¼ *cup maple syrup*
> 12 *walnut halves*

1. Preheat oven to 350° F. Lightly oil and flour 2½- to 3-quart bundt pan.

2. In a food processor or blender, purée sweet potato, the ¼ cup safflower oil, vanilla, egg yolks, and honey until smooth. Set aside.

3. Sift together nutmeg, flour, baking powder, and baking soda. Stir in ground walnuts and salt. Combine with sweet potato mixture and stir briefly. Add orange rind.

4. Beat egg whites until stiff peaks form. Carefully fold into batter and pour into prepared bundt pan. Bake until a knife tip inserted in center comes out clean (about 40 minutes). Let cool for 10 minutes, then unmold.

5. In a small saucepan over high heat, boil maple syrup for 3 minutes. Pour over top of cooled cake. Decorate with walnut halves.

Makes 1 bundt cake, 10 servings.

> *Preparation time:* 35 minutes
> *Baking time:* 40 minutes
> *Per serving:* calcium 76 mg, calories 399, carbohydrates 39 g, cholesterol 101 mg, fat 26 g, fiber 2.3 g, protein 8 g, sodium 260 mg

EASY TARTS AND PASTRIES

For those special occasions when you want to serve healthy desserts that have the flair a pastry shop could create, try these recipes. Several use filo dough in place of butter crusts to lower the total calories and fat.

SWEET DATE AND COCONUT COOKIES

These cookies may remind you of palm trees and oases—their creamy texture and sweet flavor come from a combination of chopped dates and grated fresh coconut. You can make a double batch and freeze half for tea parties or children's lunch boxes.

> *Safflower oil, for coating pan*
> ¾ *cup honey*
> 1 *egg*
> 1 *egg white*
> 1 *cup chopped, pitted dates*
> ¼ *cup grated fresh coconut*
> ½ *cup chopped almonds*
> ½ *cup raisins*
> ½ *cup whole wheat pastry or unbleached white flour*
> ½ *teaspoon baking powder*

1. Preheat oven to 350° F. Lightly oil an 8-inch-square baking pan.

2. In a large bowl combine honey, egg, egg white, dates, coconut, almonds, and raisins. In separate bowl sift together flour and baking powder. Combine contents of two bowls, mix well, and pour into prepared pan. Bake 30 minutes.

3. Let cool, then slice.

Makes about 16 squares, 8 servings.

> *Preparation time:* 15 minutes
> *Baking time:* 30 minutes
> *Per serving:* calcium 49 mg, calories 288, carbohydrates 59 g, cholesterol 31 mg, fat 6 g, fiber 3.1 g, protein 5 g, sodium 58 mg

EASY BAKLAVA

This traditional Greek dessert alternates sheets of thin filo pastry with a mixture of ground almonds, walnuts, and cinnamon. When the pastry comes out of the oven, it soaks in a lemon-flavored honey glaze.

     Safflower oil, for coating pan
 1   cup ground almonds
 1   cup ground walnuts
 1½ teaspoons cinnamon
 8   sheets filo
 ¼   cup melted unsalted butter
 1¼ cup date sugar
 2   tablespoons grated
     lemon rind
 ¼   cup lemon juice
 2   tablespoons honey

1. Preheat oven to 350° F. Lightly oil a deep 9- by 12-inch baking pan.

2. In a small bowl combine almonds, walnuts, and cinnamon. Set aside.

3. Cut each sheet of filo in half. Stack cut sheets on counter. With a large pastry brush, dot top sheet with about 1 teaspoon butter, then spread evenly to coat as much of sheet as possible (see Preparing Filo, opposite page). Lay evenly in baking pan. Sprinkle lightly with nut mixture. Repeat with remaining sheets, stacking evenly.

4. To cut baklava make 4 evenly spaced vertical cuts through the entire stack of filo. Then cut diagonally to form diamond shapes. (Four evenly spaced diagonal cuts will yield 15 to 20 pastries.) Bake for 20 minutes, then lower heat to 300° F and bake for 30 minutes more.

5. In a small saucepan over medium-high heat, simmer date sugar, lemon rind, lemon juice, and honey until thickened. Pour over cooked baklava as soon as it comes out of the oven. Let cool and then serve.

Serves 12.

Preparation time: 25 minutes
Cooking time: 50 minutes
Per serving: calcium 52 mg, calories 365, carbohydrates 44 g, cholesterol 16 mg, fat 20 g, fiber 1 g, protein 5 g, sodium 186 mg

TANGY LEMON CUSTARD TART

If you like tart lemon desserts, this one may be just the ticket. Lemon rind and juice are combined with honey and eggs to create a thick custard when baked in a whole wheat crust.

 1⅔ cup whole wheat pastry
     or unbleached white flour
 2   tablespoons date sugar
 4   tablespoons chilled unsalted
     butter or 3 tablespoons
     safflower oil
 1   egg white
 1   tablespoon apple cider
     vinegar
 3   to 4 tablespoons ice water
     Grated rind of 1 small lemon
     Juice of 2 medium lemons
 ½   cup light honey or to taste
 2   eggs

1. Preheat oven to 450° F. In a large mixing bowl, combine flour and date sugar. Make a well in center of dry ingredients and grate in butter or stir in oil. With fingers or a pastry mixer, combine butter and flour mixture until it is the texture of cornmeal. Do not overmix. Add egg white, vinegar, and enough of the ice water to form a ball of dough. Wrap in plastic wrap and refrigerate for 10 minutes.

2. In a blender or food processor, combine lemon rind, juice, honey, and eggs, and purée until smooth.

3. Lightly flour a counter or breadboard. Roll ball of dough into a 14-inch circle and press into a 9-inch tart pan (preferably one with fluted edges). Pour in lemon filling. Bake for 10 minutes, then lower heat to 350° F and bake until firm and lightly browned (about 30 more minutes).

Makes 1 nine-inch tart, 8 servings.

Preparation time: 30 minutes
Baking time: 40 minutes
Per serving: calcium 22 mg, calories 286, carbohydrates 39 g, cholesterol 82 mg, fat 13 g, fiber 2.4 g, protein 6 g, sodium 63 mg

SHAPING FILO PASTRIES

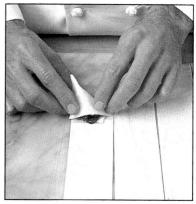

Filo triangles   *Cut 6 sheets into 2-inch strips. Place filling in lower-left corner. Fold into triangular packets.*

Filo flowers   *Press 2-inch squares (6 sheets) into lightly oiled muffin cup, spoon in 2 tablespoons of filling, crimp edges to shape.*

Filo cigars   *Place 2 tablespoons of filling at bottom edge of 3-inch strips (3 sheets), leaving ½-inch space on each side. Roll into cigar.*

APPLE-APRICOT PASTRIES

Strips of paper-thin filo are layered to make a low-calorie crust for a sweet apricot jam and apple filling, then the pastries are baked to a crisp golden color. They make great snacks when eaten right out of the oven—healthier and lower in fat than most cookie recipes—or are delicious when served as the finale to an elegant dinner party. Each pastry contains only 243 calories.

    Safflower oil, for coating
        baking pan
 2 cups thinly sliced green
        apples
 ½ cup dried currants
 2 tablespoons lemon juice
 1 teaspoon vanilla extract
 ½ cup date sugar
 ¾ teaspoon cinnamon
 ½ teaspoon nutmeg
 ¾ cup ground almonds
 8 sheets filo
 ⅓ cup melted unsalted
        butter
 ½ cup apricot preserves

1. Preheat oven to 375° F. Lightly oil a 9- by 12-inch baking pan with shallow sides.

2. In a medium saucepan over medium-high heat, cook apples, currants, lemon juice, vanilla, and date sugar until soft (about 15 minutes). Remove from heat and let cool.

3. In a small bowl mix cinnamon, nutmeg, and almonds. Set aside.

4. Sprinkle each sheet of filo with 2 teaspoons of the melted butter, then spread butter to coat filo evenly (see Preparing Filo, page 110). Sprinkle sheets with almond mixture and pile one sheet on top of another. Line prepared baking pan with stack of filo sheets, folding edges where necessary to make 1-inch sides.

5. In a small saucepan over medium heat, cook apricot preserves until soft, then spread evenly over top sheet of filo. Spoon apple mixture over preserves.

6. Bake pastry until slightly browned (about 20 minutes). Let cool, then cut into 2-inch squares.

Makes 12 squares, 12 servings.

Preparation time: 25 minutes
Baking time: 20 minutes
Per serving: calcium 33 mg, calories 243, carbohydrates 36 g, cholesterol 17 mg, fat 11 g, fiber 1.1 g, protein 3 g, sodium 116 mg

---

APPLE-CRANBERRY GEM TARTS

A perfect ending for a New Year's Eve party or Thanksgiving dinner, Apple-Cranberry Gem Tarts are mouthfuls of light, flaky pastry that contain a flavorful combination of fruits. They keep well, so you can bake them up to two days ahead of time.

 1⅔ cup whole wheat pastry or
        unbleached white flour
 2 tablespoons date sugar
        (see Note)
 4 tablespoons chilled unsalted
        butter
 3 tablespoons safflower oil
 1 egg white
 1 tablespoon apple cider
        vinegar
 3 to 4 tablespoons ice water
 ¾ cup cranberries
 2 cups sliced green apples
 ½ cup apple juice or apple
        brandy
 ¼ cup dried currants or raisins
 1 cup maple syrup
 2 tablespoons arrowroot powder
 1 tablespoon lemon juice
 ½ teaspoon cinnamon
 1 tablespoon grated lemon rind
 ½ cup ground almonds or
        walnuts

1. Preheat oven to 375° F. In a large mixing bowl, combine flour and date sugar. Make a well in center of dry ingredients and grate in butter and stir in oil. With fingers or a pastry mixer, combine butter and flour mixture until it is the texture of cornmeal. Do not overmix—or butter will melt. Add egg white, vinegar, and enough of the ice water to form 8 small balls of dough. Wrap each in plastic wrap and refrigerate for 10 minutes.

2. In a saucepan over medium-high heat, combine cranberries, apples, apple juice, currants, and maple syrup. Cook, uncovered, until berries pop. In a small bowl combine arrowroot with lemon juice and add to cranberries along with cinnamon and lemon rind. Cook, stirring frequently, until mixture thickens. Remove from heat and let cool 10 minutes.

3. Lightly flour a counter or breadboard. Roll each ball of dough into a 6-inch circle and press into a 4-inch tart pan (preferably one with fluted edges). Fill two thirds full with cranberry filling and sprinkle with ground almonds. Bake for 20 minutes. Let cool before serving.

Makes 8 tarts, 8 servings.

Note   Crunchy date sugar adds a fruity taste to the whole wheat pastry dough, but if it is not available, substitute an equal amount of maple sugar or honey.

Preparation time: 50 minutes
Cooking time: 20 minutes
Per serving: calcium 67 mg, calories 394, carbohydrates 61 g, cholesterol 19 mg, fat 17 g, fiber 39 g, protein 5 g, sodium 53 mg

---

Clockwise from top right are apple and apricot pastries, date-coconut cookies, lemon tart, baklava, and apple-cranberry tarts (see pages 110 to 112).

If you're watching your sodium intake, you won't miss the salt in this creamy carrot soup flavored with cardamom and sherry (see page 122).

Recipes for Special Diets

People suffering from, or at high risk for, high blood pressure, heart disease, diabetes, cancer, and other ailments often adopt diets that restrict the amount of fats and oils, sodium, cholesterol, or dairy products. This chapter is devoted to those people with special cooking requirements. You will find recipes that fulfill medical needs but are tasty enough to serve family and friends. Recipes such as Pasta With Miso Pesto (see page 116) or Tofu Ice Cream Parfaits (see page 119) are made without cheese or milk products, but they are difficult to distinguish from the traditional versions. Cream of Zucchini Soup (see page 116), thickened with oats and puréed vegetables, will fool everyone with its rich, creamy texture.

DAIRY-RESTRICTED DIETS

People with milk allergies or heart disease are usually instructed to avoid eating dairy products. If your doctor or nutritionist advises a dairy-free diet, you need to learn substitution tricks for your favorite cream soups, salad dressings, and desserts. Here are recipes that do not use dairy products, yet taste delicious and contain substantial amounts of protein and calcium.

PASTA WITH MISO PESTO

Savory miso paste, the by-product of the manufacture of soy sauce, is available in many supermarkets and in health-food stores. In this recipe a very small amount of miso is blended with pine nuts, garlic, and basil to make a pesto that is indistinguishable from the traditional version made with Parmesan cheese.

½ cup minced spinach leaves
½ cup minced parsley
2 tablespoons olive oil
1 teaspoon minced garlic
1 tablespoon light miso
¼ cup pine nuts, finely chopped
1 tablespoon dried basil
1 pound linguine

1. Place spinach, parsley, oil, garlic, miso, pine nuts, and basil into a blender or food processor and purée until the mixture reaches the consistency of a paste.

2. In a large pot over high heat, cook linguine in 2 quarts of boiling water until tender (7 to 8 minutes). Drain and toss with pesto. Serve hot.

Serves 4.

Preparation time: 15 minutes
Cooking time: 7 to 8 minutes
Per serving: calcium 69 mg, calories 283, carbohydrates 32 g, cholesterol 41 mg, fat 14 g, fiber 2.4 g, protein 8 g, sodium 216 mg

---

GARDEN SALAD WITH CREAMY HERB DRESSING

The secret of this delicious salad is the creamy dressing liberally laced with fresh herbs. Soft tofu is puréed to create the texture of this dairy-free dressing. You can use whatever vegetables are fresh and in season—experiment with blanched snow peas, summer squash, and whole cherry tomatoes in addition to the ingredients listed below.

1 cup peeled and julienned jicama
1 cup chopped watercress
3 cups torn red leaf lettuce
½ cup sliced radishes
2 tablespoons lime juice
¼ cup tarragon vinegar
1 tablespoon honey
½ cup soft tofu
1 teaspoon olive oil
1 teaspoon low-sodium soy or tamari sauce
1 tablespoon stone-ground mustard
2 teaspoons minced parsley
½ teaspoon chopped fresh thyme
½ teaspoon minced fresh basil

1. In a large salad bowl, toss together jicama, watercress, lettuce, and radishes.

2. In a blender purée lime juice, vinegar, honey, tofu, oil, and soy sauce until creamy. Stir in mustard, parsley, thyme, and basil, and pour over salad. Toss well and serve.

Serves 4.

Preparation time: 20 minutes
Per serving: calcium 79 mg, calories 78, carbohydrates 12 g, cholesterol none, fat 3 g, fiber .9 g, protein 3 g, sodium 143 mg

---

CREAM OF ZUCCHINI SOUP

Thickened with a mixture of cooked oats and vegetables, Cream of Zucchini Soup is a delicate, light-green purée that heralds spring or summer. The delicate flavor combines well with a simple fish dish, such as Fillet of Salmon Poached in Lemon and Wine (see page 121) or Fish Baked in Parchment With Lime and Cilantro (see page 123).

1 cup minced onion
¼ cup chopped green onion
2 teaspoons dark sesame oil
¼ cup dry sherry
¼ cup chopped parsley
1 cup chopped zucchini
¼ cup chopped celery
4 cups defatted Chicken Stock (see page 31)
⅓ cup rolled oats
1 teaspoon salt or to taste
¼ teaspoon dried thyme
¼ teaspoon white pepper
2 teaspoons chopped fresh dill

1. In a large pot over medium-high heat, sauté onion and green onion in sesame oil and sherry for 5 minutes, stirring frequently. Add parsley, zucchini, and celery, and cook 10 minutes, stirring occasionally.

2. Pour in stock, and add oats, salt, thyme, white pepper, and dill. Bring soup to a boil, then lower heat to medium and simmer, covered, for 20 minutes.

3. Transfer soup to a blender in small amounts and purée until thick and smooth. Return to pot. Taste for seasoning, reheat, and serve.

Serves 6.

Preparation time: 20 minutes
Cooking time: 35 minutes
Per serving: calcium 35 mg, calories 75, carbohydrates 8 g, cholesterol 2 mg, fat 2 g, fiber .85 g, protein 4 g, sodium 500 mg

---

CURRANT AND ORANGE MUFFINS

This recipe is made with rice flour instead of wheat and contains no milk products. The batter uses a creamy nut milk made from almonds puréed with orange juice and is sweetened with a small amount of maple syrup and honey.

Safflower oil, for coating muffin tin
1 *cup rice flour*
1 *tablespoon baking powder*
1 *teaspoon baking soda*
½ *cup rolled oats, ground*
¼ *cup honey*
1 *tablespoon maple syrup*
¼ *cup safflower oil*
½ *cup ground almonds*
½ *cup orange juice*
1 *teaspoon grated orange rind*
2 *eggs*
½ *cup dried currants*

1. Preheat oven to 400° F. Lightly oil a 12-hole muffin tin.

2. In a large bowl combine rice flour, baking powder, baking soda, and ground oats. In a separate bowl combine honey, maple syrup, and the ¼ cup oil until very smooth. In a blender or food processor, purée almonds and orange juice, then strain. Add almond liquid to honey mixture along with orange rind.

3. Separate eggs. Stir yolks into honey mixture. Beat egg whites until stiff peaks form.

4. Combine dry and wet ingredients, then stir in currants. Fold in egg whites. Spoon into prepared muffin cups, filling each three fourths full. Bake until muffins spring back when pressed lightly in center (about 20 minutes).

Makes 1 dozen muffins, 12 servings.

Preparation time: 25 minutes
Baking time: 20 minutes
Per serving: calcium 41 mg, calories 186, carbohydrates 25 g, cholesterol 42 mg, fat 8 g, fiber .53 g, protein 3 g, sodium 192 mg

Basics

LOW-CALORIE SUBSTITUTIONS FOR HIGH-FAT DAIRY PRODUCTS

If you need to restrict your intake of high-fat dairy products, try creamy, low-fat substitutes for your favorite recipes. Be sure, though, to look for a good alternative source of calcium, such as leafy greens or certain seafoods, when eliminating dairy products from your diet (see page 86).

Nonfat Yogurt

Use nonfat yogurt in place of buttermilk, whole milk, or sour cream in salad dressings and baked goods—just add in the same amount. Use it in "cream" sauces and serve over fish or vegetables (add yogurt at the end and cook as little as possible since it tends to separate).

Low-Fat Cheeses

Look for labels that read *low fat* or *part skim*—usually found on packages of mozzarella, ricotta, farmer, and certain cream cheeses. Low-fat cheeses taste just as good as and, in some cases, have less than half the calories of whole-milk products.

Tofu and Soy Cheeses

Creamy or soft tofu can be used as a substitute for cream cheese or whipped cream toppings. Add lemon juice to blended soft tofu to create a mock sour cream for creamy salad dressings and baked potatoes. Firm tofu can replace ricotta cheese in lasagna. Or, try one of the new soy cheeses on top of your next baked pasta dish—just grate it as you would regular cheese and add the same amount to recipe.

Mock Cream Cheese Topping
Blend 8 ounces soft tofu with 1 tablespoon maple syrup and ½ teaspoon nutmeg until very smooth. Serves 4.

Calories per serving: 54 (compared to 189 for cream cheese)

Mock Sour Cream Blend 4 ounces soft tofu with 2 teaspoons lemon juice, or to taste, until very smooth. Makes 4 ounces.

Calories per ounce: 21 (compared to 61 for whole-milk sour cream)

Mock Ricotta Cheese Crumble 8 ounces firm tofu and combine with 2 tablespoons Italian herbs or Italian seasoning. Add herbal salt substitute to taste. Makes 8 ounces.

Calories per ounce: 20 (compared to 49 for whole-milk ricotta cheese)

Tofu Ice Cream Parfaits, laced with strawberries and bananas, will be a healthy hit with children or at any fun gathering.

CARROT MUFFINS

Light as a feather, Carrot Muffins are a savory combination of carrots, almond milk, egg whites, whole wheat flour, pineapple, and honey. They are perfect for brunch or as a light, low-sugar dessert. They also freeze well, so plan on making a double batch to keep for impromptu entertaining.

> *Safflower oil and flour, for coating muffin tin*
> ⅓ cup almonds
> ⅓ cup water
> 2½ cups whole wheat pastry or unbleached white flour
> 2 teaspoons cinnamon
> 2 teaspoons baking soda
> 2 cups grated carrots
> 1 cup crushed pineapple, drained
> ¼ cup safflower oil
> ½ cup honey
> ½ cup chopped, pitted dates
> 3 egg whites

1. Preheat oven to 350° F. Lightly oil and flour a 12-hole muffin tin.

2. Place almonds and the water in a blender and purée, then strain milk into a bowl. Set aside.

3. In a large bowl sift together flour, cinnamon, and baking soda. In a separate bowl combine almond milk, carrots, pineapple, the ¼ cup safflower oil, honey, and dates. In a smaller bowl beat egg whites until stiff peaks form.

4. Mix dry and wet ingredients, stirring briefly to combine. Fold in egg whites. Spoon batter into muffin tin and bake for 35 minutes. Let cool, then remove from muffin tin.

Makes 1 dozen muffins, 12 servings.

> *Preparation time:* 25 minutes
> *Baking time:* 35 minutes
> *Per serving:* calcium 39 mg, calories 230, carbohydrates 40 g, cholesterol none, fat 7 g, fiber 3.6 g, protein 5 g, sodium 169 mg

ALMOND COOKIES

Rich tasting but dairy free, Almond Cookies are a good choice to end a Chinese menu. They can be made the night before, then wrapped well to keep them from drying out. Besides adding protein, almonds add calcium, potassium, and phosphorus to your diet.

Safflower oil, for coating baking sheet
2¾ *cups whole wheat pastry or unbleached white flour*
½ *cup date sugar*
1 *teaspoon baking powder*
¾ *cup honey*
½ *cup safflower oil*
¼ *cup soy margarine, softened*
1 *beaten egg*
1 *tablespoon almond extract*
1 *cup whole almonds*

1. Preheat oven to 300° F. Lightly oil a large baking sheet.

2. In a large bowl combine flour, date sugar, and baking powder. In a separate bowl combine honey, the ½ cup safflower oil, margarine, egg, and almond extract until very smooth.

3. Mix contents of 2 bowls to form dough. Roll in small balls about 2 inches in diameter. Press into circles and place on cookie sheet about 2 inches apart. Press an almond into center of each cookie.

4. Bake cookies for 12 minutes, watching carefully as they tend to brown quickly. Remove from cookie sheet and let cool on rack.

Makes 24 to 30 cookies, about 8 servings

Preparation time: 25 minutes
Baking time: 12 minutes
Per serving: calcium 18 mg, calories 163, carbohydrates 19 g, cholesterol 8 mg, fat 9 g, fiber 1.2 g, protein 3 g, sodium 64 mg

TOFU ICE CREAM PARFAITS

When the fresh, soft variety of tofu is flavored and blended into a purée, it is hard to distinguish from sour cream or yogurt. In Tofu Ice Cream Parfaits, tofu absorbs the flavor of the banana and vanilla to create a delicately creamy dessert that is especially elegant when layered with fresh fruit. Tofu is a low-fat source of protein and provides as much calcium as an equal amount of milk.

2 *cups soft tofu*
2 *tablespoons maple syrup*
½ *ripe banana*
1 *teaspoon vanilla extract*
3 *cups sliced strawberries or kiwifruit*

1. In a blender or food processor, purée tofu, maple syrup, banana, and vanilla until very smooth and creamy. Pour into a shallow pan and freeze overnight or for 8 hours.

2. Just before serving, cut frozen tofu mixture into small chunks and quickly blend to the consistency of ice cream. Spoon into dessert glasses, alternating layers with sliced strawberries. Serve immediately.

Serves 6.

<u>Note</u> Although the banana is hard to replace since it adds creaminess and masks any telltale soy taste, almost any fresh fruit in season can be substituted for the strawberries or kiwifruit. Try blackberries, peaches, pears, and apricots for variety.

Preparation time: 15 minutes
Freezing time: 8 hours
Per serving: calcium 126 mg, calories 110, carbohydrates 15 g, cholesterol none, fat 4 g, fiber 1.6 g, protein 7 g, sodium 8 mg

FAT- AND CHOLESTEROL-RESTRICTED DIETS

Many people who have heart conditions and high blood cholesterol, or who simply want to prevent heart problems in the future, are advised to follow a diet low in fat and cholesterol. The following recipes give you a variety of flavors without including excess fat. Many are also very low in calories—an added bonus for weight loss or maintenance.

CHINESE HOT-AND-SPICY ASPARAGUS SALAD

This spicy salad has a cooling effect when served in summer and works well with any Chinese menu. Adjust the spiciness to your taste by increasing or decreasing the cayenne pepper, garlic, and gingerroot. Serve it warm or chilled.

1 *pound asparagus*
1 *tablespoon minced garlic*
1 *tablespoon grated gingerroot*
½ *teaspoon salt or herbal salt substitute*
½ *teaspoon honey*
2 *tablespoons low-sodium soy or tamari sauce*
1 *teaspoon dark sesame oil*
1 *tablespoon rice vinegar*
¼ *teaspoon cayenne pepper*
¼ *teaspoon hot-pepper flakes (optional)*

1. Bring a large pot of water to a boil over high heat. Trim ends of asparagus and slice each stalk diagonally into 3-inch pieces. Steam until tender (8 to 10 minutes). Drain.

2. In a large bowl combine garlic, gingerroot, salt, honey, soy sauce, sesame oil, vinegar, cayenne, and hot-pepper flakes. Toss with asparagus. Chill or serve warm.

Serves 4.

Preparation time: 10 minutes
Cooking time: 8 to 10 minutes
Chilling time (optional): 2 hours
Per serving: calcium 22 mg, calories 38, carbohydrates 6 g, cholesterol none, fat 1 g, fiber .7 g, protein 2 g, sodium 453 mg

... ON SKIMMING FAT

Fat adds flavor and texture to foods, so few people relish the thought of eliminating fat from their diets. However, it is not difficult to cut out unnecessary fat. Here are some tips to become a more fat-conscious cook and to defat recipes easily.

☐ If allowed to sit for a short time, fats reveal themselves in cooked foods and can be skimmed off. Invest in a gravy separator or use a bulb baster or slotted spoon to skim fats from cooking liquids.

☐ Float a piece of bread on top of soups or broths to absorb the fat; then discard bread.

☐ One quick way to defat chicken stock is to place the stock in the refrigerator for one hour, then peel off the congealed fat that forms on the top.

☐ When buying meats, choose the leanest cuts. At home, trim all excess fats from the sides of steaks, chops, and cutlets. Avoid processed meats such as cold cuts, sausage, bacon, and hot dogs. Choose lean turkey, turkey ham, and smoked chicken breast.

☐ Use nonstick pans for sautéing and stir-frying, broiling, and baking whenever the recipe calls for oiling or buttering the pan.

☐ Choose roasting pans with oven racks so that the fat drips off.

☐ Buy a carbon steel wok or omelet pan and season it, so you can cook stir-fries and egg dishes without excessive oil.

☐ Select the least fatty fish, such as whitefish, cod, flounder, haddock, and scrod. Buy tuna packed in water rather than in oil.

MIXED RICE PILAF

Mixed Rice Pilaf combines wild, basmati, and brown rices with onion, garlic, red bell pepper, and celery. Sherry, instead of oil, is used to sauté the vegetables, which considerably lowers the fat content of this dish.

- 1 cup chopped onion
- 2 teaspoons minced garlic
- ⅓ cup minced red bell pepper
- ½ cup minced celery
- ½ cup dry sherry or white wine
- 2 cups long-grain brown rice
- ½ cup wild rice
- ½ cup basmati rice
- 4 cups defatted Chicken Stock or Vegetarian Stock (see page 31)
- ½ teaspoon dried thyme
- ¼ teaspoon dried sage
- 1 tablespoon low-sodium soy or tamari sauce

1. In a heavy pot over medium-high heat, sauté onion, garlic, red bell pepper, and celery in sherry until vegetables are soft (5 to 10 minutes).

2. Add brown, wild, and basmati rices. Cook, stirring, for 3 minutes. Add stock, thyme, and sage, and bring to a boil. Lower heat to medium and cook, uncovered, for 15 minutes.

3. Lower heat to low, cover pot, and let pilaf steam until rice is tender (about 25 minutes). Stir in soy sauce.

Serves 6.

Preparation time: 25 minutes
Cooking time: 55 minutes
Per serving: calcium 50 mg, calories 346, carbohydrates 69 g, cholesterol none, fat 2 g, fiber 5.7 g, protein 10 g, sodium 1004 mg

CHINESE STIR-FRIED VEGETABLES OVER RICE

This easy stir-fry recipe gets its rich flavor from sherry, Chinese five-spice powder, garlic, and gingerroot, and eliminates the fat from cooking oils. The selection of fresh vegetables can change with the season and availability of produce. Try marinating a few of the vegetables in the sherry, garlic, and gingerroot for several hours before adding to the wok.

- 1 cup thinly sliced onion
- 1 teaspoon minced garlic
- 1 teaspoon grated gingerroot
- ¼ cup dry sherry
- 1 cup sliced bok choy
- ½ cup broccoli florets, broken into small pieces
- ½ cup sliced mushrooms
- ½ cup julienned red bell pepper
- ¼ cup defatted Chicken Stock (see page 31)
- 1 cup mung bean sprouts
- ½ teaspoon Chinese five-spice powder
- 1 tablespoon low-sodium soy or tamari sauce, or to taste
- 1 tablespoon arrowroot powder

1. In a wok or large skillet over medium-high heat, sauté onion, garlic, and gingerroot in sherry for 5 minutes, stirring frequently. Add bok choy, broccoli, mushrooms, bell pepper, and broth. Cover and steam until vegetables are tender-crisp (about 5 minutes).

2. Add bean sprouts and cook 1 minute. In a small bowl combine five-spice, soy sauce, and arrowroot. Add to stir-fry and cook until mixture thickens (about 1 minute). Serve hot.

Serves 6.

Note Chinese five-spice powder, a blend that typically includes fennel seed, cloves, Szechuan peppercorn, cinnamon, and anise, is available in Chinese markets.

Preparation time: 20 minutes
Cooking time: 12 minutes
Per serving: calcium 54 mg, calories 71, carbohydrates 12 g, cholesterol none, fat 1 g, fiber 3.2 g, protein 3 g, sodium 164 mg

FILLET OF SALMON POACHED IN LEMON AND WINE

A simple but elegant main dish, and one very low in fat, fillet of salmon is also rich in omega-3 oils, which many medical professionals believe help lower cholesterol (see Reducing the Cholesterol in Your Diet, page 63). For a variation on this recipe, try marinating the salmon in the lemon and wine poaching liquid for several hours and grilling it over hot mesquite charcoal.

- ⅓ cup lemon juice
- ½ cup dry white wine
- 4 large salmon fillets
- 2 tablespoons minced parsley

1. In a large skillet over medium-high heat, bring lemon juice and wine to a boil. Lower heat to medium. Add salmon and cover skillet.

2. Poach salmon until it flakes when pressed with a fork (5 to 8 minutes). Remove from poaching liquid and serve immediately, sprinkled with parsley.

Serves 4.

Preparation time: 5 minutes
Cooking time: 5 to 8 minutes
Per serving: calcium 420 mg, calories 211, carbohydrates 2 g, cholesterol 47 mg, fat 7 g, fiber .1 g, protein 27 g, sodium 118 mg

BAKED PEAR GRATIN

Baked Pear Gratin is a simple dessert of baked pears, ground almonds, and date sugar. When it is baked, then broiled, the date sugar turns the pears a rich golden color.

- Safflower oil, for coating baking dish
- 4 medium-sized winter pears, such as Bosc
- 1 tablespoon lime juice
- 2 tablespoons dark rum
- 2 tablespoons ground almonds
- ½ teaspoon cinnamon
- 1 tablespoon date sugar

1. Preheat oven to 375° F. Lightly oil a large baking dish.

2. Peel, core, and thinly slice pears and layer in bottom of baking dish. Sprinkle with lime juice and rum.

3. Combine almonds, cinnamon, and date sugar. Sprinkle over pears. Cover pan with aluminum foil and bake for 40 minutes. Remove aluminum foil and place pan under broiler. Broil to a light golden brown (3 to 5 minutes), and serve immediately.

Serves 6.

Preparation time: 20 minutes
Cooking time: 45 minutes
Per serving: calcium 19 mg, calories 105, carbohydrates 19 g, cholesterol none, fat 2 g, fiber 3.0 g, protein 1 g, sodium 7 mg

The complementary flavors of lemon, dry white wine, and parsley combine in this easy poached salmon entrée—as low in fat as it is high in nutrients and flavor.

SODIUM-RESTRICTED DIETS

Many people with hypertension or who have a family history of high blood pressure or heart disease are restricting the sodium in their diet. The recipes in this section contain little or no added salt. Instead, they are seasoned with herbs and spices and use cooking techniques that enhance the natural flavors in fruits, vegetables, lean meats, and chicken. If you tend to reach for the salt shaker without thinking, you will be pleasantly surprised by the rich flavor of such easy-to-prepare recipes as Low-Sodium Chicken Soup With Vegetables (see below) or Vegetarian Chili (see page 123).

CARROT SOUP WITH SHERRY AND CARDAMOM

Carrots, a good source of vitamin A and minerals, give this soup a rich golden orange color. The subtle seasonings include sherry, cardamom, and orange rind. Served warm, it is a hearty soup for a family-style dinner; chilled, it makes a good soup for a dinner party.

    1 cup chopped onion
    1 tablespoon minced garlic
    1 teaspoon safflower oil
    ⅓ cup dry sherry
    2 cups chopped carrots
    4 cups defatted Chicken Stock
      (see page 31)
    1 teaspoon cardamom
    ½ cup nonfat plain yogurt
    ½ teaspoon nutmeg
    ½ teaspoon grated orange rind

1. In a large stockpot over medium-high heat, sauté onion and garlic in oil and sherry for 10 minutes. Add carrots and cook 5 minutes. Add stock and bring to a boil.

2. Lower heat to medium and cook soup for 20 minutes. Purée in batches in a blender and return to pot. Add cardamom, yogurt, nutmeg, and orange rind. Heat through and serve.

Makes 6 to 7 cups, 6 servings.

> *Preparation time:* 25 minutes
> *Cooking time:* 35 minutes
> *Per serving:* calcium 62 mg, calories 83, carbohydrates 10 g, cholesterol 1 mg, fat 1 g, fiber 1.1 g, protein 4 g, sodium 177 mg

LOW-SODIUM CHICKEN SOUP WITH VEGETABLES

Very different from traditionally salty chicken soups, this Middle Eastern soup recipe is pared down to include only 246 milligrams of sodium per serving. The secret to its wonderful flavor is the liberal use of herbs and sherry. Since the alcohol cooks off before serving, the recipe is also very low in calories. Add the optional chile for a spicy twist. Traditionally, the chicken pieces are left whole and the soup is served as a main course with bread and salad.

    1 frying chicken (3 lb),
      skinned and cut into
      serving pieces
    ½ cup dry sherry
    ½ cup chopped green onions
    2 cups chopped tomatoes
    1 cup corn kernels
    ½ cup diced sweet potatoes
    ½ cup shelled peas
    2 tablespoons minced
      fresh chives
    1 teaspoon minced fresh basil
    ½ teaspoon minced fresh
      tarragon
    1 small jalapeño chile, seeded
      and minced (optional)
    6 cups defatted Chicken
      Stock (see page 31)
    6 cups water

1. In a large stockpot or Dutch oven over medium-high heat, sear chicken pieces in sherry by sautéing rapidly on both sides until browned (about 10 minutes). Remove from pot and set aside.

2. Add green onions, tomatoes, corn, and sweet potatoes, and sauté for 5 minutes in cooking liquid left in stockpot. If pot becomes dry, add a small amount of water.

3. Add peas, chives, basil, tarragon, and chile and cook 5 minutes. Add stock, the water, and chicken pieces. Bring to a boil, then lower heat to medium, cover pot, and cook for 45 minutes.

Serves 8.

<u>Note</u>   For an even tastier soup, make this recipe the night before, let cool, and then refrigerate overnight. The rich aroma and flavor of the herbs will intensify.

> *Preparation time:* 20 minutes
> *Cooking time:* 65 minutes
> *Per serving:* calcium 37 mg, calories 249, carbohydrates 13 g, cholesterol 76 mg, fat 7 g, fiber 1.9 g, protein 29 g, sodium 246 mg

VEGETARIAN CHILI

You will not believe that this chili is meatless—it is thick and hearty and perfect for football weather or winter lunch boxes. For an even richer texture, you can add tempeh, a savory soy product that contributes good low-fat protein. Vegetarian Chili freezes well, so make extra for easy weekend lunches.

> 1 cup minced onion
> ½ cup minced celery
> ⅓ cup minced green bell pepper
> 1 tablespoon minced garlic
> ½ cup dry red wine
> ½ cup diced canned green chiles
> 3 cups chopped tomatoes
> 3 cups cooked pinto beans
> 2 teaspoons cumin
> 1 teaspoon chopped cilantro
> 1 tablespoon chili powder
>   or to taste
> 2 teaspoons dried oregano
> 2 cups water
> 3 tablespoons tomato paste
>   Herbal salt substitute
>   (optional)

1. In a large stockpot or Dutch oven over medium-high heat, cook onion, celery, bell pepper, and garlic in red wine for 10 minutes. Add chiles and tomatoes and cook 3 minutes.

2. Add beans, cumin, cilantro, chili powder, oregano, the water, and tomato paste. Raise heat to high, bring to a boil, then lower heat to medium. Cover pot and cook until chili is thick (45 minutes to 1 hour).

3. Taste for seasoning, add salt substitute if needed, and serve hot.

Makes 8 to 10 cups, 8 servings.

Preparation time: 25 minutes
Cooking time: 1 hour to 1 hour and 15 minutes
Per serving: calcium 72 mg, calories 144, carbohydrates 27 g, cholesterol none, fat 1 g, fiber 10 g, protein 8 g, sodium 36 mg

FISH BAKED IN PARCHMENT WITH LIME AND CILANTRO

Lime and cilantro add a Caribbean flavor to this easy, salt-free entrée. Choose fillets of red snapper, cod, flounder, or orange roughy. You can even marinate the fish in the poaching liquid overnight before cooking.

> *Safflower oil, for greasing parchment*
> 4 *large fillets of red snapper, cod, flounder, or orange roughy*
> 1 *teaspoon grated gingerroot*
> 2 *tablespoons sake or rice wine*
> 1 *tablespoon lime juice*
> 1 *teaspoon grated lime rind*
> 2 *tablespoons minced cilantro*
> 1 *teaspoon dark sesame oil*

1. Preheat oven to 350° F. Lightly oil 4 sheets parchment paper.

2. Place 1 fillet on the center of each sheet of parchment. In a small bowl combine gingerroot, sake, lime juice, lime rind, cilantro, and sesame oil. Spoon an equal amount over each fish fillet.

3. Roll edges of parchment together, forming a packet around fish. (See Healthy Ideas With Parchment Cooking, page 50.) Bake for 12 minutes.

4. To serve, unroll parchment packets and slide fish onto plates. Spoon poaching liquid over fish and serve immediately.

Serves 4.

Preparation time: 15 minutes
Cooking time: 12 minutes
Per serving: calcium 20 mg, calories 113, carbohydrates 1 g, cholesterol 57 mg, fat 2 g, fiber .1 g, protein 21 g, sodium 71 mg

SEASONINGS BEYOND SALT

Salt is needed for many essential functions in the body, and it occurs naturally in many healthy foods. However, excess sodium has been linked to hypertension (high blood pressure) by many research studies. Despite these findings, many people still salt their food routinely before tasting it.

About one fourth of your salt intake comes from the salt you add to food, the rest from salt added in manufacturing. Pickles and sauerkraut are salted in the preserving process; ketchup, condiments, and sauces often contain large amounts of sodium; snack foods are notorious for their salt content. Many prepared seasonings—celery and garlic salt, chili sauce, barbecue sauce, Worcestershire sauce—contain additional sodium. Even baking powder and baking soda, used in most packaged bakery products, contain salt.

How do you reduce the excess salt in your diet? If you are interested in cutting sodium intake, the first step is doing away with the salt shaker. Your taste buds may object for a few months, but they will eventually reawaken from the desensitizing that salt engenders.

Meanwhile, you can season foods effectively without salt, using fresh and dried herbs and spices, sauce reductions, and wines. A few drops of lemon juice can bring out the flavor in many foods—try this on your next serving of steamed asparagus, for example. Rub fresh garlic or gingerroot on lean meats and chicken before barbecuing, rather than dousing with salt and pepper. Try seasoning salad dressings with such herbs and spices as tarragon, cumin, basil, thyme, and oregano. Add a dash of nutmeg and cinnamon to fruit desserts, a bit of saffron or curry to rice or other grain dishes.

INDEX

Note: Page numbers in italics refer to photographs separated from recipe text.

U.S./METRIC MEASURE CONVERSION CHART

		Formulas for Exact Measures			Rounded Measures for Quick Reference		
	Symbol	When you know:	Multiply by:	To find:			
Mass (Weight)	oz	ounces	28.35	grams	1 oz		= 30 g
	lb	pounds	0.45	kilograms	4 oz		= 115 g
	g	grams	0.035	ounces	8 oz		= 225 g
	kg	kilograms	2.2	pounds	16 oz	= 1 lb	= 450 g
					32 oz	= 2 lb	= 900 g
					36 oz	= 2¼ lb	= 1,000g (1 kg)
Volume	tsp	teaspoons	5.0	milliliters	¼ tsp	= 1/24 oz	= 1 ml
	tbsp	tablespoons	15.0	milliliters	½ tsp	= 1/12 oz	= 2 ml
	fl oz	fluid ounces	29.57	milliliters	1 tsp	= 1/6 oz	= 5 ml
	c	cups	0.24	liters	1 tbsp	= ½ oz	= 15 ml
	pt	pints	0.47	liters	1 c	= 8 oz	= 250 ml
	qt	quarts	0.95	liters	2 c (1 pt)	= 16 oz	= 500 ml
	gal	gallons	3.785	liters	4 c (1 qt)	= 32 oz	= 1 liter
	ml	milliliters	0.034	fluid ounces	4 qt (1 gal)	= 128 oz	= 3¾ liter
Length	in.	inches	2.54	centimeters	⅜ in.	= 1 cm	
	ft	feet	30.48	centimeters	1 in.	= 2.5 cm	
	yd	yards	0.9144	meters	2 in.	= 5 cm	
	mi	miles	1.609	kilometers	2½ in.	= 6.5 cm	
	km	kilometers	0.621	miles	12 in. (1 ft)	= 30 cm	
	m	meters	1.094	yards	1 yd	= 90 cm	
	cm	centimeters	0.39	inches	100 ft	= 30 m	
					1 mi	= 1.6 km	
Temperature	°F	Fahrenheit	5/9 (after subtracting 32)	Celsius	32°F	= 0°C	
					68°F	= 20°C	
	°C	Celsius	9/5 (then add 32)	Fahrenheit	212°F	= 100°C	
Area	in.²	square inches	6.452	square centimeters	1 in.²	= 6.5 cm²	
	ft²	square feet	929.0	square centimeters	1 ft²	= 930 cm²	
	yd²	square yards	8361.0	square centimeters	1 yd²	= 8360 cm²	
	a.	acres	0.4047	hectares	1 a.	= 4050 m²	